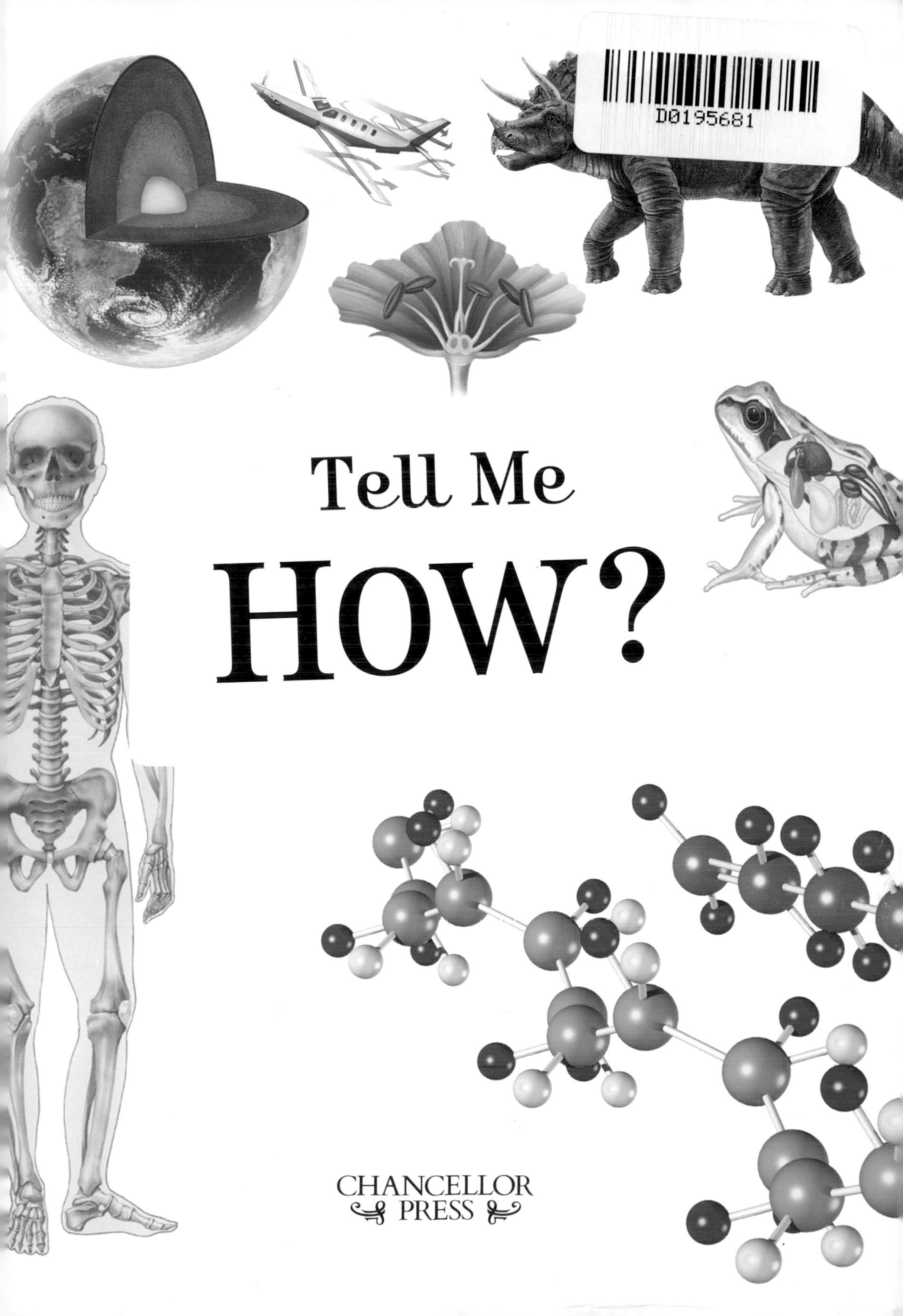

Tell Me HOW?

CHANCELLOR PRESS

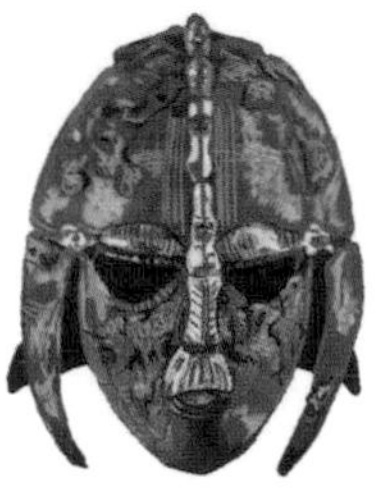

First published in 2001 by Chancellor Press,
an imprint of Octopus Publishing Group Ltd,

Reprinted 2003 (twice), 2004 (three times), 2005 (three times),
2006 (three times), 2007 (twice), 2008, 2009 (twice)

New edition published in 2010 by Chancellor Press,
an imprint of Octopus Publishing Group Ltd,
189 Shaftesbury Avenue,
London WC2H 8JY
www.octopusbooks.co.uk

Reprinted 2011 (twice)

An Hachette UK Company
www.hachette.co.uk

ISBN: 978-0-753720-92-9

A CIP catalogue record for this book is available from the British Library

Produced by Omnipress, Eastbourne

Printed in China

CONTENTS

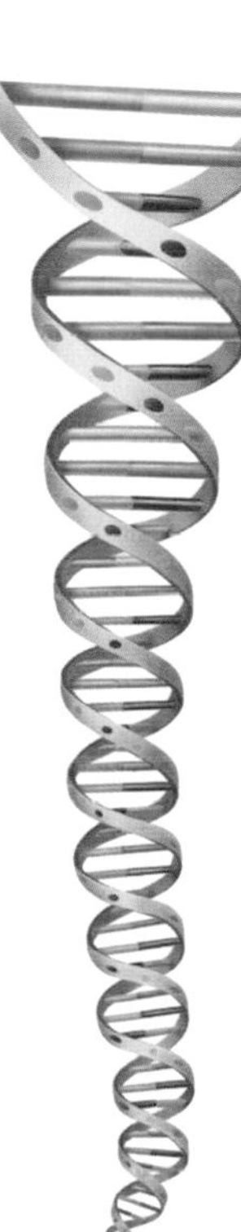

THE HUMAN BODY

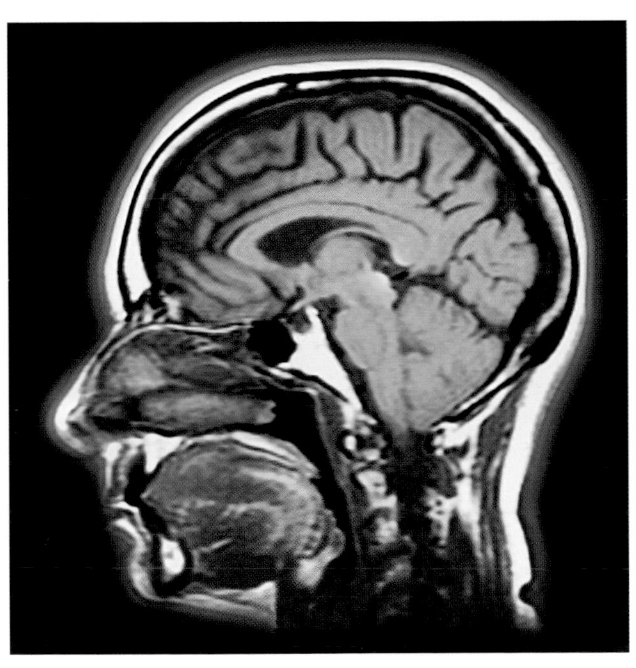

Contents

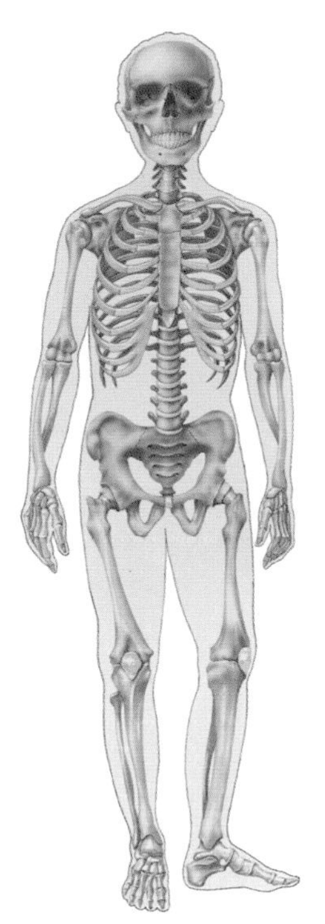

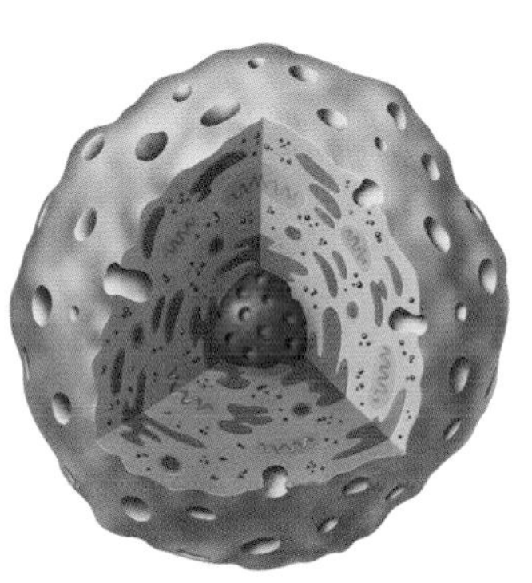

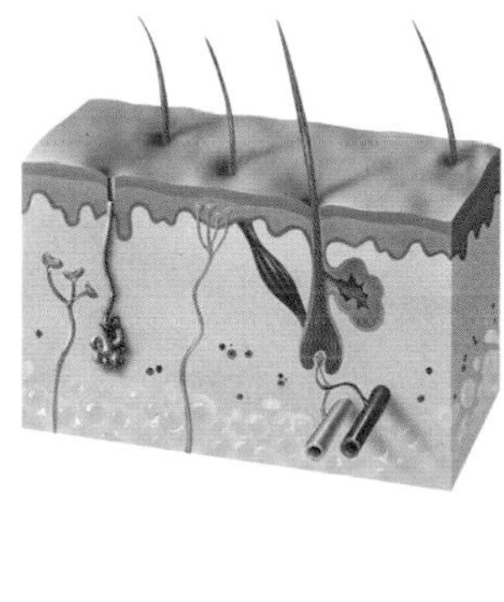

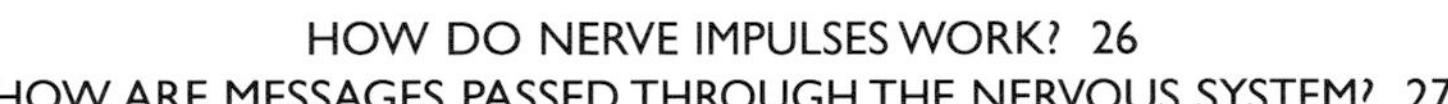

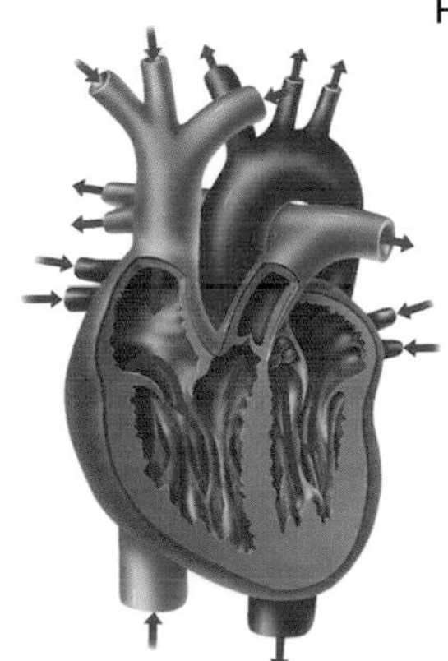

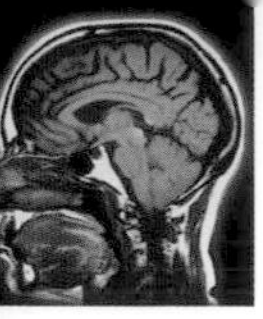

How do the kidneys work?

The kidneys work by effectively removing the majority of waste products from our blood, and are vital to our health. We each have two kidneys, which lie on the back wall of the abdomen. From the inner side of each kidney a tube called the ureter runs down the abdominal cavity entering the bladder.

Blood is pumped through groups of tiny tubes inside the kidneys, and harmful waste material passes out through the walls of these vessels and down the ureter into the bladder. Here it is ready to be discharged from the body as urine.

The kidneys also work by producing certain hormones which help to regulate blood pressure.

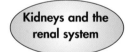

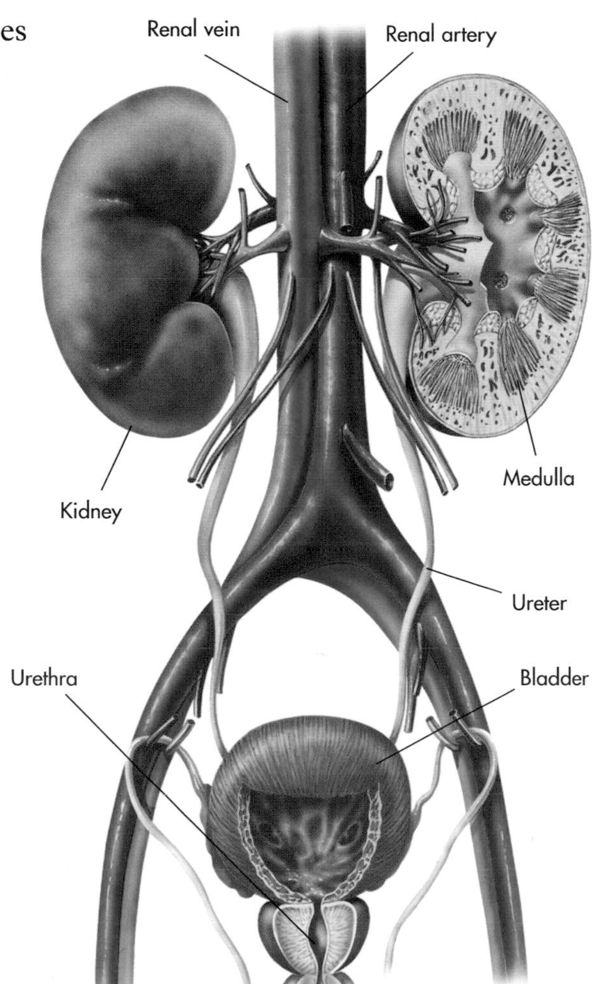

Kidneys and the renal system

FACT FILE

Cells consist of jelly-like cytoplasm, surrounded by a membrane, through which nutrients pass.

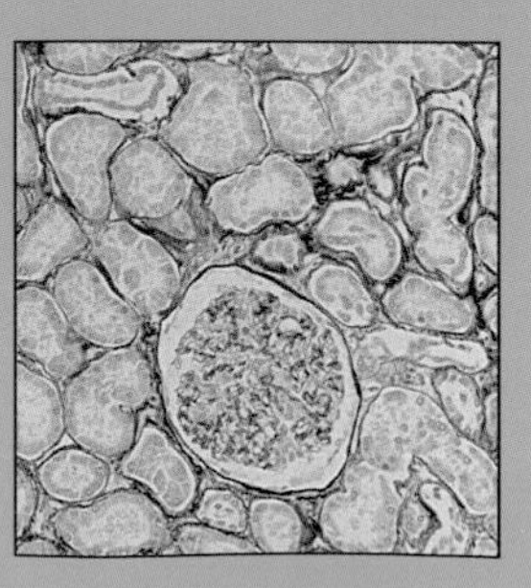

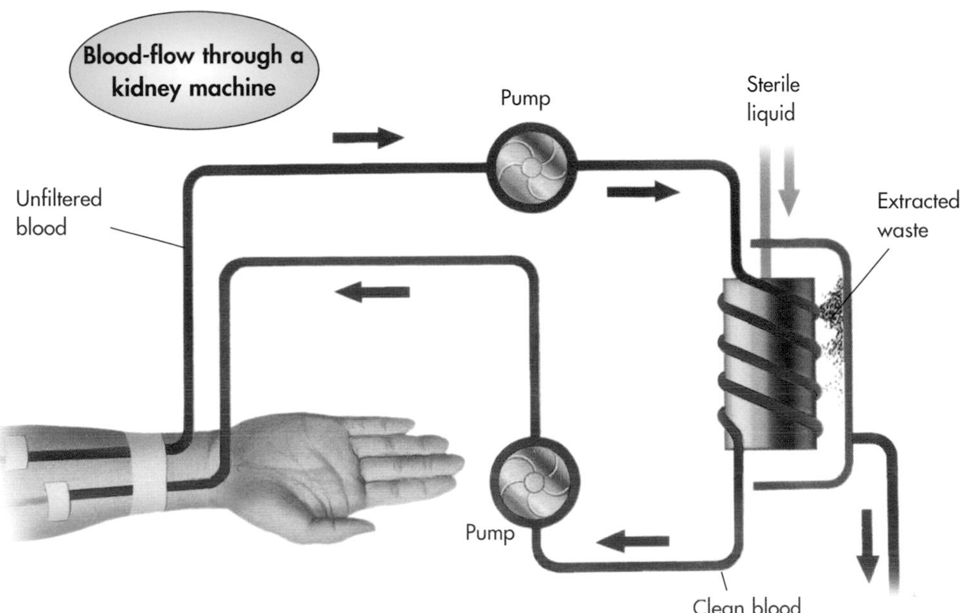

How do kidney machines work?

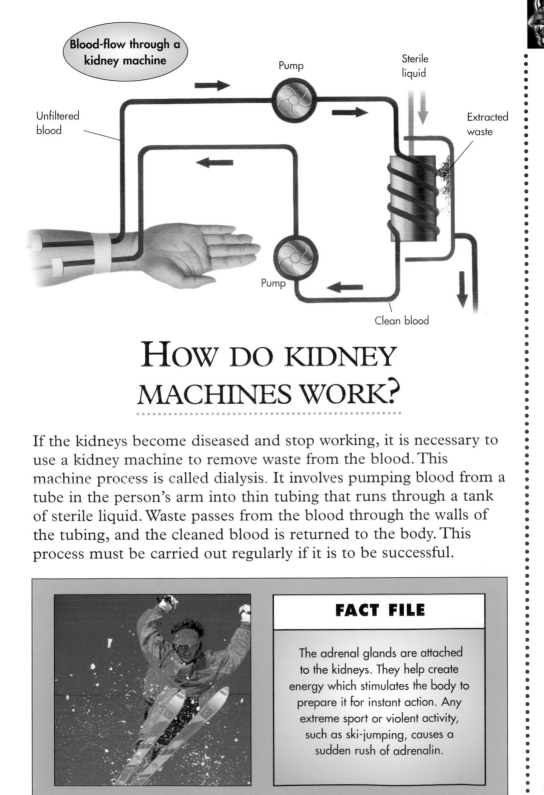

If the kidneys become diseased and stop working, it is necessary to use a kidney machine to remove waste from the blood. This machine process is called dialysis. It involves pumping blood from a tube in the person's arm into thin tubing that runs through a tank of sterile liquid. Waste passes from the blood through the walls of the tubing, and the cleaned blood is returned to the body. This process must be carried out regularly if it is to be successful.

FACT FILE

The adrenal glands are attached to the kidneys. They help create energy which stimulates the body to prepare it for instant action. Any extreme sport or violent activity, such as ski-jumping, causes a sudden rush of adrenalin.

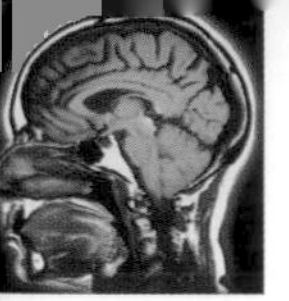

How does our body grow?

The most important forces that cause growth lie inside a living thing from the beginning. Thesc forces are called its heredity. The human body has stages of growth: embryo and foetus, infant, child, youth, mature adult and old age. People's bodies grow faster in the early weeks of life than at any other time. Even before the end of the first year, they are growing less rapidly. Through the whole period of childhood, they grow at a moderate rate. Then growth starts to speed up again. All human beings are much alike in their growth. But there are important differences. Boys and girls all follow the same general pathway of growth, but each one follows it in his own way.

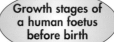

Growth stages of a human foetus before birth

4 weeks

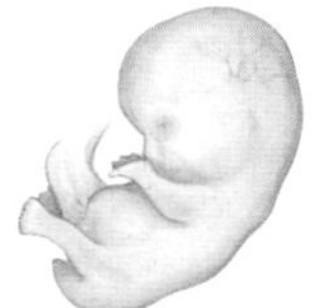

8 weeks

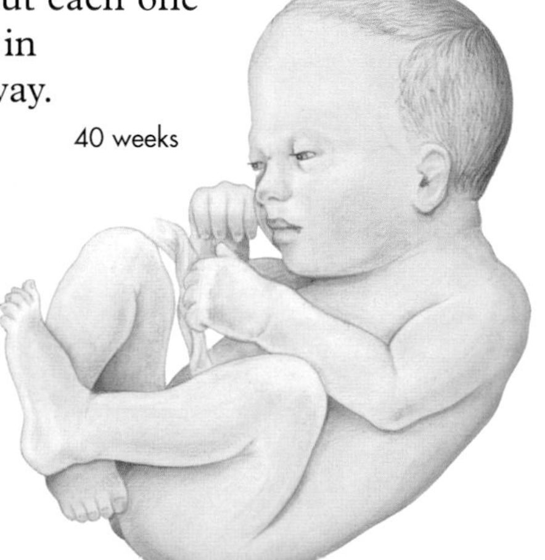

40 weeks

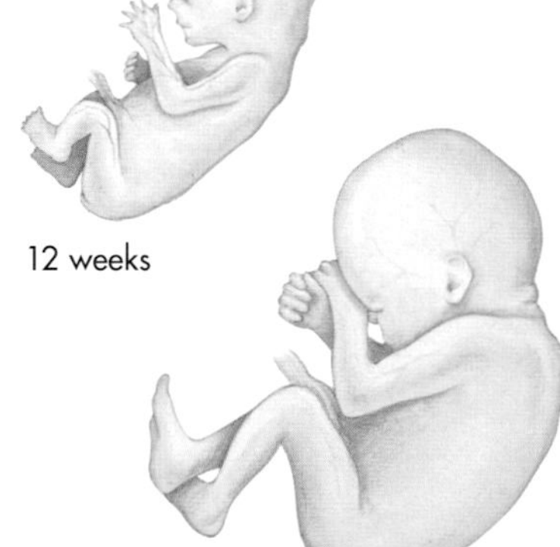

12 weeks

20 weeks

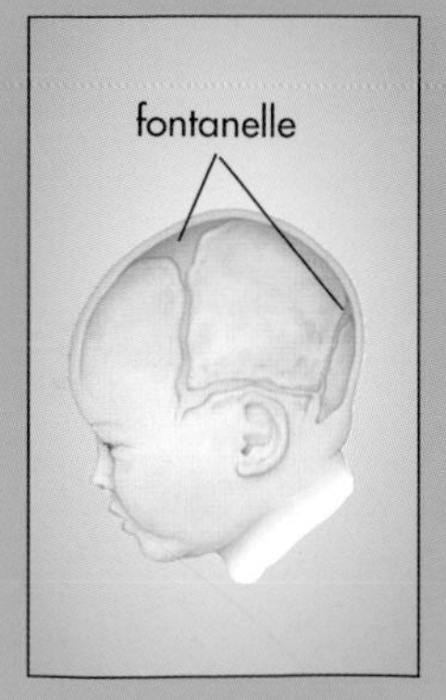

FACT FILE

The bones of a baby's head are not fully fused at birth, making the skull flexible enough to pass through the mother's birth canal. The bones eventually join, but a gap in the skull, called the fontanelle, may not close up for several months.

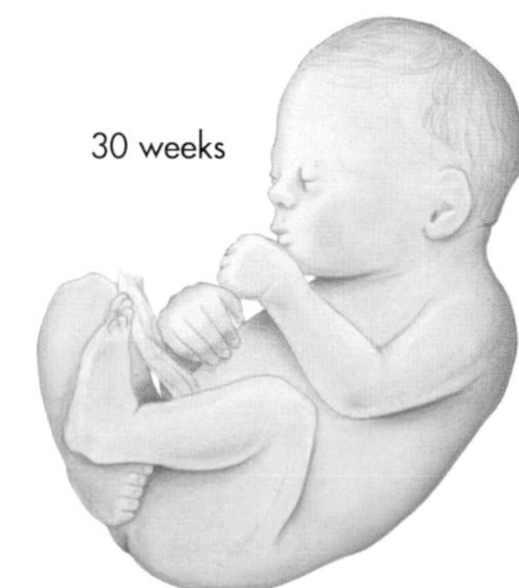

30 weeks

How do people age?

Ageing is a result of the gradual failure of the body's cells and organs to replace and repair themselves. This is because there is a limit to the number of times that each cell can divide. As the body's cells begin to near this limit, the rate at which they divide slows down. Sometimes the new cells that are produced have defects or do not carry out their usual task effectively. Organs can then begin to fail, tissues change in structure, and the chemical reactions that power the body become less efficient. Sometimes the blood supply to the brain is not effective. The brain cells become starved of oxygen and nutrients, leading to forgetfulness. For most old people memories bring great pleasure. Strangely, even though recent events may be forgotten, old people often clearly remember events that took place in their childhood.

FACT FILE

The skin becomes looser as people age. As skin sags it forms into wrinkles and creases because the fibres of collagen that normally provide support to the skin become weaker.

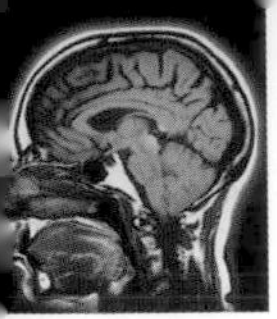

HOW DO MUSCLES WORK?

There are 639 muscles in the human body, each comprising around ten million muscle cells. Each of these cells is like a motor containing ten cylinders arranged in a row. The cylinders are tiny boxes that contain fluid and when a muscle contracts the brain sends a message to these tiny boxes. For a fraction of a second, the fluid in the tiny box congeals; then it becomes fluid again. It is this action that causes the muscle to move. When a muscle is stimulated into action, it reacts quickly – it may contract in less than one tenth of a second. But before it has time to relax, another message comes along. It contracts again and again. All these contractions take place so quickly that they become fused into one action with the result that the muscle performs one smooth, continuous action.

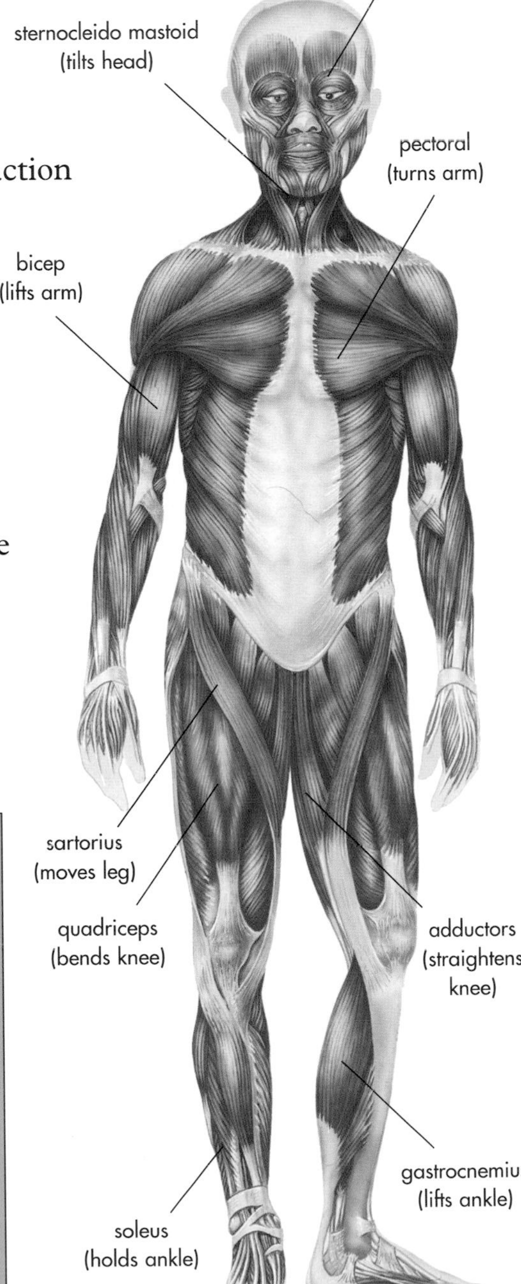

FACT FILE

When two muscles work against each other, they are always slightly contracted. This is called muscle tone. Active people tend to have better muscle tone.

How do joints work?

The human body has more than 100 joints. Some joints move like a simple hinge, such as those in the elbows and knees. Other joints move in all directions, such as the shoulder joint or the base of the thumb. Joints in the spine allow only a small amount of movement. The ends of most bones are covered with tough rubbery cartilage, which cushions them from impact as we move. Many joints are lubricated with an oily liquid called synovial fluid so they can bend freely. Synovial fluid is held in a bladder between the layers of cartilage on the ends of the bone. These lubricated joints can move freely and without friction.

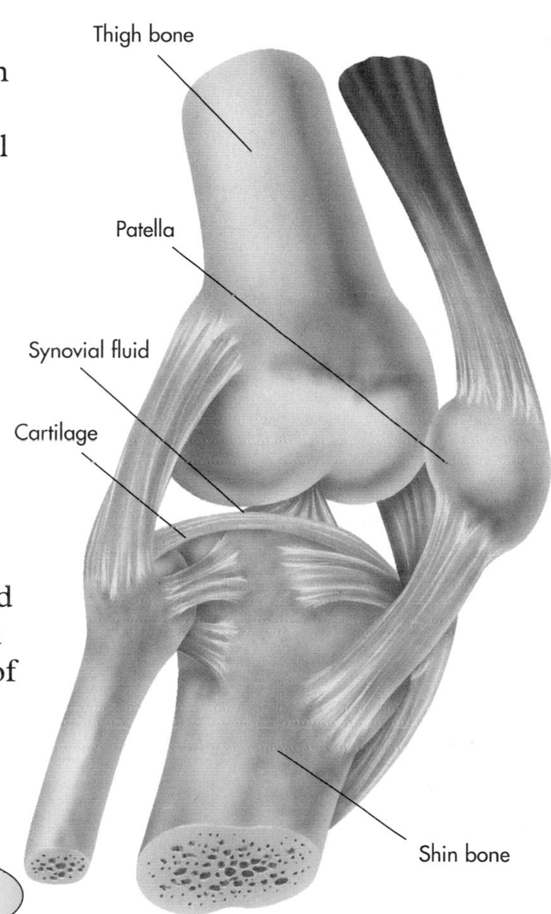

The knee joint

FACT FILE

Regular exercise improves muscle strength and endurance, and keeps the body supple. It can also improve your body shape and posture as well as strengthening your heart and improving your blood flow. It will generally make you feel much better and help you to sleep soundly.

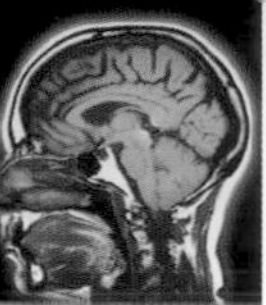

How do we digest food?

Taking food into our bodies is not enough to keep us alive and growing. The food must be changed so that it can be used by the body, this process is called digestion. In the mouth, the saliva helps break down starches. When food has been moistened and crushed in the mouth, it travels to the stomach. Here, the juices from the stomach wall are mixed with the food, helping to break down proteins into simpler forms to aid digestion. The starches continue to break down until the material in the stomach becomes too acid.

The materials in the stomach are churned about to mix digestive juices well throughout the food. When the food becomes liquified it enters the small intestine. In the first part of the small intestine, the duodenum, digestion continues. Juices from the pancreas and liver help to further break down the foods. The breakdown of proteins is finished here, fats are split into finer parts, and starch digestion is completed here. It is also in the small intestine that digested food is absorbed into the blood and lymph. Finally, in the large intestine, water is absorbed and the contents become more solid, so they can leave the body as waste material.

FACT FILE

Cholesterol is a fatty substance found in blood and some fatty foods. It can be deposited on the walls of arteries, making them more narrow. This reduces blood flow in the arteries and can cause blockages.

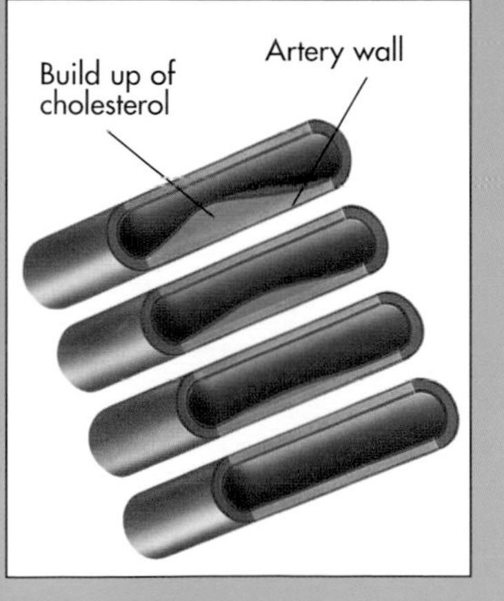

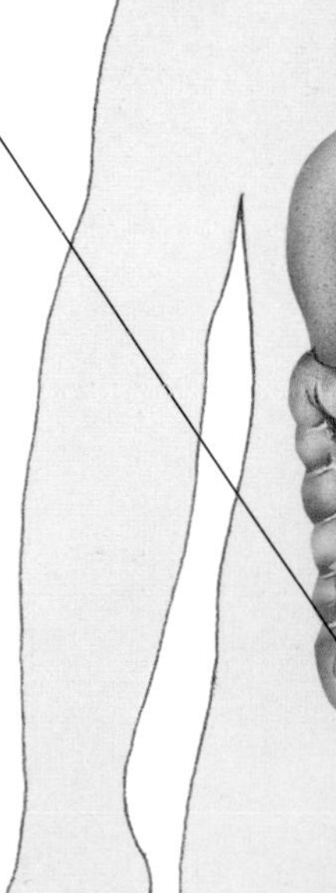

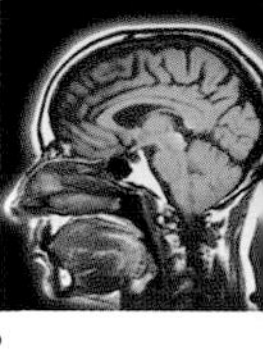

WHAT MAKES US HUNGRY?

When we need food, our body begins to crave for it. But how do we know that we are feeling 'hunger'? How does our mind receive the message and make us feel 'hungry'? Hunger has nothing to do with an empty stomach, it begins when certain nutritive materials are missing in the blood. When the blood vessels lack these materials, a message is sent to a part of the brain called the hunger centre. This hunger centre works like a brake on the stomach and intestine. As long as the blood has sufficient food, the hunger centre slows up the action of the stomach and the intestine. When the food is missing from the blood, the hunger centre makes the stomach and intestine more active. That is why a hungry person often hears his stomach rumbling.

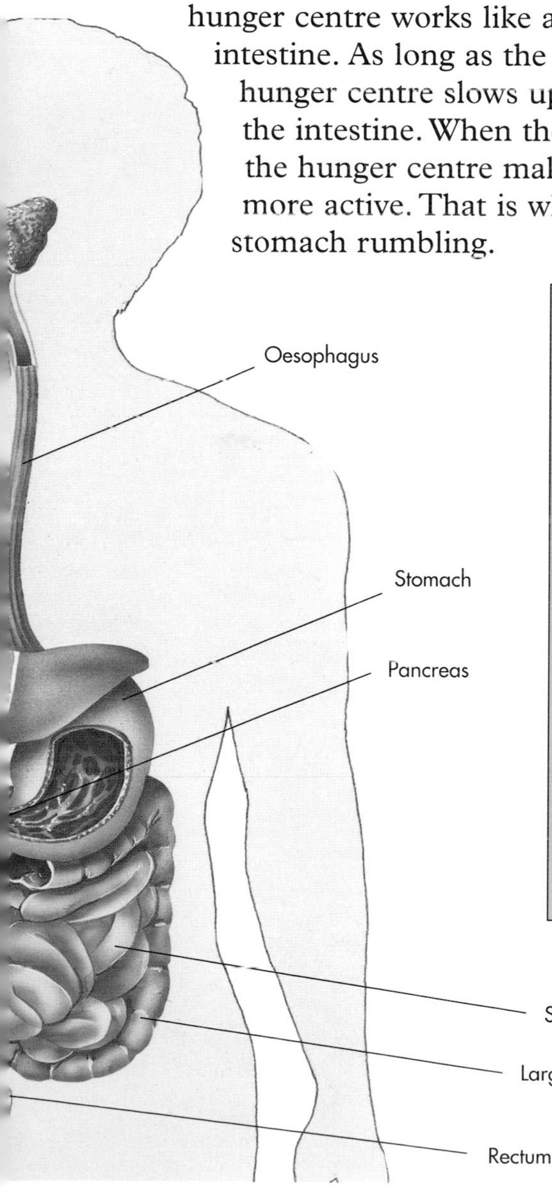

Oesophagus

Stomach

Pancreas

Small intestine

Large intestine

Rectum

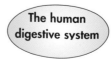

The human digestive system

FACT FILE

The thyroid is a large butterfly-shaped gland located in the throat. Its hormones accelerate the release of energy from food and help control our metabolism.

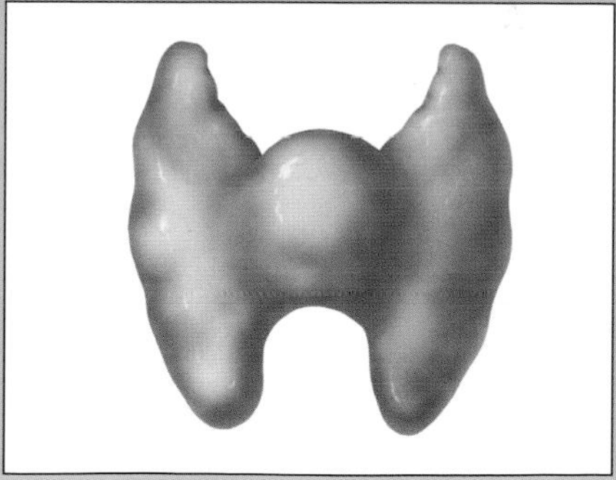

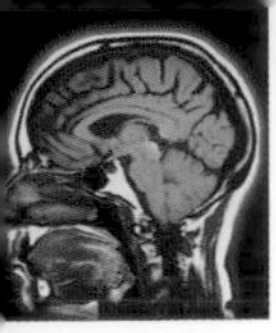

HOW DOES THE IMMUNE SYSTEM WORK?

Unlike most of the other body systems, the immune system is scattered throughout the body. The main defences against invaders such as bacteria and viruses are white blood cells called lymphocytes which are stored in the body's lymphatic system. This is a network of thin tubes running throughout the body. It contains a watery liquid called lymph, which it drains from the tissue and returns to the blood.

At intervals along the length of the lymph vessels are small lumps called lymph nodes. Lymphocytes are stored in these lymph nodes. Waves of lymphocytes are released when the body is injured, or when invaders are detected, and the lymphocytes swarm to the damaged area to protect and repair it.

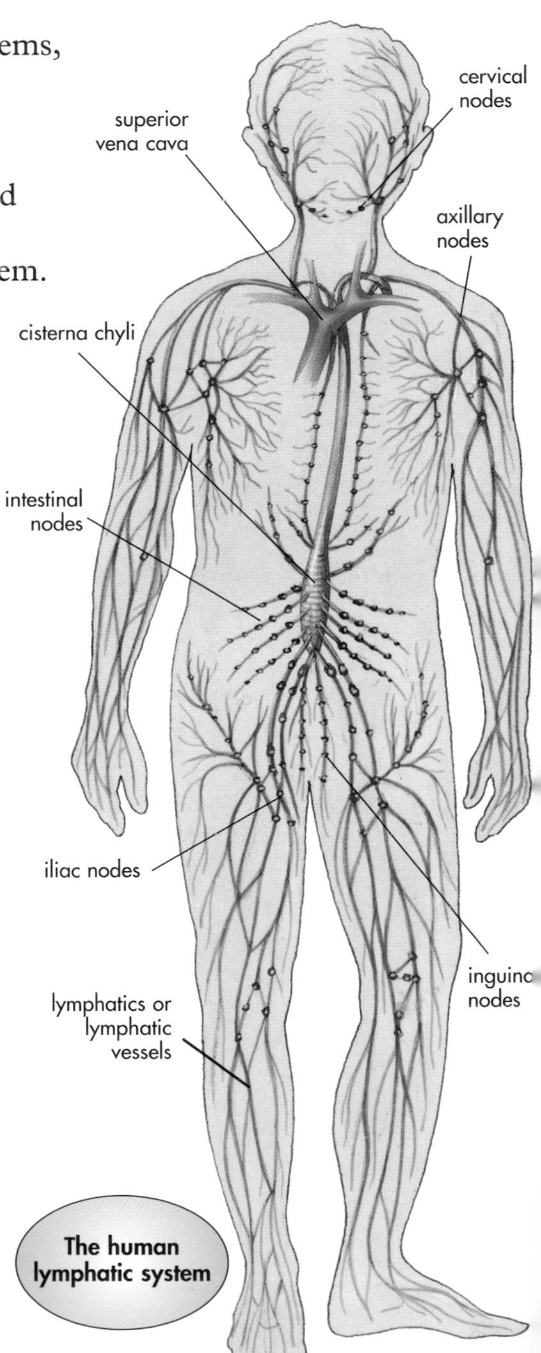

The human lymphatic system

FACT FILE

Newborn babies are fed on their mother's milk which contains special antibodies, helping to boost the baby's immune system.

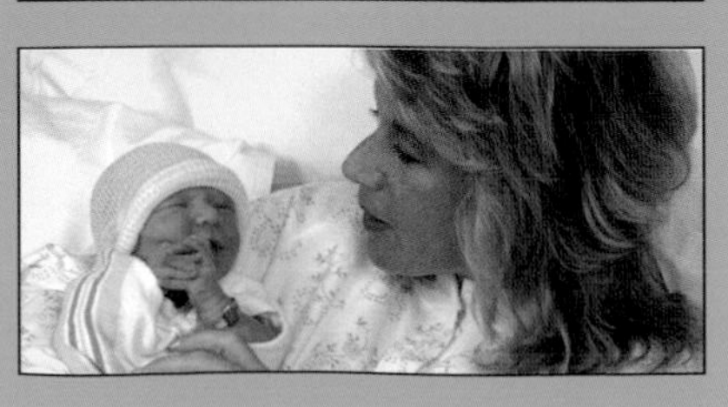

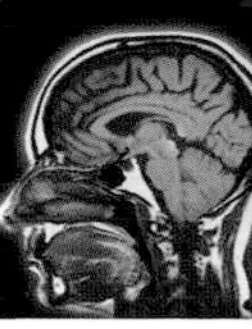

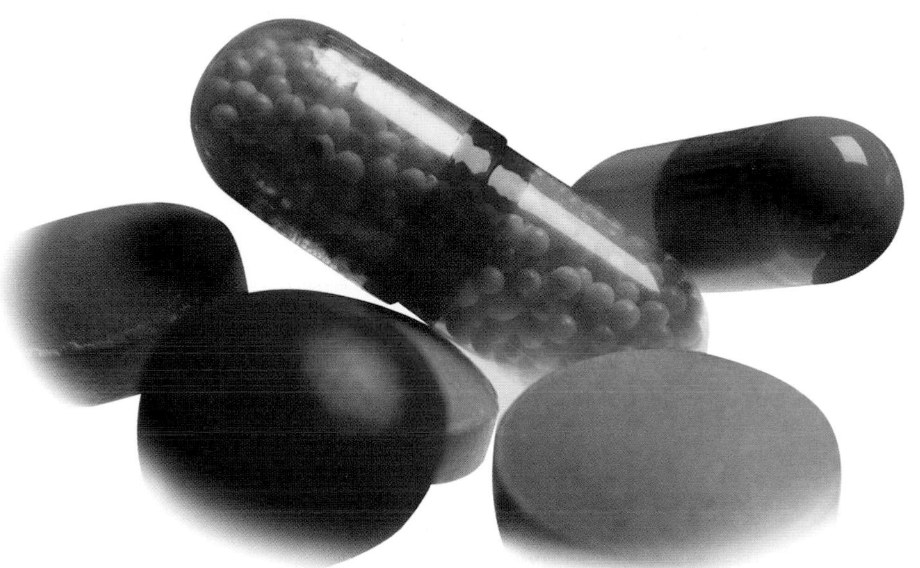

How do antibiotics work?

Antibiotics are chemicals that help your body to fight diseases caused by bacteria and fungi. They are manufactured naturally by some microbes in order to protect themselves, but are now made synthetically. Different antibiotics work in different ways: some stop bacteria reproducing by preventing the formation of cell walls, while others prevent them from absorbing nutrients. Antiobiotics have no effect on viruses.

Broad-spectrum antibiotics work against many bacteria and those that work against specific microorganisms are called selective antibiotics. Overuse of antibiotics in human medicine and in animal feed has led some bacteria to mutate into forms that are resistant, such as strains of tuberculosis and the so-called 'superbugs'

FACT FILE

As viruses invade a cell (1) they shed their outer layer (2) and take over the genetic material in the host cell in order to reproduce themselves (3). They begin to construct protein coats around the new viruses (4) and eventually burst out of the host cell (5) or leave it in an envelope (6) ready to infect new cells.

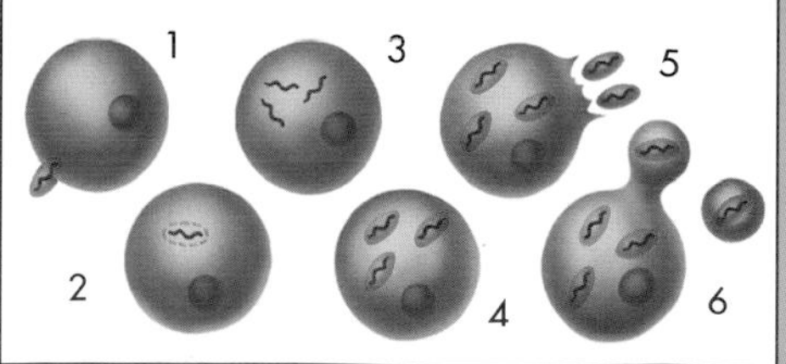

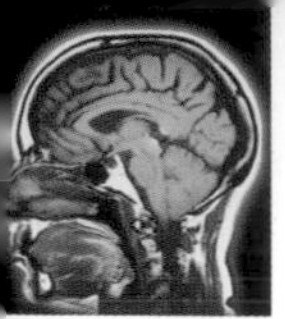

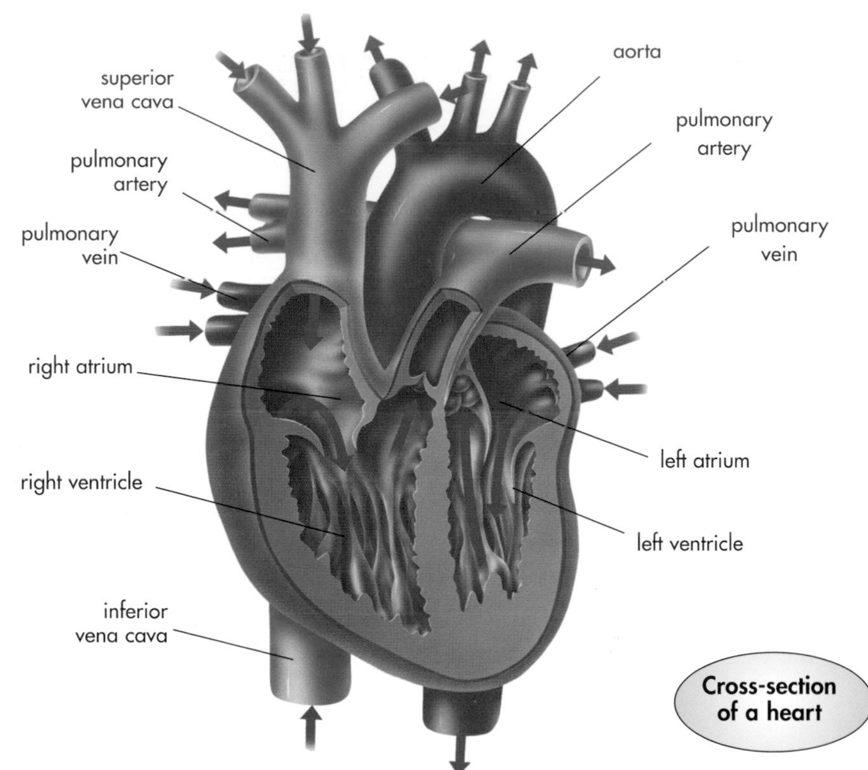

Cross-section of a heart

HOW DOES THE HEART WORK?

The heart is a fist-sized muscular organ that pumps blood around the body. It is actually two pumps that are joined together. At the top of each side of the heart is a thin-walled chamber called the atrium which receives blood that returns to the heart through the veins. Once the atrium is filled, it contracts and squeezes its blood into a much more muscular chamber called the ventricle. The ventricle contracts in turn and forces blood at high pressure along the arteries and off to the lungs or the rest of the body. A system of one way valves stops the blood from leaking back into the heart. The left side of the heart pumps blood to the lungs to collect more oxygen.

FACT FILE

An electrocardiogram, or ECG, measures the electrical signals that the heart produces as it beats. These signals change when a person suffers from certain medical conditions that affect the heart. They are measured by attaching wires to the chest near the heart. A doctor can study results as printed information.

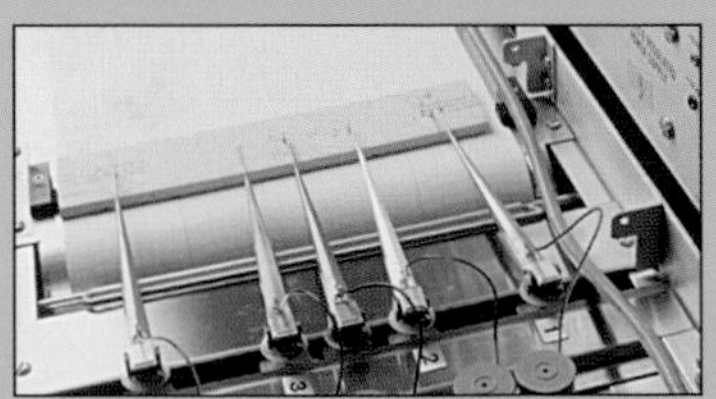

How does our blood circulate?

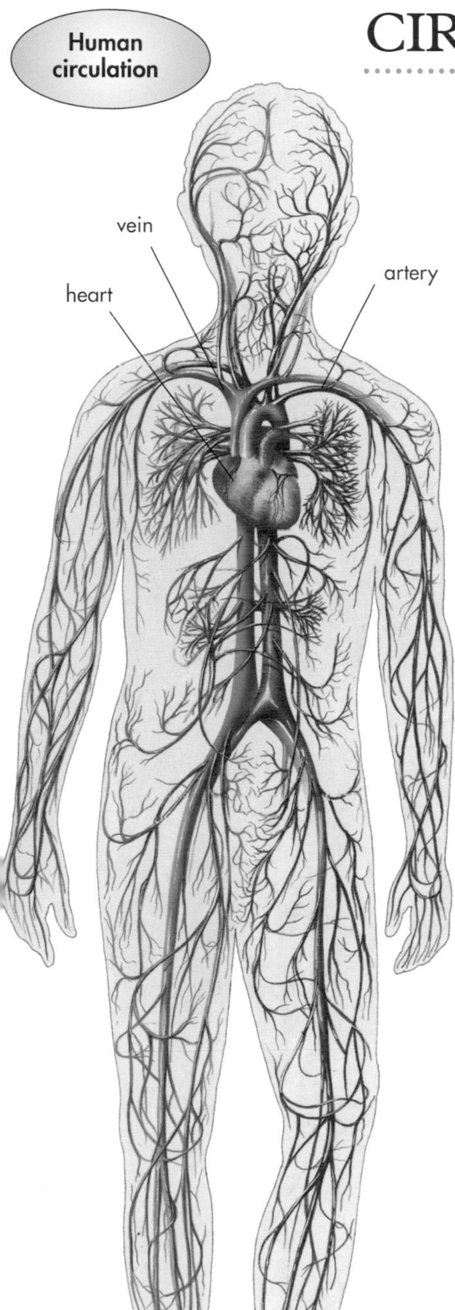

Blood is pumped in a continuous flow from the heart. Blood flows inside a network of tubes called blood vessels – arteries, veins and capillaries.

The blood in arteries comes straight from the heart and is pumped under pressure, so the artery walls are thick and muscular. Blood moves from arteries to veins through tiny capillaries, which are about one-tenth the thickness of a human hair. Capillaries are so narrow that red blood cells have to squash themselves up to pass through. Veins return blood to the heart, and because the pressure is lower, they have thinner walls than arteries.

FACT FILE

Each day the heart beats about 100,000 times – that's more than 36 million times a year! A woman's heart beats faster than a man's. The heart can pump 7 litres (14 pints) of blood around your body in just one minute; this heart rate can be increased by exercise.

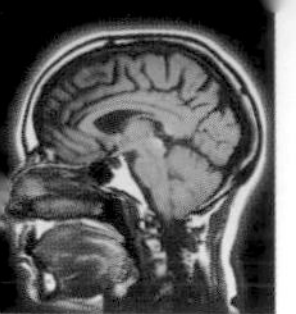

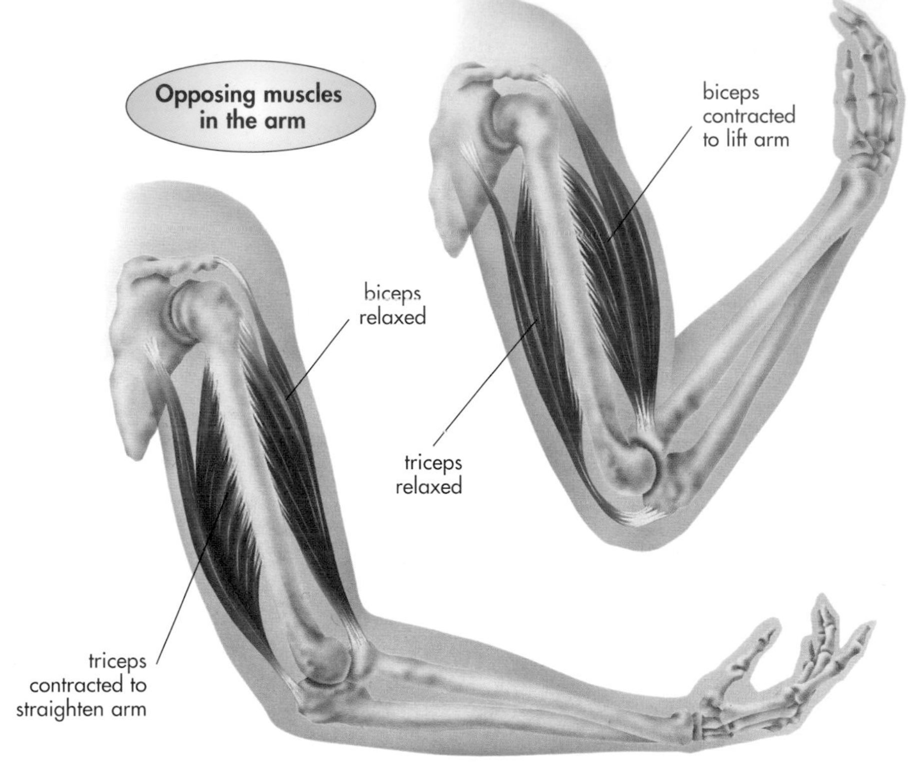

HOW CAN MUSCLES WORK IN PAIRS?

Muscles actually work in pairs. A muscle can only pull in one direction so it needs another muscle to pull in the opposite direction in order to return a bone to its original position. When you lift your forearm, the biceps muscle shortens to lift the bone. When you straighten your arm, the triceps muscle pulls it back again and the biceps relaxes. The same action takes place in your legs when you walk and run, and when you move your fingers and toes.

FACT FILE

Our metabolism is the sum of all chemical activity in our cells which break down the food we take in. Our metabolic rate increases with vigorous exercise, which means that we use the energy produced by food much more efficiently.

How do muscles respond to exercise?

Muscles are made up of long, thin cells called muscle fibres. But muscles differ in what they do and how they do it. When a muscle contracts, it produces an acid known as lactic acid. This acid is like a poison, with the effect of making you feel tired, by making the muscles feel tired. If the lactic acid is removed from a tired muscle, it stops feeling tired and you can go right to work again!

But, of course, lactic acid is not removed normally when you exercise and various toxins are produced when muscles are active. They are carried by the blood through the body and cause tiredness throughout the entire body, especially in the brain. So feeling tired after exercise is really the result of a kind of internal poisoning.

However, the body needs this feeling of tiredness so that it will want to rest. During rest, waste products are removed, the cells recuperate, nerve cells of the brain recharge the batteries and the joints replace their supplies of lubricant they have used up. So while exercise is good for the body and muscles – rest is just as important!

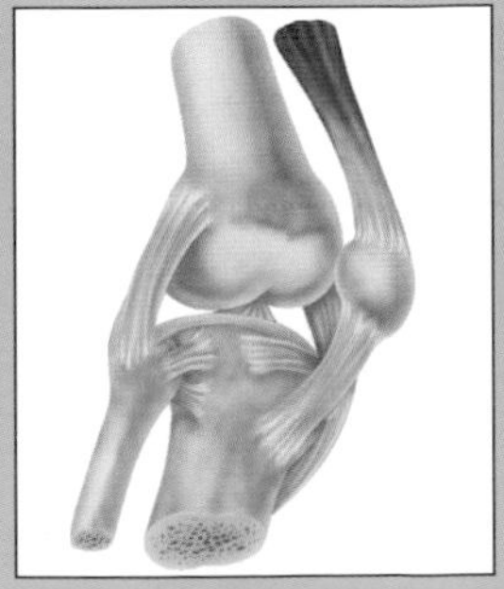

FACT FILE

The knee is a typical load-bearing joint. The ends of the bone are cushioned by a pad of cartilage to protect them from impact. Wear and tear is minimized by a lubricant called synovial fluid.

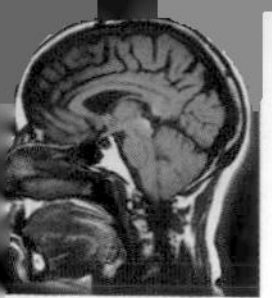

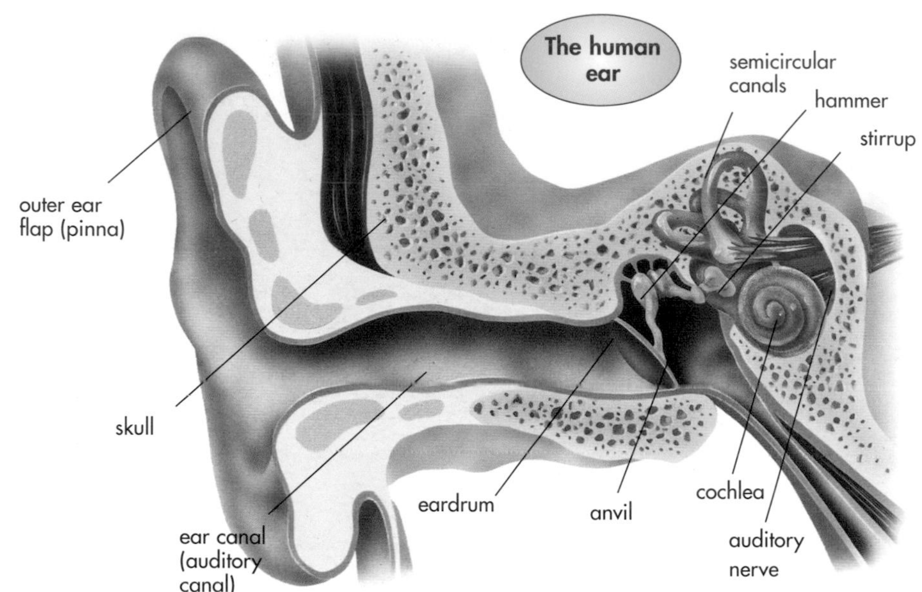

HOW DO WE HEAR?

The ear is made up of three main parts: the fleshy outer ear, the middle ear and the inner ear. Sound waves are funnelled by the outer ear through the ear canal to set up vibrations in the eardrum, a thick, tightly stretched membrane. The vibrations are transferred to the three tiny bones of the middle ear: the hammer, anvil and stirrup and through them to the fluid of the shell-shaped part of the inner ear, the cochlea. In the cochlea, hair cells detect the motion in the fluid and translate it into nerve impulses they send via the auditory nerve to the brain, which interprets the impulses. One common form of hearing loss occurs when the hair cells in the cochlea gradually lose sensitivity or are destroyed through exposure to loud noise as they cannot be replaced.

FACT FILE

Our ears and eyes are sometimes deceived. When we see lightning and hear thunder, it is never at the same time. This is because light travels faster than sound. Our ears always register the sound of thunder after our eyes have seen the lightning.

How sensitive is my hearing?

Sound is measured in decibels (dB). We can hear sounds ranging from a low rumble up to a high-pitched whistle.

The lowest sounds can sometimes be felt in the chest, while very shrill sounds may be so high that we cannot actually hear them. A bat's squeak is at the limit of what human beings can hear, and many people cannot hear this noise at all.

Our hearing is not very sensitive compared to animals such as dogs, who can hear very high-pitched sounds. Dogs are able to respond to a supersonic whistle that cannot be heard by humans at all.

FACT FILE

When you fly in a plane your ears may pop as the air inside them expands. If this did not happen your eardrum would burst as the air trapped inside your ear expanded.

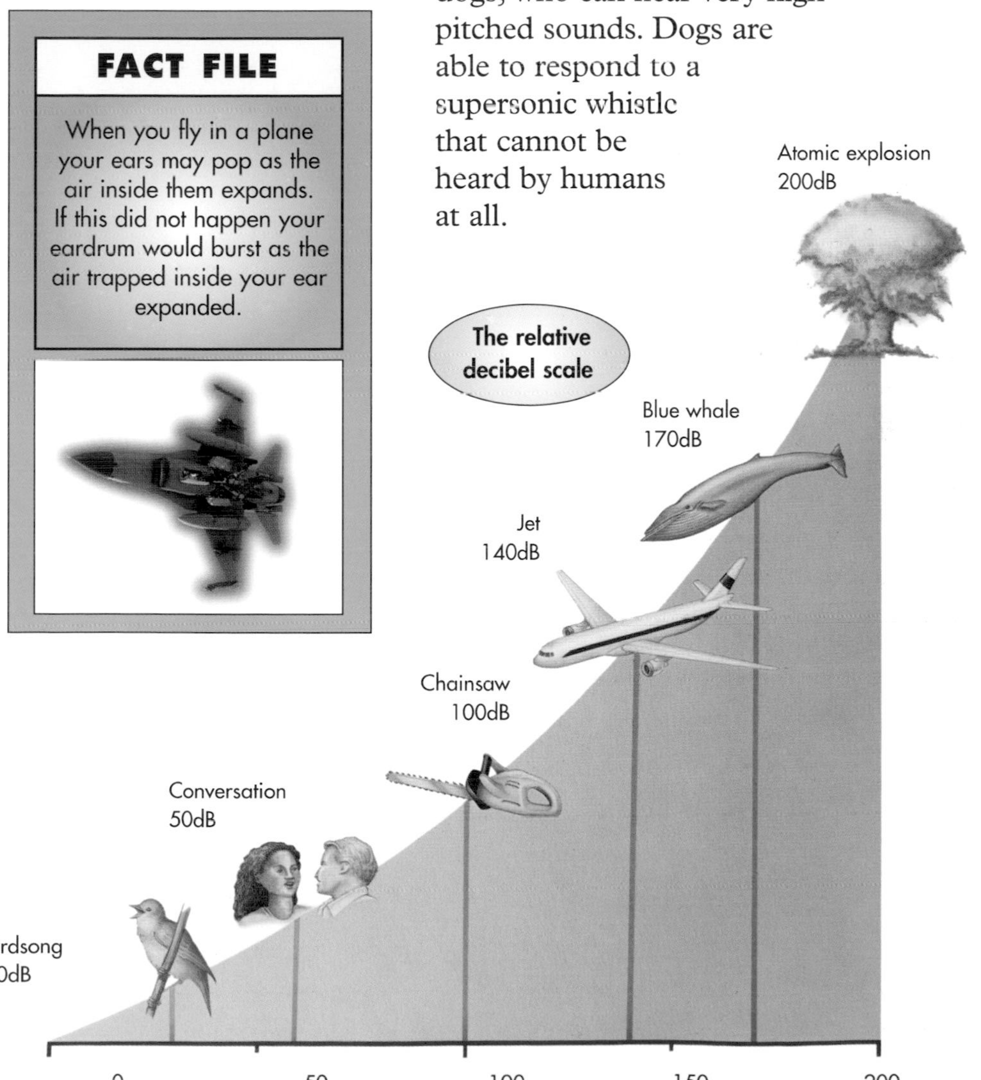

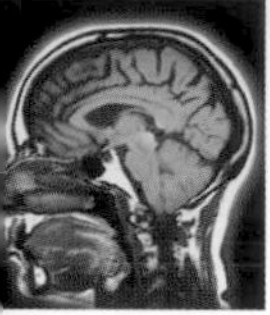

How do we taste things?

There are distinct regions on the tongue where the main tastes are recognised.

The tongue is covered with small bumps, called taste buds, that are grouped together in areas with different functions. These taste buds react to simple tastes and pass messages to the brain.

Taste buds on the tip of the tongue detect sweet tastes, and those at the back of the tongue detect bitter tastes. Groups of taste buds at the side of the tongue measure sour and salty tastes. The taste of any food is a combination of these four basic tastes.

These taste buds, or 'flavour receptors', transmit the different taste information as a message to the brain. It is the brain which processes the information and tells us what food is actually in our mouths.

We each have around 10,000 taste buds on our tongues. As we grow older our taste buds become less sensitive. This is one of the reasons why elderly people may no longer enjoy their food so much.

Hot foods taste better because the heat causes more of the pleasant smells to rise into the nose. These abundant smells contribute to the total taste of the food.

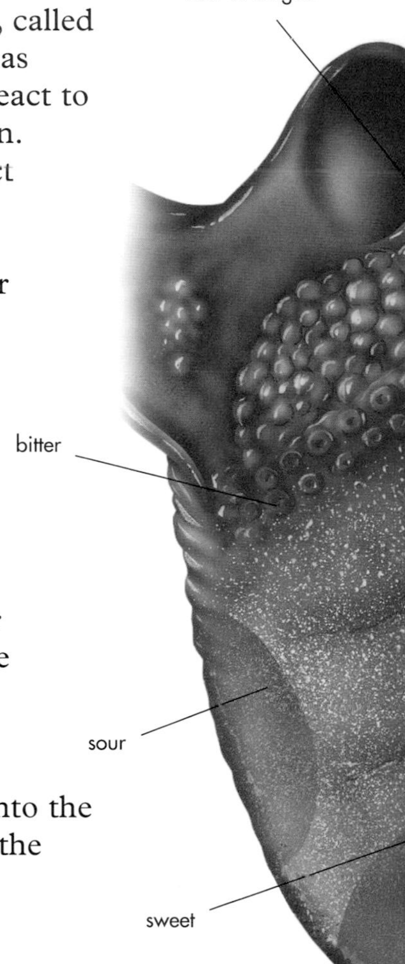

FACT FILE

Smells enter the back of the nose when you inhale. They also rise up from the back of the mouth as you eat, which is why smell is such an important part of tasting and enjoying food.

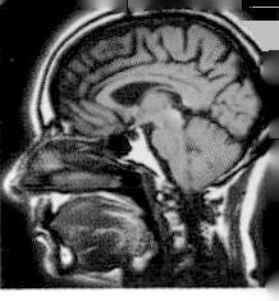

How similar are taste and smell?

When we taste food it is a mixture of both taste and smell. As you eat, tiny food particles drift up into the passages of the nose from the back of the mouth.

The smell of the food contributes to the simple tastes detected by the tongue. This explains why food tastes odd when we have a cold because the nasal organs become inflamed and therefore the sense of smell is temporarily smothered.

When we eat spicy foods, such as curry or chilli, mild pain also forms a part of the characteristic taste. If these foods did not burn the mouth slightly, they would not taste like curry or chilli at all.

If we were to lose our sense of smell, almost all taste sensation would be lost as well, meaning that we would not enjoy the taste of our food nearly so much.

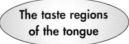

The taste regions of the tongue

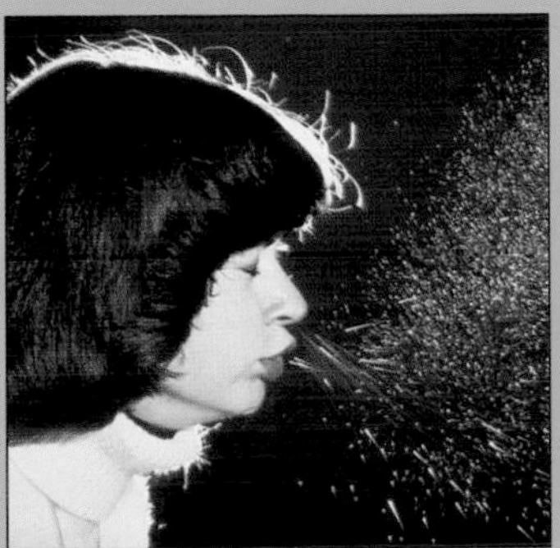

FACT FILE

When we sneeze a cloud of tiny water droplets is ejected violently through the mouth and nose carrying with it any microbes present in your lungs. This is how colds and influenza are spread.

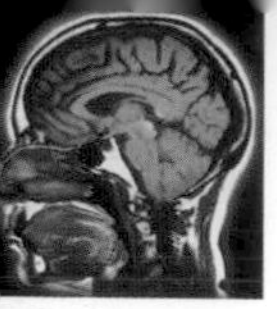

HOW IS THE EYE MADE?

The eye is very like a camera. It has an adjustable opening to let in the light (the pupil), a lens which focuses the light to form an image, and a sensitive film (the retina) on which the image is recorded.

Inside each human eye are about 130,000,000 light-sensitive cells. When light falls on one of these cells it causes a chemical change. This change starts an impulse in the eye fibre which sends a message through the optic nerve to the 'seeing' part of your brain. The brain has learned what this message means so that we know exactly what we are seeing.

The eye itself is shaped like a ball with a slight bulge at the front. In the middle is a hole called the 'pupil', which appears black because it opens into the dark inside of the eye. Light passes through the pupil to the lens. The lens then focuses the light forming a picture at the back of the eyeball.

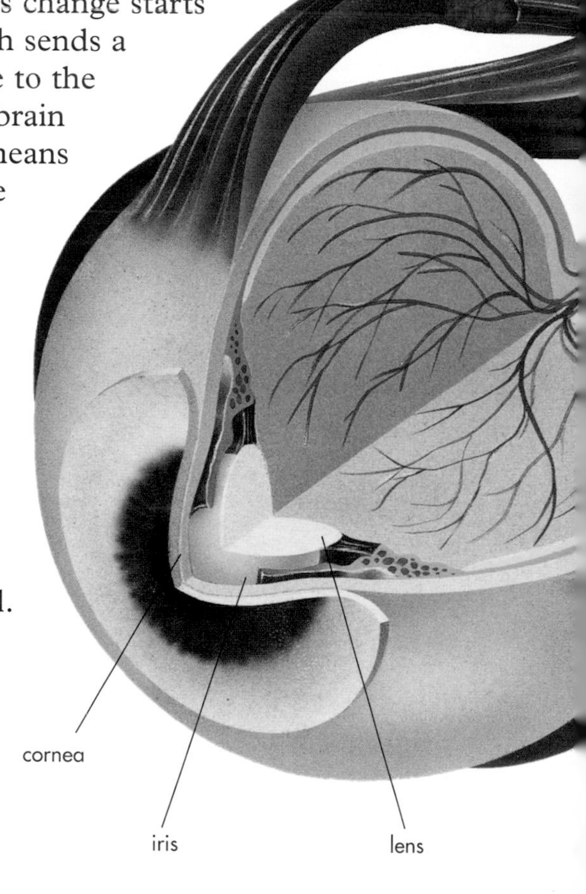

A cross-section of the human eye

FACT FILE

People with normal vision will be able to see two shapes in this diagram. Those who are colour-blind will only be able to see coloured dots.

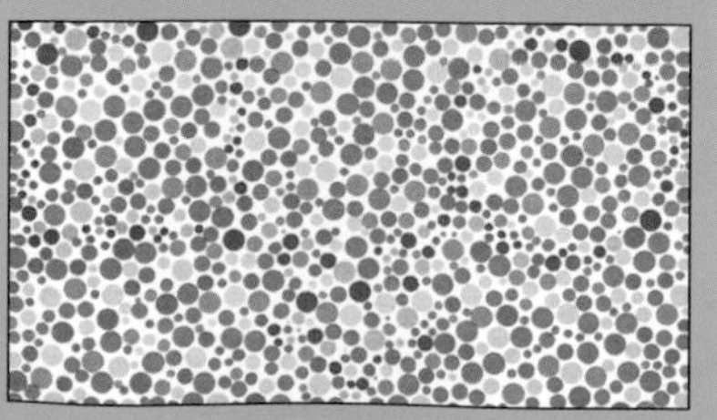

How do I see in colour?

The retina is filled with a layer of tiny cells called rods and cones. These cells contain coloured substances that react when light falls on them, triggering a nerve impulse.

Rods are slim cells that are responsible for us seeing in black and white. They work even if the light is very poor, seeing everything in shades of grey.

Cone cells give us colour vision. They contain different light-sensitive substances that respond to either red, yellow-green or blue-violet light. Together with the grey images produced from the rods, cone cells give you the coloured picture that you see.

Cones can only work in bright light which is why colours are so hard to see in dim light. You have 125 million rod cells and 7 million cone cells in each eye.

optic nerve

retina

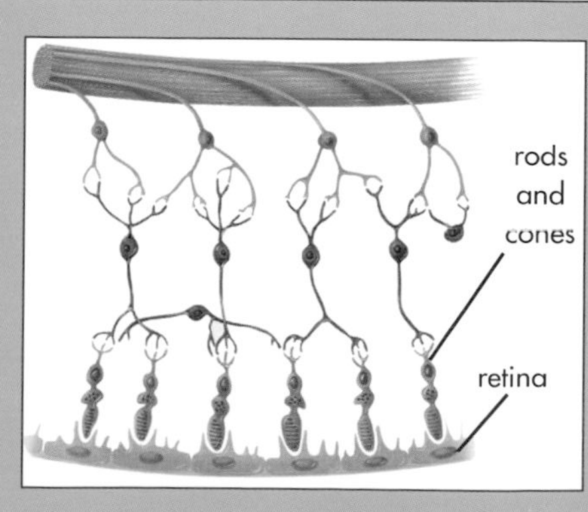

FACT FILE

The rod and cone receptor cells are buried in the retina. They are attached to nerves in order to pass on information as they detect light when it falls on them. The mass of rod and cone cells in our eyes is like an organised network of electrical wiring.

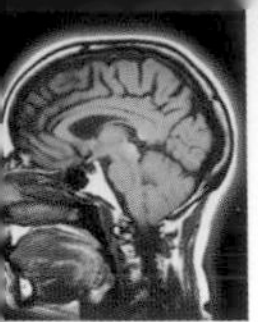

HOW DO NERVE IMPULSES WORK?

A nerve impulse is like a very simple message: either on or off. Because there are so many neurones which are connected to one another, this simple signal is enough to carry the most complicated messages throughout the whole of the body's nervous system. As a nerve impulse arrives at the junction between two nerve cells, it is carried across the gap or synapse by chemicals called neurotransmitters. These contact sensitive areas in the next nerve cell, and the nerve impulse is carried along.

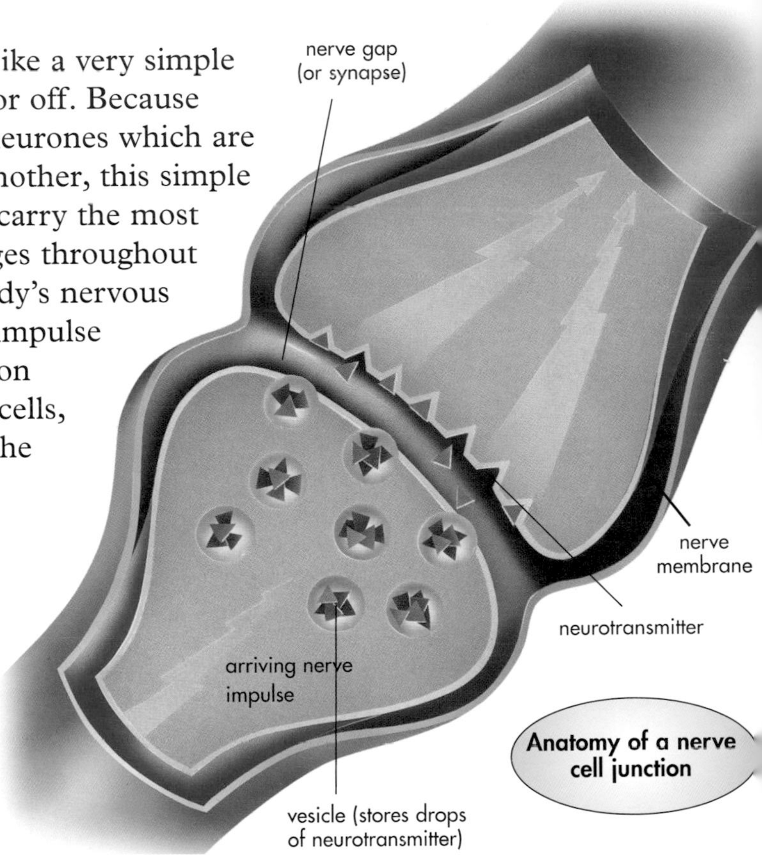

Anatomy of a nerve cell junction

FACT FILE

Scientists have produced maps showing how electrical activity in one part of the brain can cause a movement or other reaction. This mapping has been done during brain surgery. As there are no sense organs in the brain it is possible to operate on people who are fully conscious, without them feeling any pain. This enables doctors to know which part of the brain has been damaged after an accident.

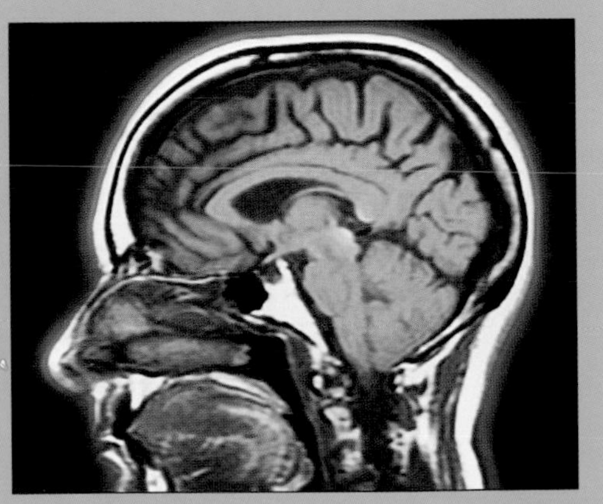

How are messages passed through the nervous system?

Nerve impulses that pass through the nervous system are able to jump from one neurone to the next. Inside the nerve fibre, the nerve impulse travels as an electrical signal. When it reaches the end of the long fibre, it jumps across to the next neurone by means of a chemical transmitter. This chemical is released from the branched ends of the fibre. As this transmitter substance contacts the next neurone, it starts another nerve impulse. This whole process is very fast, and nerve impulses travel along the largest nerve fibres at 90m per second.

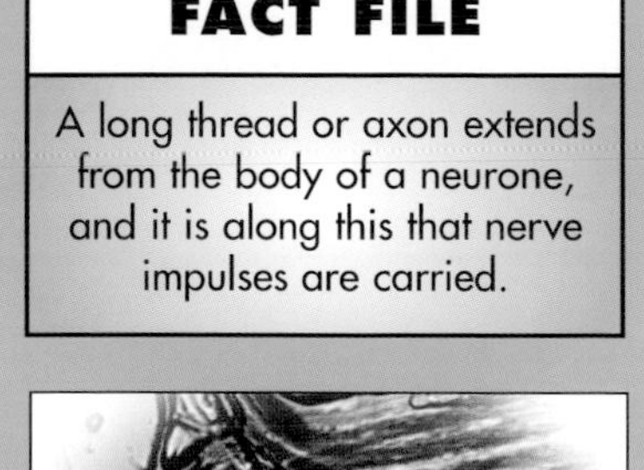

FACT FILE

A long thread or axon extends from the body of a neurone, and it is along this that nerve impulses are carried.

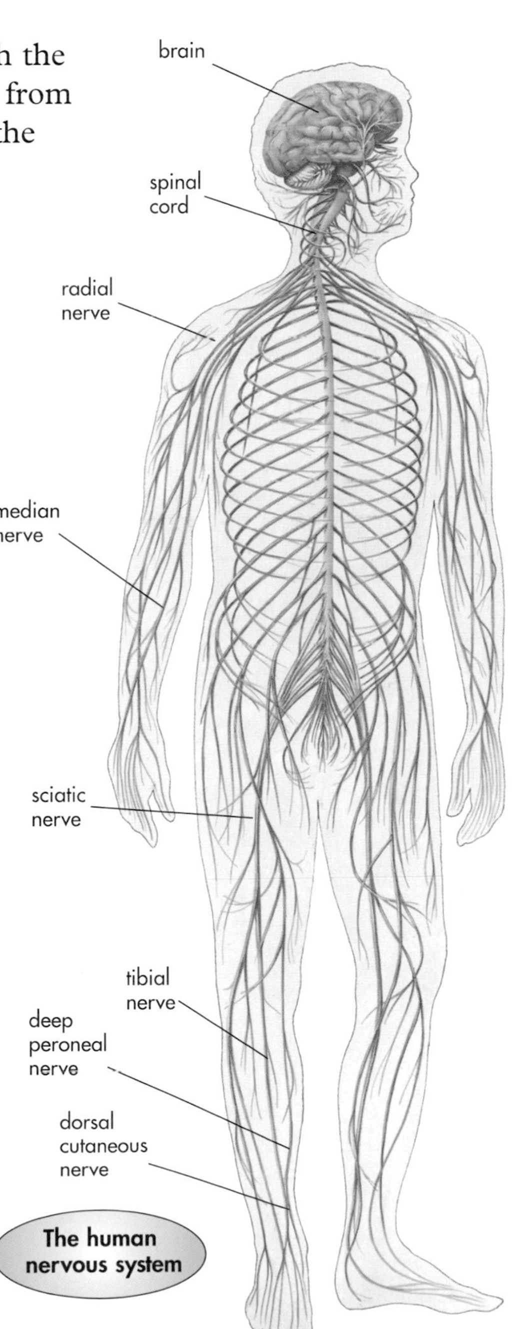

The human nervous system

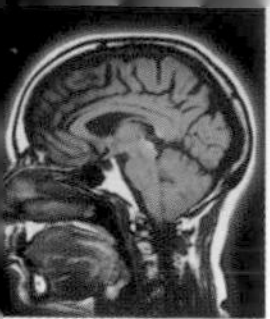

HOW DOES A BROKEN BONE HEAL?

Mending a broken bone is somewhat like mending a broken saucer, except the doctor doesn't have to apply any glue. This is produced by connective tissue cells of the bone itself. Bone tissue has an amazing ability to rebuild itself. When bone is broken, bone and soft tissues around the break are torn and injured. Some of the injured tissue dies. The whole area containing the bone ends and the soft tissue is bound together by clotted blood and lymph.

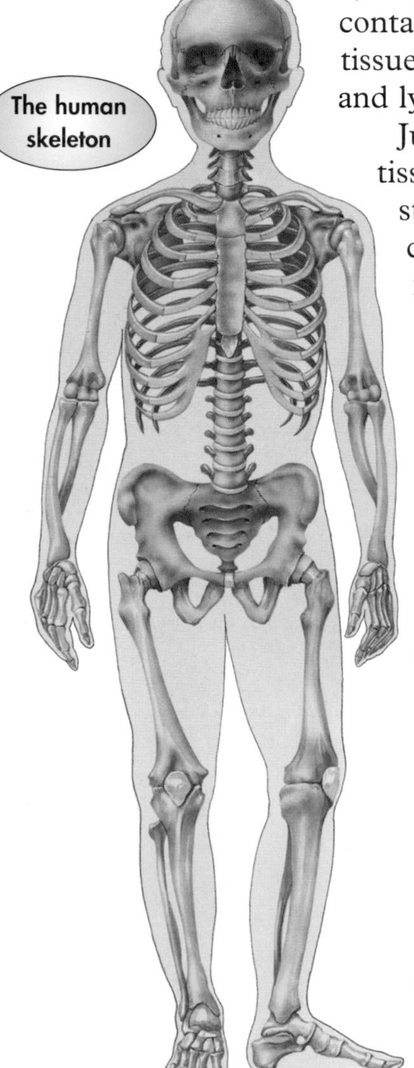

Just a few hours after the break, young tissue cells begin to appear – the first step in repairing the fracture. These cells multiply quickly and become filled with calcium. Within 72 to 96 hours after the break, these cells form a tissue which unites the ends of the bones. More calcium is deposited in this newly formed tissue, which eventually helps form hard bone, developing into normal bone over a period of months. A plaster cast is usually applied to the broken limb in order not to move the bone and keep the edges in perfect alignment.

FACT FILE

Constant use helps to keep the bones strong. Lack of exercise is one of the main reasons why elderly people's bones can become so weak and prone to easy breakage.

The human healing process

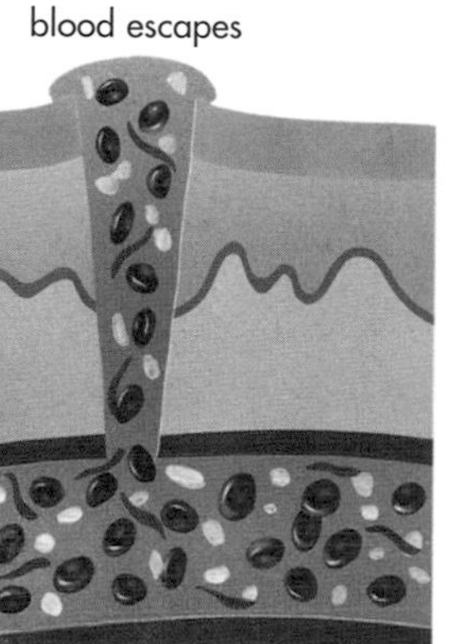

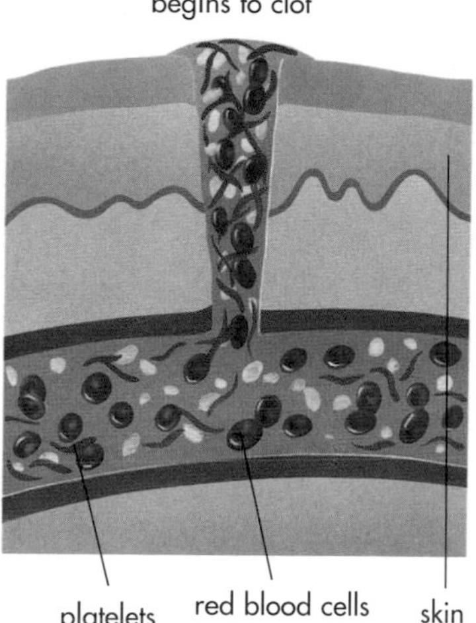

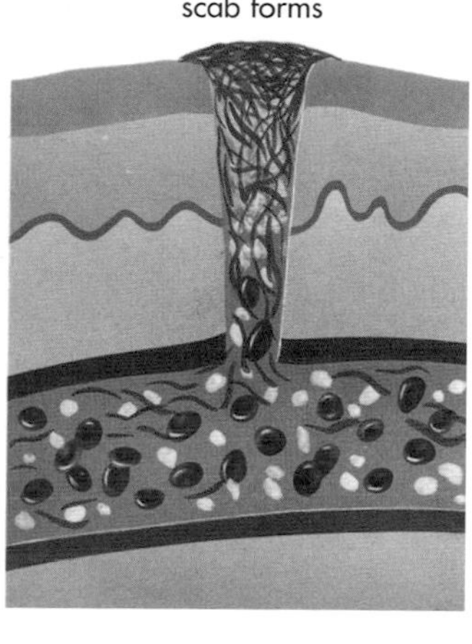

HOW DO CUTS AND GRAZES HEAL THEMSELVES?

When we cut or graze ourselves, the body is able to heal itself. When the skin incurs a wound, platelets in the blood congregate at the site of the wound to form a temporary clot. This usually happens as soon as a wound is exposed to the air. This quickly plugs the wound.

White blood cells gather around the wound site to kill invading microbes, helping to prevent infection.

New cells eventually grow into the wound replacing the damaged tissue. For a small cut or graze, this usually takes a couple of days. Soon the clotted material, which has formed a scab, falls off to reveal clean, new skin underneath. Sometimes we protect our grazes and cuts with plasters whilst our bodies deal with the repair.

FACT FILE

Cells need food, oxygen and water in order to survive. Food and water are supplied by the blood and other body fluids, which also carry away wastes. Blood also contains food substances and chemicals needed by the cell.

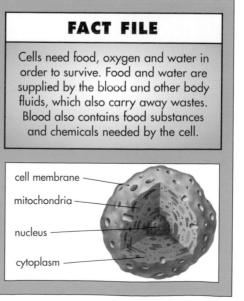

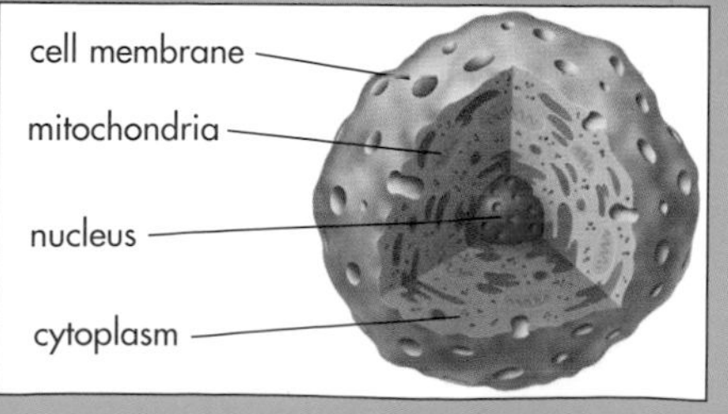

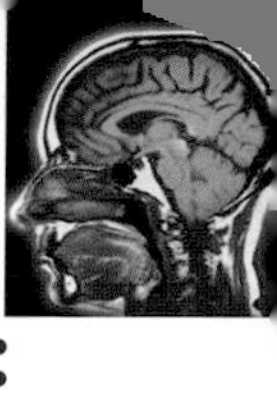

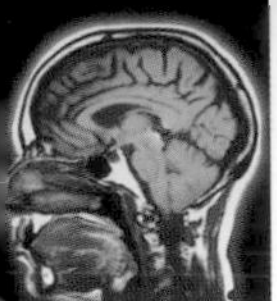

Straight hair grows from rounded hair follicles.

Hair growing from oval follicles will be wavy

Flattened hair follicles cause the hair to be very curly

How fast does hair grow?

For men who are becoming a little bald, hair doesn't grow fast enough! But in the case of a young boy, the hair seems to grow too fast! The rate at which hair grows has actually been measured and found to be about 1.5cm (half an inch) a month. The hair doesn't grow at the same rate throughout the day but seems to follow a kind of rhythm. At night, the hair grows slowly, but as day begins, this is speeded up. Between 10 and 11am, the speed of growth is at its greatest. Then the hair grows slowly again. It picks up speed between 4 and 6pm, and then the growing slows up again.

Of course, these variations in the speed of growth are so tiny that you cannot possibly notice them. So don't expect to stand in front of the mirror at 10am and be able to watch your hair sprouting up! Not all people have the same amount of hair. Blond people tend to have finer hair, but more profuse than dark people. Red-haired people have the coarsest and fewest hairs.

FACT FILE

Hair is straight or curly depending on the shape of the follicle from which it grows. Straight hair grows from completely round follicles, while wavy hair comes from oval follicles. Very curly hair grows from flattened follicles.

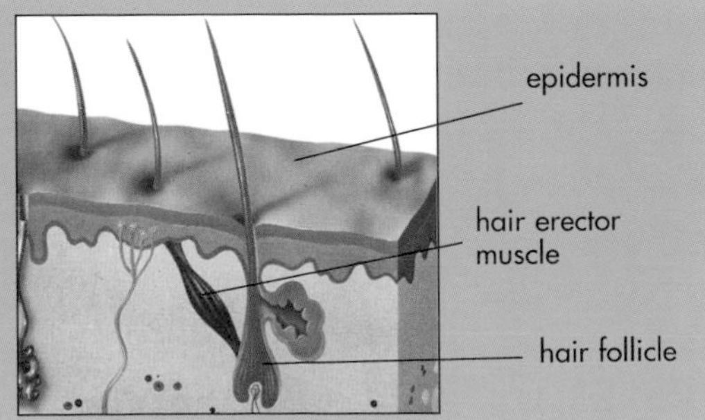

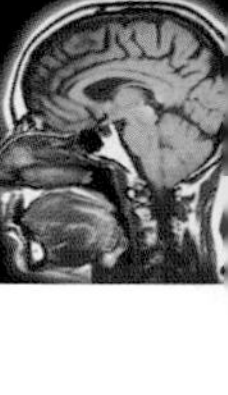

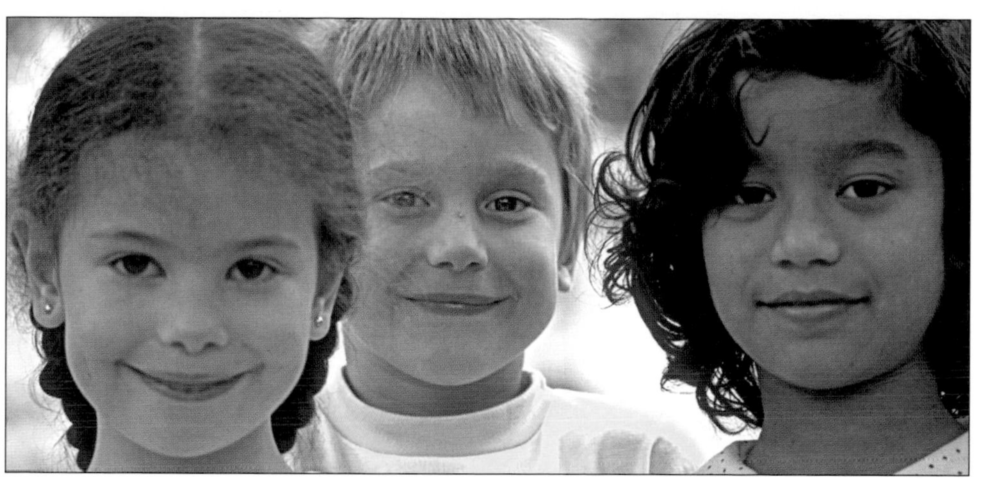

How does skin colour differ?

There are certain colour bases in the tissues of the skin called chromogens, which in themselves are colourless. When certain ferments or enzymes act on these colour bases, a definite skin colour results. The base colour of skin is creamy white. A yellow pigment is present in the skin, which is added to the base. Tiny granules of a substance called melanin are also present and although they are brown in colour, when there is a quantity present, they appear to be black.

A further tone is added to the skin by the tinge of red blood circulating in tiny blood vessels. The colour of a person's skin depends on the proportions in which these colours are combined.

Genetics plays a part too, but essentially, all the skin colours of the human race can be obtained by different combinations of these ingredients, which each and every one of us possesses.

FACT FILE

Skin develops extra melanin when it is exposed to strong sunlight. Tiny grains are produced in the skin cells and spread to produce an even suntan which helps protect against Sun damage. You can get sunburnt if you are exposed too long so always wear protective sun cream and cover your head.

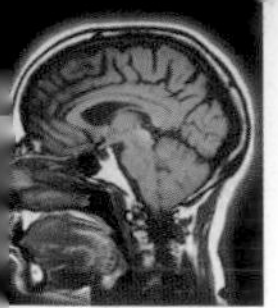

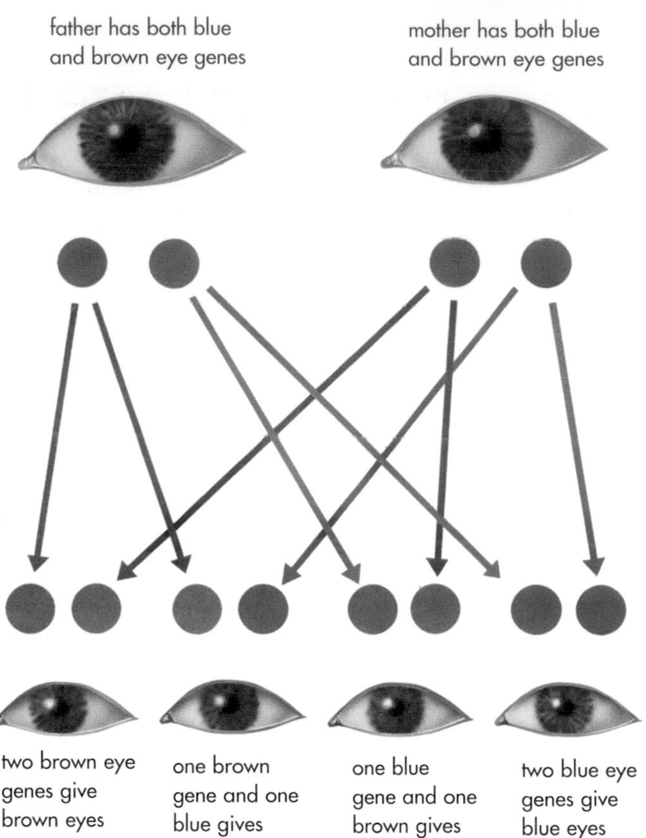
father has both blue and brown eye genes
mother has both blue and brown eye genes
two brown eye genes give brown eyes
one brown gene and one blue gives brown eyes
one blue gene and one brown gives brown eyes
two blue eye genes give blue eyes

How do we get brown eyes?

FACT FILE

This DNA molecule is shaped like a ladder twisted into a spiral. The pattern in which these are formed is the code built into the DNA molecule and groups of these forms genes.

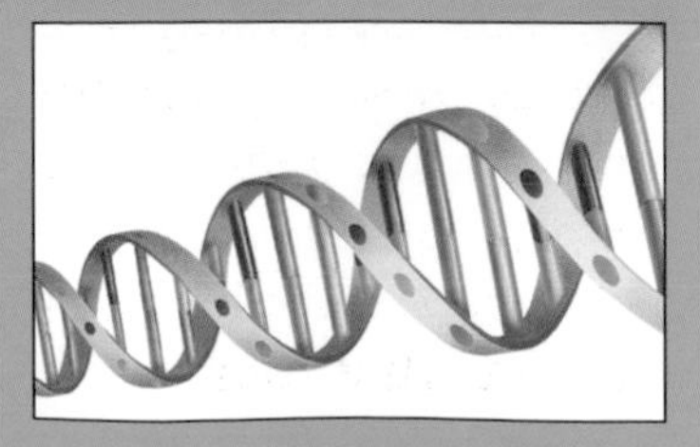

At fertilization, the embryo receives genes from both parents. However, not all genes are equal and the 'dominant' genes override the characteristics carried by the rest, which are called 'recessive'.

The gene for brown eyes is always dominant, so if a child receives one gene for blue eyes and one for brown, from each parent, the child will always have brown eyes.

It is possible for two brown-eyed parents to have a child with blue eyes, if each carries the recessive blue-eyed gene from their parents.

How do teeth differ?

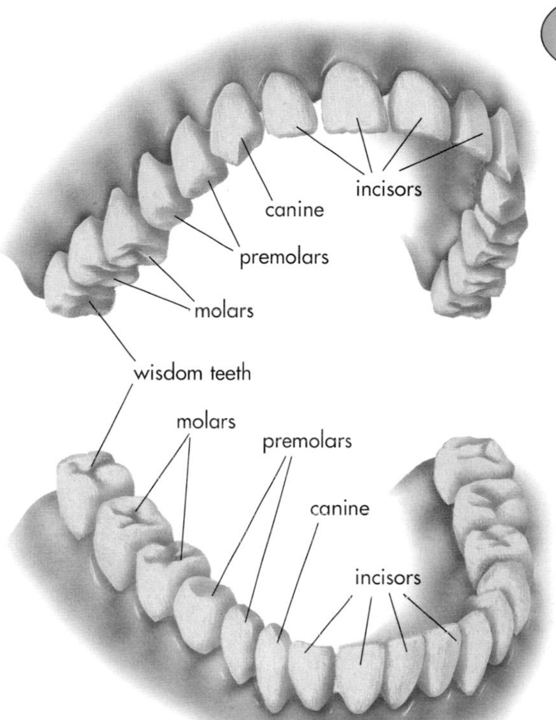

A set of human teeth

Your first set of teeth are called milk teeth. These teeth grow beneath the gum and have to force their way out. This process is called teething, and can be very painful. You only have 20 milk teeth.

Later another set of teeth form in the gum, under the first set. This second set of teeth gradually pushes the milk teeth out until there are 32 permanent teeth.

Teeth have different shapes so that they can carry out different jobs. Incisor teeth at the front of the mouth are flat and shaped like chisels. You use them to cut your food. The canines are the pointed teeth just behind the incisors, and you use them to tear food.

The back teeth, called molars and premolars, are flattened so they can grind the food into small pieces ready for swallowing. Wisdom teeth are a mystery as no-one has discovered exactly why humans have them and what their purpose is.

FACT FILE

Babies are usually born without teeth, as they survive on only milk for the first few months of their lives.

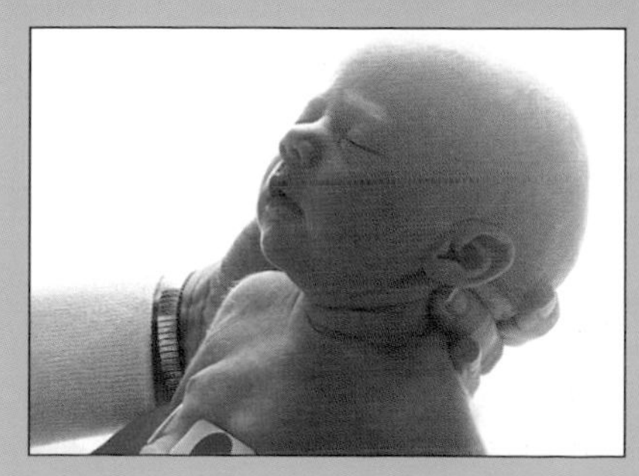

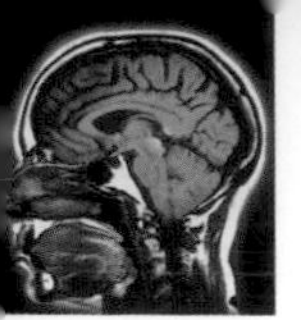

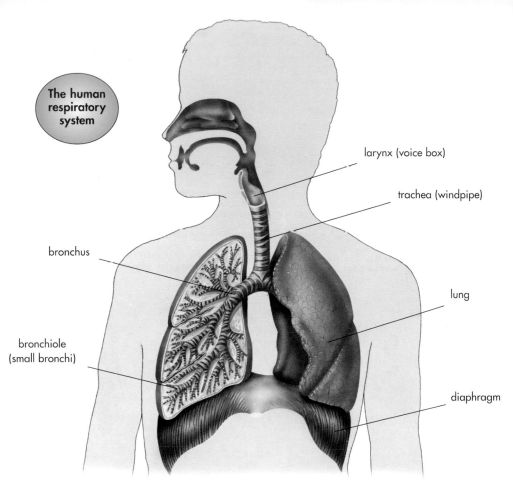

The human respiratory system

larynx (voice box)
trachea (windpipe)
bronchus
lung
bronchiole (small bronchi)
diaphragm

HOW DO WE BREATHE?

When we breathe we draw air in through the nose and mouth and into the lungs. Air travels down a tube called the trachea that forks into other tubes called bronchi, which lead into the lungs. From here the air passes into a series of smaller air passages and eventually into tiny air sacs, or bladders, called alveoli. Oxygen is absorbed through the thin walls of the alveoli into the blood and carbon dioxide is released to be breathed out as a waste product.

FACT FILE

Smoking damages the natural cleaning mechanism of the lungs and also poisons the cells that line the lungs. Regular smokers often suffer from lung diseases like bronchitis.

How do we smell?

Our sense of smell is probably the oldest of the five senses. As you breathe in, air passes through a cavity behind the nose which contains patches of millions of smell receptors called olfactory cells. Sensory hairs stick out from the surface of these receptor cells and these hairs detect smells and pass information along nerve fibres to the brain.

Substances that you can recognize as having an odour dissolve in the layer of mucus covering the sensory cells, stimulating them to produce a signal. Most people are able to detect about 4,000 different smells. However, people whose work is based on their ability to smell, such as chefs, perfume makers and wine tasters, can distinguish as many as 10,000 different smells.

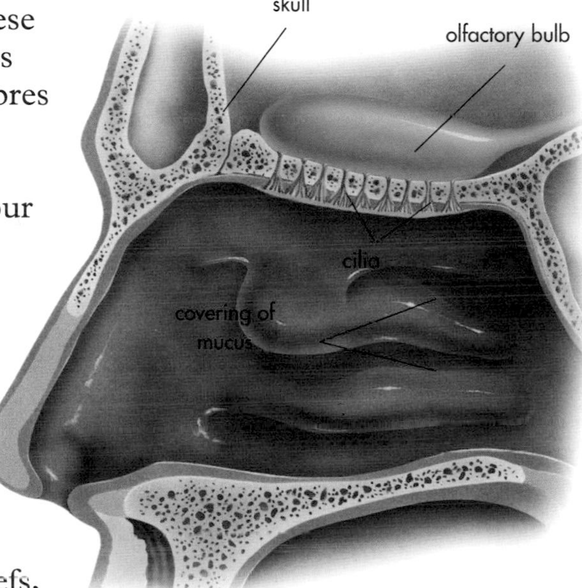

The nasal passages

FACT FILE

The sense of smell in dogs is very highly developed. Some dogs are able to identify and follow the smell of a person's perspiration even though it may be several days old. These 'sniffer' dogs are often used to find people buried under an avalanche or in houses destroyed by earthquakes. They are also trained to sniff out drugs and work in conjunction with the police.

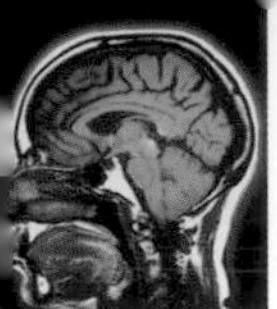

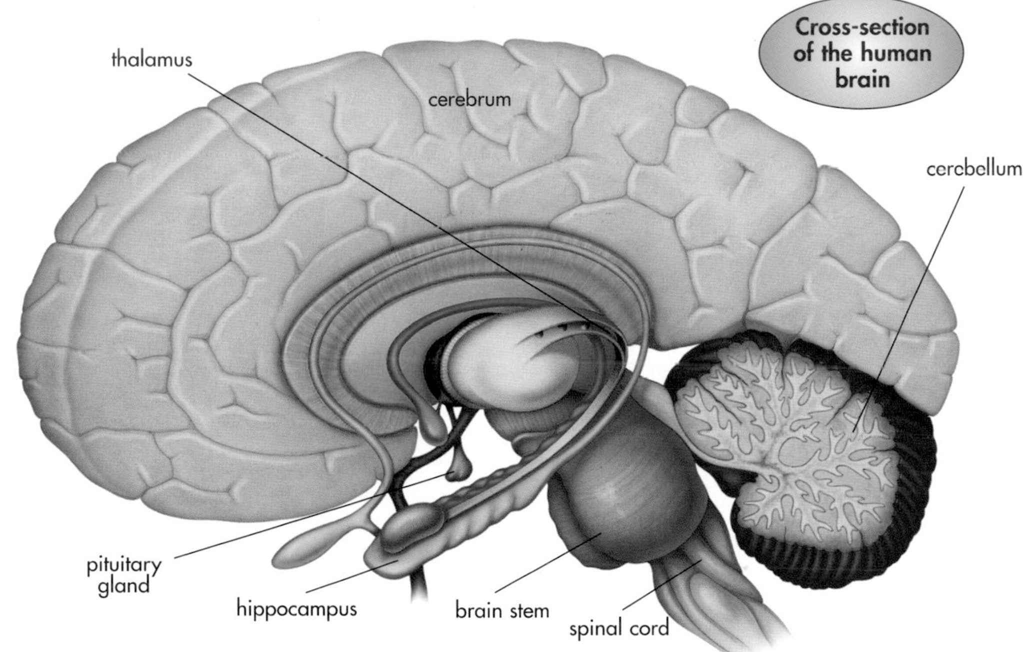

HOW DOES THE BRAIN WORK?

The brain is the body's control centre. It coordinates all the messages that pass through the nervous system, giving us the ability to learn, reason and feel. It also controls the body's automatic functions such as breathing, heartbeat, digestion, growth and blood pressure.

The brain is divided into three main regions each with a different function. The large part at the top is the cerebrum, where most of our thinking, reasoning and memory is controlled. The cerebellum is a smaller area at the back where both accurate movement and coordination are controlled. The brain stem is a small region at the base where most of our automatic body functions are processed and controlled.

FACT FILE

Each side of the brain controls the opposite side of the body. Usually the left side controls speaking, writing and logical thought, while the right controls artistic abilities. This musician is using the right side of his brain.

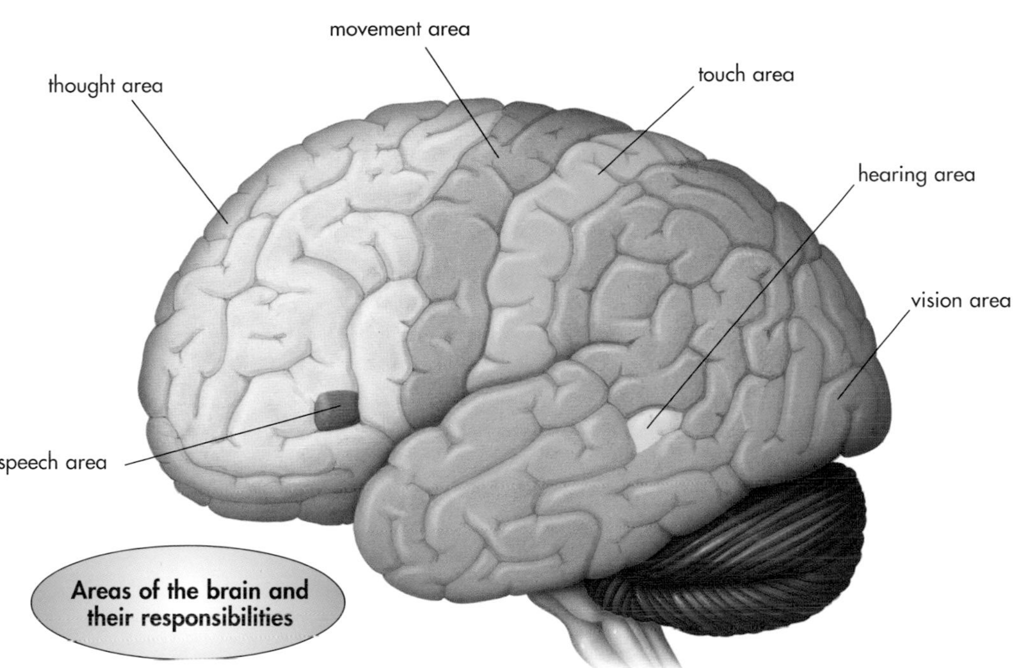

HOW DOES MY MEMORY WORK?

FACT FILE

The sense of smell has powerful effects in retrieving memories. Often a smell, like the burning of a bonfire, can suddenly trigger a memory from many years ago.

Memory is the ability to store things that you experience and learn, ready for use in the future. Some things are remembered easily, such as dramatic events in our life. However, more ordinary things need to be rehearsed in the mind several times before they 'stick'.

There are three different ways of storing memory. Sensory memory, which is very brief, tells you what is happening around you and allows you to move without bumping into things. Short-term memory, which lasts for only about 30 seconds, and allows you to remember a phone number and dial it, but after a minute or so it will vanish. Finally long-term memory, for things that you have carefully memorized and learned.

The Natural World

Contents

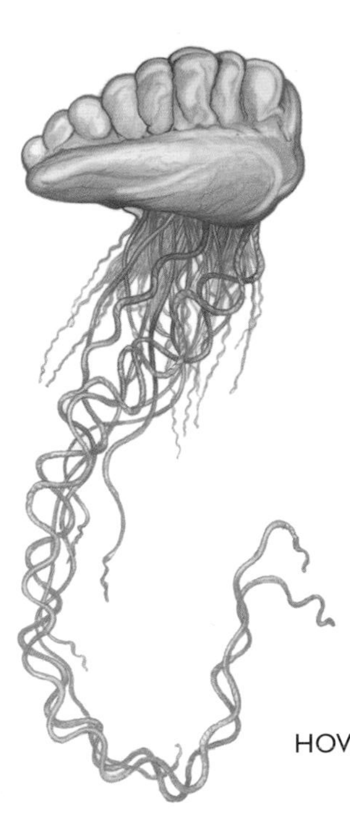

How do trees grow ?

Trees need nourishment to grow. They obtain water and minerals from the soil and carbon dioxide from the air. Chlorophyll in their leaves harnesses the energy of the sun's rays to make sugar, starch and cellulose.

Between the wood of a tree and its bark, there is a thin band of living cells called the cambium. New cells are formed here; those which develop on the wood side of the cambium grow as wood and those on the bark side mature as bark. In this way, as the tree grows older it increases in diameter.

Trees grow in height as well as in diameter. At the end of each branch or twig there is a group of living cells. During periods of active growth, these cells multiply to form new leaves and stem length.

A cross section of a tree shows alternating bands of light and dark wood. The lighter bands have bigger cells and were formed in spring; the dark bands consist of small, tightly packed cells made in the autumn.

FACT FILE

Trees are the largest living organisms on Earth. The biggest tree, the Californian giant redwood, is nearly 100m high and has a trunk that is 11m thick. The total weight of one of these trees is more than 2,000 tonnes. These ancient trees have very few branches and leaves, and are often scarred by fire and lightning strikes.

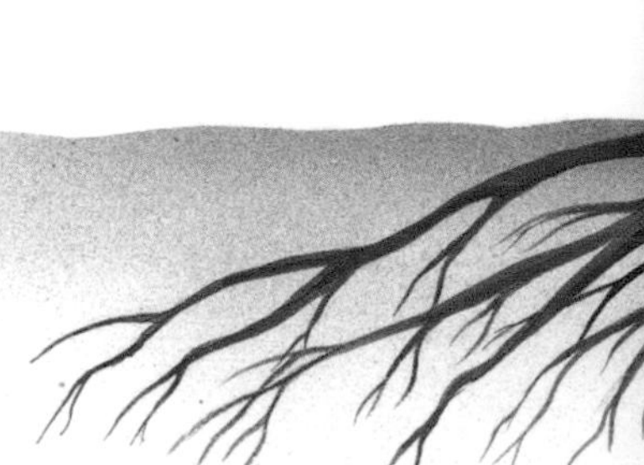

HOW DO LEAVES GROW?

Green plants and trees have to manufacture their food. The leaves are the food factories for plants and trees.

Leaves of fruit trees manufacture food that helps them to make fruit. For example, peaches are sweet. So peach tree leaves make sugar. By a process called photosynthesis, leaves manufacture sugar from the water and carbon dioxide. Leaves are able to carry out these processes because of chloroplasts, which contain chlorophyll, inside their cells.

The roots of a plant or tree take water from the soil that eventually reaches the veins of the leaves. These veins carry back food the leaves have made. Carbon dioxide enters the tree's cells through the leaves and when the sun is shining, leaves manufacture the sugar. In doing so, oxygen is produced which exits the tree through its leaves.

Leaves give off water, too. Part of the water taken in through the root is used to make sugar. The rest is given off through the surface of the leaves.

FACT FILE

Energy from the Sun evaporates water from the leaf surface, through the stomata. This reduces pressure in the channels carrying water from the roots, so more water is drawn up the stem.

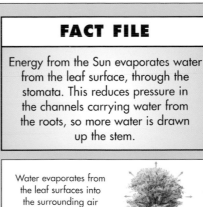

Water evaporates from the leaf surfaces into the surrounding air
More water is taken up by the roots from the soil

How do you define an amphibian?

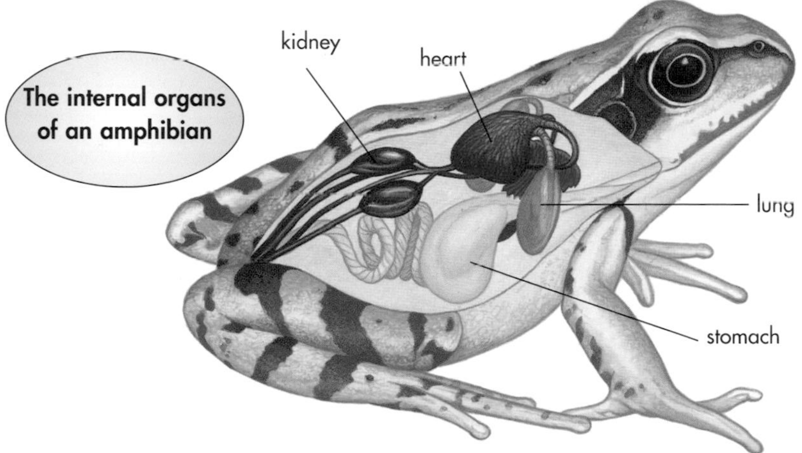

FACT FILE

Some brightly coloured amphibians produce poison in glands on their skin. The bright colours warn birds and animals not to eat them. The poisons are among the most powerful known to humans. In South America, poison from the poison arrow frog is added to the arrow tips used by the Indians for hunting.

From an evolutionary point of view, amphibians are halfway between fish and reptiles. There are 4,400 living species of amphibian. Frogs, toads, newts and salamanders are all amphibians. Many live mainly on land, but most spend at least some of their lives in water.

Frogs and salamanders are able to breathe through their damp skins to a certain extent, both in the water and on land, but toads must rely largely on their lungs and cannot remain in water for long. Toads and frogs are similar in many ways, although toads usually have rougher, drier skins and may waddle rather than hop as frogs do. Some toad spawn is produced in strings, like necklaces, rather than the mass of eggs laid by a frog.

The largest amphibian, the Chinese giant salamander, is 1.8m (6ft) long.

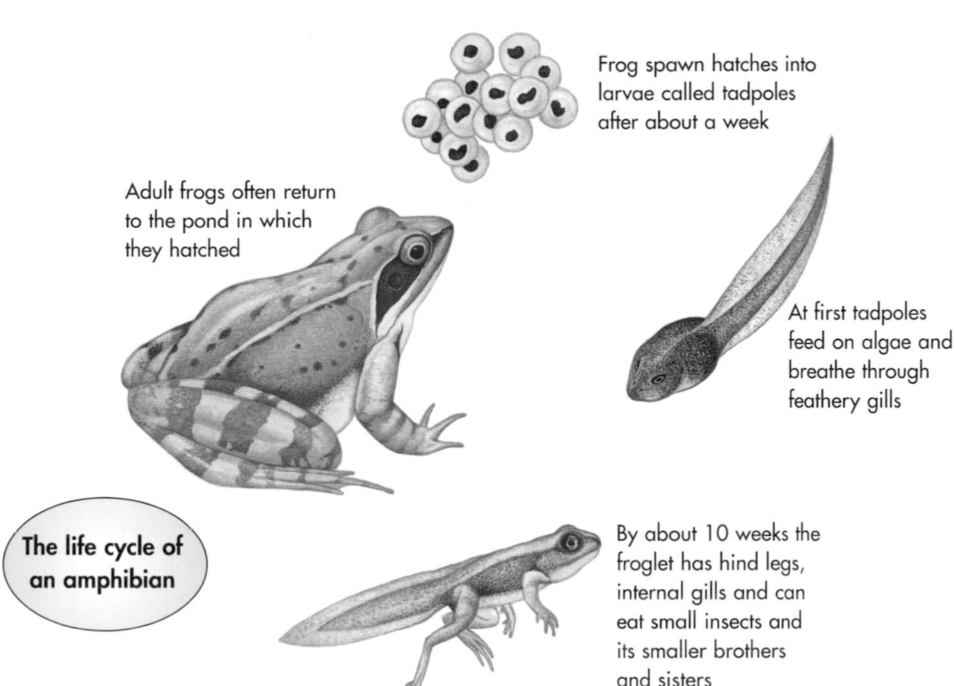

Frog spawn hatches into
larvae called tadpoles
after about a week
Adult frogs often return
to the pond in which
they hatched
At first tadpoles
feed on algae and
breathe through
feathery gills
The life cycle of
an amphibian
By about 10 weeks the
froglet has hind legs,
internal gills and can
eat small insects and
its smaller brothers
and sisters

How do frog eggs hatch?

Most amphibians lay their eggs in water. Frogs' eggs are called spawn. They are protected from predators by a thick layer of jelly. Inside this a tadpole develops. When it hatches out, it is able to swim, using its long tail, and breathes through gills. As a tadpole grows, first hind legs and then fore legs begin to grow. Lungs develop, and the young frog is able to begin to breathe with its head above water. Gradually the tail shortens until the young frog resembles its adult parents.

FACT FILE

The tree frog lives in the rain forests of South America and uses the pools of water in the centre of certain tropical plants. Although it can swim, it spends much of its life out of water, among the leaves of trees where there are plenty of insects for food. It has sticky toes that enable it to climb.

How do birds fly?

The bodies of birds are specially modified to give them the power of flight. Their bones are hollow to keep them light. Their bodies are also extremely lightweight, allowing them to glide and fly with the minimum of effort. For example, an eagle has a wing span of more than 2 metres and yet it weighs less than 4 kilograms. Birds also have air sacs linked to their lungs to give them extra oxygen as they flap their wings.

However, flying is not just a matter of flapping wings up and down. It is a mixture of gliding and powered flight. When the wings are flapped they move in a complicated way, scooping air downwards and backwards. The wing actually twists so that the air is pushed back in the right direction to give lift. The wings are twisted again on the forward stroke so that they slide easily through the air without slowing down the bird's flight. A bird's feathers, which help to reduce wind resistance in flight, are ideal because they are very light, yet also strong and flexible.

FACT FILE

The falcon is a bird of prey which feeds on other birds and small animals. It is equipped with powerful talons and a sharp beak in order to kill and dismember its prey. When the falcon dives on its prey it closes its enormous wings and drops like a stone to pick up speed. Powerful muscles in the bird's legs help to cushion the huge impact of the strike.

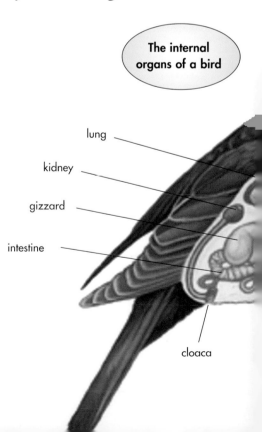

The internal organs of a bird

lung
kidney
gizzard
intestine
cloaca

How fast can birds fly?

It is easy to assess the speed of horses and people in races because there is a start and a finish line, but it is much harder to measure the speed of a bird in flight.

Many figures have been published about the speed in flight of various birds but most authorities doubt these statistics.

In general, the heavier the bird is, the faster it needs to fly in order to stay in the air. One expert believes that the fastest recorded flight for a bird was that of a homing pigeon going at 94.2 miles per hour.

Here are the estimated speeds that some birds fly at. The peregrine falcon can fly at about 65 to 75 miles per hour and the next fastest are ducks and geese who can go at about 65 to 70 miles per hour.

The European swift, golden plover and dove can reach 60 to 65 miles per hour, while hummingbirds reach speeds of 55 to 60 miles an hour. Starlings fly at about 45 to 50 miles and swallows usually at about 25 miles per hour.

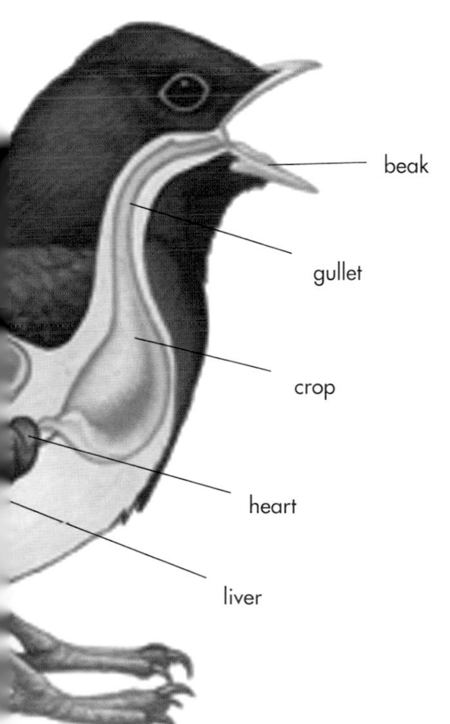

FACT FILE

Some birds cannot fly at all. Such birds include penguins who use their wings in water, enabling them to swim very fast. The penguin shown below is a rare Yellow-eyed species. There are only about 3,000 of them left in the world.

The sidewinder

HOW DO SNAKES MOVE?

Snakes have several ways of moving about. The most common way is to throw their body into loops and move forward by pressing against anything solid.

Another way in which a snake moves is by contracting its muscles, which pushes the body along rather like a concertina being squeezed open and shut.

The desert-living sidewinder moves by throwing a loop out to one side, then sliding its body towards the loop while throwing another loop sideways at the same time. The sidewinder looks like a spring rolling along the sand, but this is an effective way of moving on this soft surface. Most snakes are able to swim effectively by using a wriggling motion.

FACT FILE

Snakes and crocodiles are both reptiles. A reptile is an air-breathing animal with a body structure between that of an amphibian and a mammal. Living reptiles include crocodiles, tortoises and turtles, snakes and lizards.

How do snakes inject their poison?

A venomous snake is one who has saliva glands which produce a substance that is poisonous to its prey. This substance is called the snake's venom. Some snakes' venom is so powerful it could kill an elephant. About two hundred venomous snakes (out of 412 species) can be considered dangerous to people.

Two of these are African snakes called the boomslang and the bird snake. Their fangs are in the rear of their mouths and are greatly enlarged and have grooves running down one side. Just above these fangs is an opening that leads to the venom-producing gland. When a rear-fanged snake bites, venom drips down the grooves into the wound made by the fangs. In cobras, however, the fangs are at the front of the mouth, one on each side of the upper jaw. A muscle surrounds the venom gland so that when the snake bites the muscles press on the gland and force the venom down into the fang and out through the tip. The spitting cobra can spray venom from its fangs the way water is squirted from a toy gun.

The cobra

FACT FILE

Giant snakes have been reported in many parts of the world. The largest recorded snake is the anaconda which can reach a length of 9 metres.

How many kinds of fish are there?

Fish, like all creatures that existed thousands of years ago, have undergone many changes in their development. There were fish in the oceans before humans ever appeared on the Earth. In the world today there are more living species of fish than of any other class of backboned animals. There are around forty thousand different kinds of fish which live in every kind of water from mountain torrents and tiny ponds to the depths of the Earth's oceans.

Fish are divided into three general types: the cartilaginous fish which includes sharks, skate and rays. The second type is the bony fish, which have a complete bony skeleton and are covered with bony scales. This group of fish are the most common and account for over 90% of all fish. Finally there are the lungfish, which are a special type of fish because they have two sets of breathing equipment, possessing both gills and lungs.

Cross-section of a fish

FACT FILE

Salmon breed in small freshwater streams but spend most of their life in rivers and seas. To breed, they return to the stream where they hatched. They even leap up waterfalls in order to reach their spawning grounds.

How can fish breathe underwater?

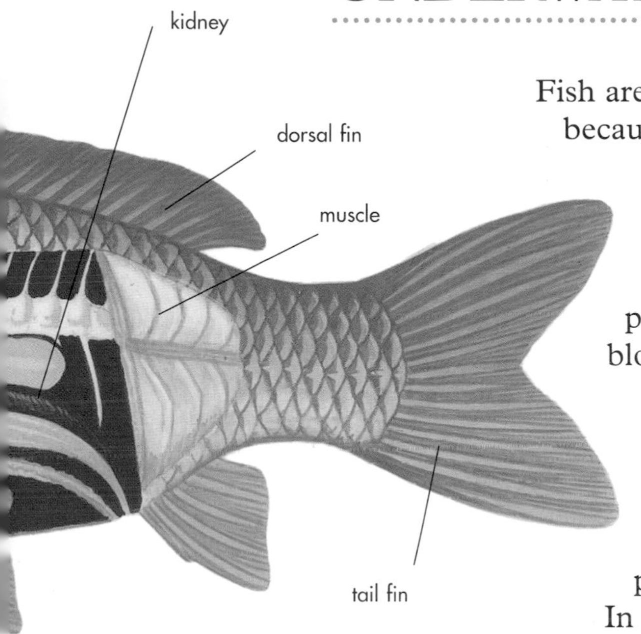

Fish are able to breath underwater because they have special organs called gills. Gills are bars of tissue at the side of the fish's head. They have masses of finger-like projections that contain tiny blood vessels. Water goes into the fish's mouth and flows over its gills. The gill filaments take in oxygen (which is dissolved) from the water and pass it into the fish's blood. In this way the gills have the same function as the lungs of air-breathing animals. If water is contaminated, fish need to take oxygen from another source. Some attempt to come to the surface of the water and take in oxygen from the air. However, their gills are neither suitable nor adept at processing oxygen from the air.

Fish are able to smell, although they do not use their gills for this. They have two small nostrils on their heads which act as organs of smell. The sense of smell is much more developed in some fish than it is in others. Sharks, for example, rely on their keen sense of smell to hunt down and catch other animals to feed on.

FACT FILE

Piranhas are very aggressive fish and can be dangerous in large numbers. Piranhas are supposed to be able to strip all the flesh from a pig or cow in a few minutes, but they are probably not dangerous to humans unless attracted to blood.

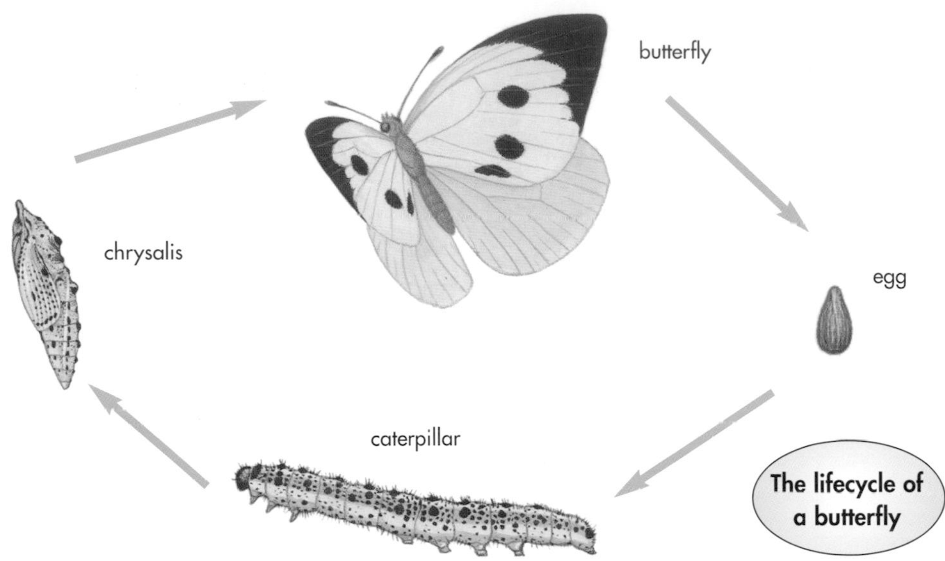

The lifecycle of a butterfly

HOW DOES A CATERPILLAR BECOME A BUTTERFLY?

During her lifetime a female butterfly can lay from 100 to several thousand eggs. She is very careful to lay these eggs near the kind of plant that will be useful to her offspring later.

These eggs will hatch into tiny, wormlike grubs called 'caterpillar larvae' which begin to feed and grow immediately. They will shed their skins several times.

When the caterpillar feels it is time for a change, it spins a little button of silk to which it clings. It lands head down and sheds its caterpillar skin. It then appears as a pupa or chrysalis.

The pupa or chrysalis may sleep for some weeks During this time it is undergoing a change, so that when it emerges from its chrysalid skin, it is a butterfly. It will spread its wings so that they can dry and become firm before it will attempt to fly.

FACT FILE

This hover fly mimics a wasp, though it has no sting. It is an excellent flyer and can hover or fly backwards or sideways if necessary. It feeds on flower nectar.

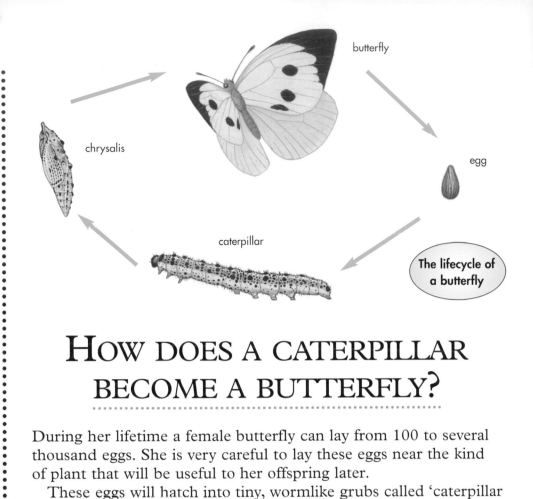

How do spiders make their webs?

A spider lies in wait for insects

Spiders spin their web from silk which is pumped out from tiny nozzles at the back of the abdomen, called spinnerets. As the silk is stretched by the spider into a thread it hardens and becomes proportionately stronger than steel.

Some of these threads are quite sticky, while others simply support the web. The spider is able to feel the vibrations of the web when an insect flies into it and it then runs quickly across the web to capture its prey.

Usually the insect is wrapped in silk before being eaten by the spider.

FACT FILE

Ants are called arthropods, which means they have a hard outer shell to protect their organs and joints to allow for free movement.

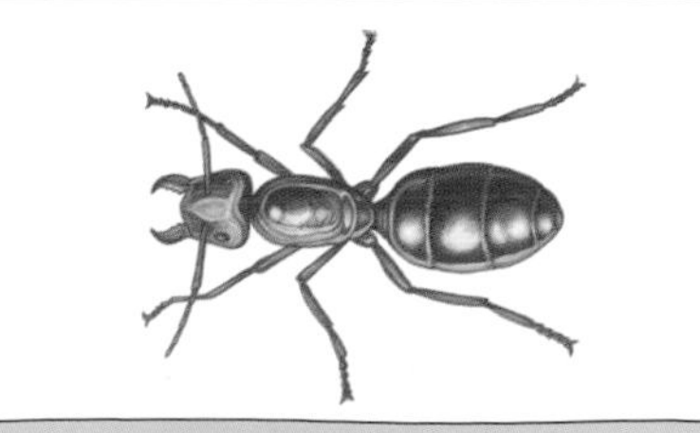

HOW DANGEROUS ARE JELLYFISH?

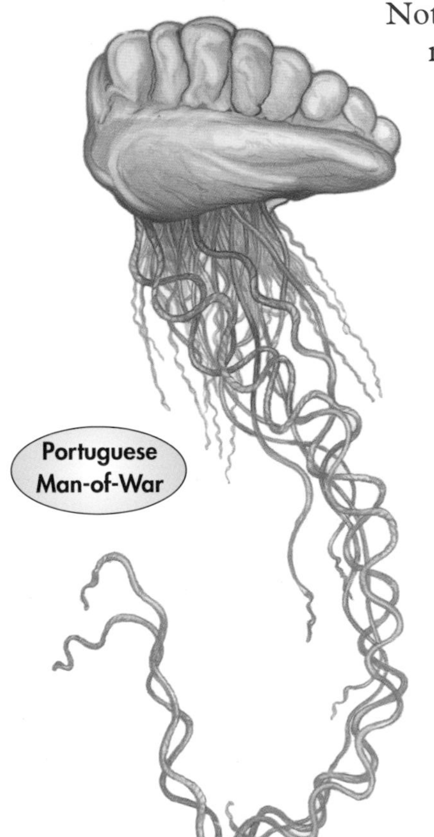

Not all jellyfish are dangerous, but many can cause severe pain and the stings of several can be fatal without rapid treatment. Among the most dangerous is the box jellyfish that lives in vast swarms in the southern oceans.

The body of most jellyfish is shaped like an upturned bowl, and has a thick layer of a jellylike substance between two layers of body cells. The dangerous part of the jellyfish is the long stinging tentacles. When the stinging cells come into contact with prey, they inject poison into it to paralyse or kill it. They eat fish, plankton and smaller jellyfish.

The Portuguese Man-of-War, which drifts on the surface of warm oceans round the world is not a true jellyfish, but a colony of modified jellyfish and other creatures with specialist functions such as capturing and digesting food. The blue 'head' is one member of the colony which has become a float filled with gas. The members of the colony share a common digestive system. The tentacles may reach as much as 60 feet in length.

FACT FILE

The octopus belongs to a group of animals called 'cephalopods' which means they are 'head-footed' because the foot is divided into long armlike tentacles that grow out from the head. The octopus has eight such tentacles.

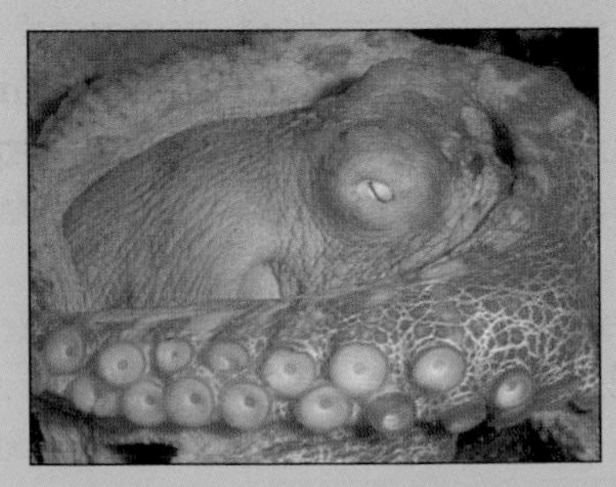

HOW DO STARFISH SEE?

There are about 2000 species of starfish in the world. They do not have eyes as we think of them but at the end of each arm is a light-sensitive red eye spot surrounded by a circle of spines. Starfish do not see colour but can detect if, for instance, something dark is moving in front of a pale background. They frequently raise the tips of their arms to spot their prey. They also have a tiny tentacle at the end of each arm that can detect chemical changes and vibrations in the water.

Many starfish eat molluscs, which they pull apart with their suckered arms. Then they push their stomach out through their mouth and injest the mollusc.

The crown of thorns starfish eats coral, and has caused serious damage to the Great Barrier Reef off the coast of Australia.

FACT FILE

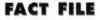

Coelenterata are a group of small animals including sea anemones and corals. Most of them live in the sea and have arms covered with stinging cells. They feed on plankton.

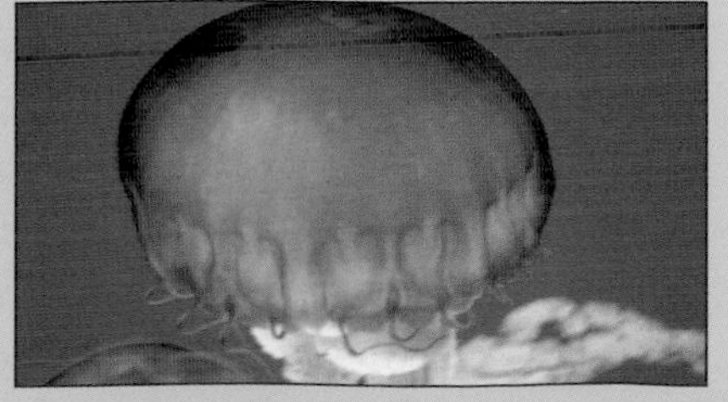

FACT FILE

Caribou usually live in relatively small numbers. However, when the time comes for them to migrate in search of food, they have been known to form herds of up to 3,000.

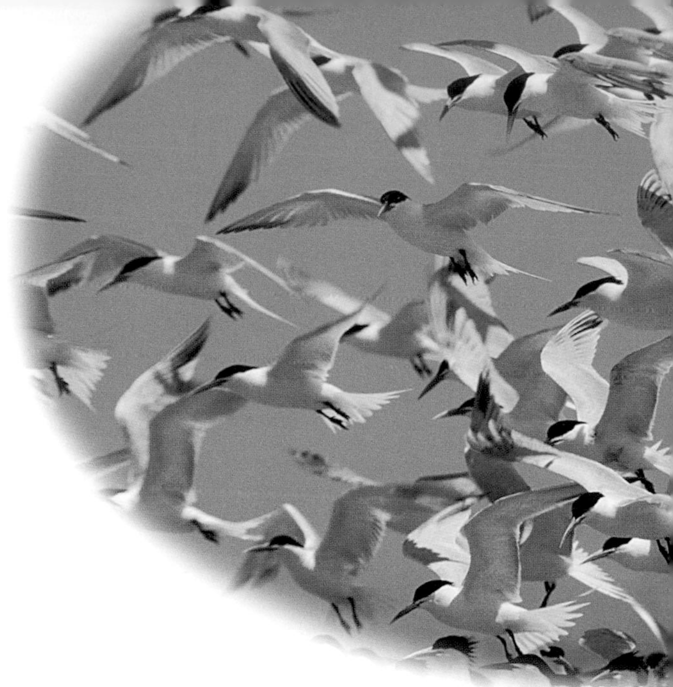

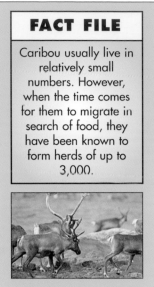

HOW DO BIRDS KNOW WHEN TO MIGRATE?

Man has been fascinated by the migration of birds since the very beginning of history – did you know it is even mentioned in the Bible?

And yet, so many thousands of years later, we still don't have all the answers. By migration, we mean the movement of birds south in the autumn and north in the spring, or moving from lowlands to highlands, or from inland to the coast.

We know that some go to warmer climates because they couldn't survive winter conditions. Also those birds that feed on certain insects, or small rodents, wouldn't find any food in winter. Whatever the reason is, how do they actually know when to make this long flight? It is believed that birds can tell when the days get shorter (and longer in spring) and this acts as an 'alarm clock' to tell them that it is time to move along.

So it is the change in the length of the day and the disappearance of food that tell the bird to head to warmer places. There are many other factors involved, of course, and many things we still don't understand, but these are certainly the main reasons why birds migrate.

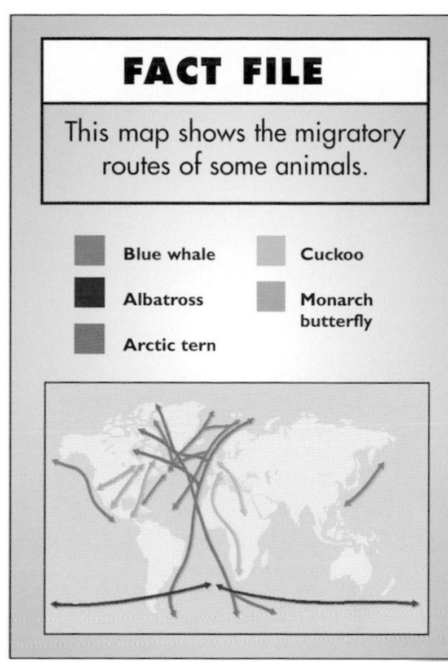

HOW FAR DO BIRDS MIGRATE?

Now we know why birds migrate, the next question is how far do they actually fly to find better conditions.

The champions among birds that migrate are the arctic terns. This amazing bird will travel as many as 35.4 km (22,000 mi) during the course of a year, going back and forth. It nests over a wide range from the Arctic Circle to as far south as Massachusetts.
It will take this bird about twenty weeks to make its trip down to the antarctic region and it averages about 1.6 km (1,000 mi) a week.

Most land birds only make short journeys during their migrations. But there is one bird, the American golden plover, that makes a long nonstop flight over the open ocean. It may fly from Nova Scotia directly to South America, a distance of about 3.8 km (2,400 mi), without even stopping.

We are not certain that birds start and end their migrations on exactly the same day each year. But there is one bird who comes pretty close to it. It is said that the famous swallows of Capistrano, California, are thought to leave on October 23 and return on March 19, but of course their date of departure and arrival has been found to vary from year to year.

How do plants live in the desert?

To start with there are many kinds of deserts. Some are the familiar ones with bare rock and shifting sand, upon which the hot sun beats down, but others, such as the Gobi, have bitterly cold winters. So a desert is a region where only special forms of life can exist and they have adapted themselves accordingly.

A good example of this is the cactus. This has adapted extremely well to hot, arid conditions. They have thick, fleshy stems which store water. Little or no leaf surface prevents too much evaporation of water from the plant's surface. Many desert plants have thorns, spines, or a horrible taste and smell which discourages animals from eating them.

Desert plants usually lie dormant during the dry or cool season, or drop seeds that can survive such a period.

FACT FILE

When a rock is exposed to the action of wind, rain and frost it breaks up into smaller particles. If the particles are small enough, these particles are then called 'sand'.

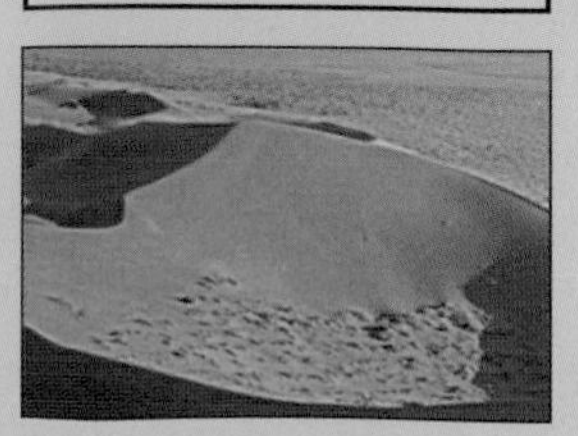

A desert cactus

HOW LONG CAN A CAMEL GO WITHOUT WATER?

The most important part of the camel is its hump. When that hump is empty, it loses its firm shape and flops to one side. The purpose of the hump is to serve as a storage place for food.

The camel can also take its own water supply along. The camel has three stomachs. It uses the first one to store food while it is grazing and to form it into cud. In the second stomach are the digestive juices and in the third the chewed cud is digested. In the walls of the first two stomachs, there are pockets for storing water. Muscles holds these pockets closed when they are full. Whenever the camel needs some water, these muscles open and close to let out as much water as it needs.

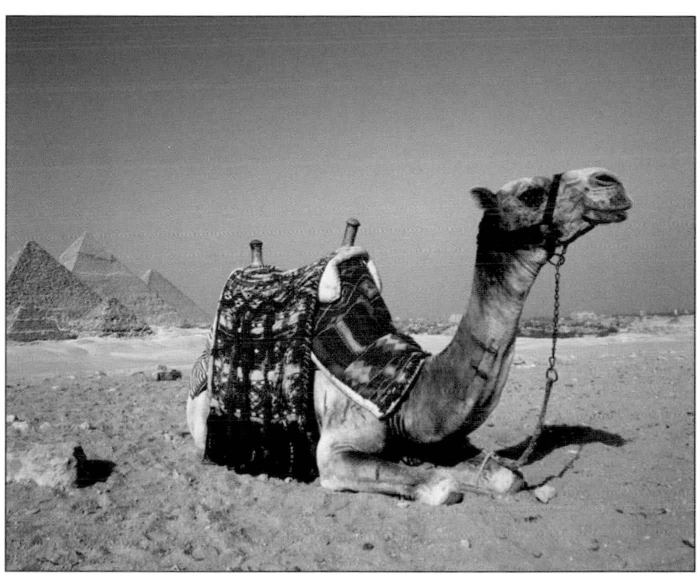

If a camel travels slowly and with a light load, the water in its stomach can last anything from six to ten days.

FACT FILE

Plants can also store food and water over the winter or in very dry conditions. Underground storage organs develop from roots, stem or leaf bases. The Venus Flytrap has a trap which looks and smells like a flower to insects. When they land on it they touch a trigger hair which slams the trap shut and they are then digested by the plant.

HOW DO FERNS REPRODUCE?

Ferns do not reproduce in the same way as other plants. They have fronds instead of true leaves, and some ferns grow into a tree-like form that can be 24 m (78.7 ft) tall.

Microscopic spores are produced on the underside of the fronds and these are scattered by the wind. When these spores land in a suitably damp place, they will sprout and grow into a tiny flat plant that develops small reproductive structures.

Sperms fertilize the egg cell, which begins to grow as the tiny plant shrivels up and dies. This is when the complete fern begins to develop.

The fern's reproductive parts are very delicate and can only survive in a moist atmosphere, so these plants will only grow in damp places.

FACT FILE

Algae are the most primitive form of plant life. Most algae are aquatic and range in size from microscopic single-celled organisms to seaweed that is several metres long. They do not have roots but grip to the surface with an organ called a holdfast.

How do mushrooms grow?

Mushrooms are very remarkable plants. They have no roots, no stems and no leaves. They grow so fast that you almost feel as if you can see them growing. They are known as fungi, which means they have no chlorophyll to manufacture their own food.

The part of the mushroom that you see above the ground is only the fruiting part of the fungus.

The rest of the plant lies under the surface in the form of a mass of dense white tangled threads. These threads are called mycelium or spawn.

The mycelium threads grow from little spores which are tiny dust-like particles shed from the fully-grown mushroom. On these threads small whitish knobs of tissue bud out and push upwards to expand and finally break out into an umbrella shape. Underneath the umbrella there are little radiating gills which are set very close together. It is on these gills that the tiny spores are developed. The spores then drop out and are carried away by the wind. When the spores fall on surfaces suitable for growth, they develop into new plants.

FACT FILE

Lichens are peculiar organisms in which algae and fungi both live together. Many grow like a mat, while others look like a small branched plant. They often grow on roofs, rocks or tree branches and are frequently brightly coloured.

How do flowers develop their scent?

A flower has a fragrance when certain essential oils are found in the petals. These oils are produced by the plant as part of its growing process. They are very complex and under certain conditions this substance is broken down or decomposed and is formed into a volatile oil. This oil evaporates and when this happens we can smell the fragrance it gives off.

The type of scent a flower gives off depends on the different chemicals in the volatile oil. Various combinations produce different fragrances. These same oils can also be found in leaves, bark, roots, fruit and seeds. As an example, oranges and lemons have them in their fruit, almonds in their seeds and cinnamon in its bark.

The Arabians were the first to distill rose petals with water to produce rose water. This was 1,200 years ago, and we still extract perfume from flowers today.

FACT FILE

The hummingbird is the world's smallest bird. It can hover backwards as it feeds on flower nectar.

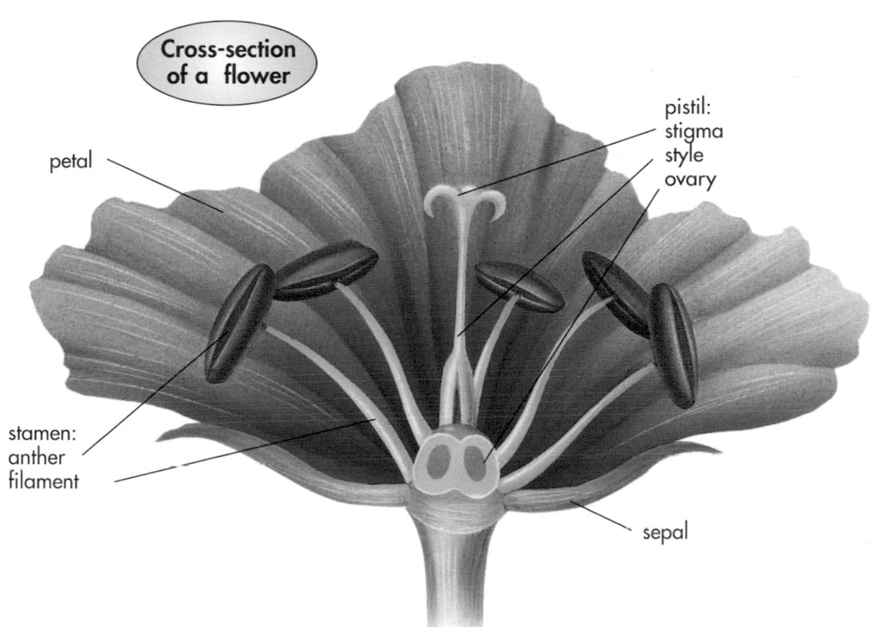

How do new flowers grow?

A flower has four main parts. There is a green outer cup made up of leaflike sepals. Within the sepals are the petals. Within the petals are the reproductive organs necessary for producing seeds.

In the middle of the flower are one or more pistils. Around the pistils is a ring of stamens. The pistil is the female part of the flower. The bottom of this is enlarged and it is called the ovary. Inside the ovary are little round ovules which later form into seeds. But they can only become seeds if they are fertilized by the contents of a pollen grain. Pollen grains are produced by the stamens, the male organs of the flower. The grains must go through the top of the pistil and reach the ovules at the bottom. This fuses with the egg cell and completes the process of fertilization.

Pollen can also be carried by the wind or by insects feeding on the nectar.

FACT FILE

Pollen is the plant's equivalent of an animal's sperms. It carries the male reproductive genes. Pollen grains have a pattern, allowing the plant to be identified.

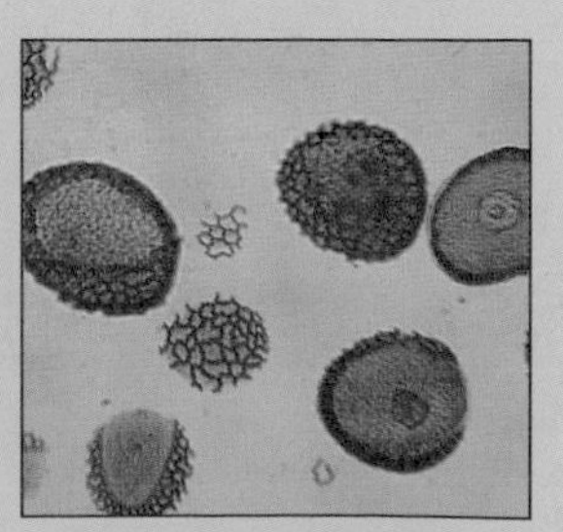

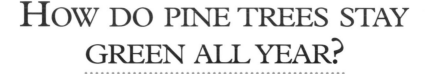

How do pine trees stay green all year?

Corsican Pine

Leaves have several functions and one of them is to make food for the tree. Leaves take in carbon dioxide from the air and water and minerals from the soil. The chlorophyll in the leaves absorbs energy from the sun. Sunshine forces the chlorophyll to change the carbon dioxide and water into sugar. The sugar made in the leaves is the tree's basic foods.

Leaves also give off enormous quantities of water. Certain trees, however, like pines and firs have different kinds of leaves. They have narrow, needlelike leaves with a thick, waxy outer covering which prevents the evaporation of water. Consequently the leaves on such trees remain for several years. When the leaves do fall, new ones grow at the same time and the branches never look bare. That is why these types of trees are called evergreens.

FACT FILE

Fertilizers are used to make crops grow larger and faster. Crops are also regularly sprayed with pesticides and herbicides. There are fears that the chemicals could cause health problems.

Norway Spruce

How can leaves change their colour?

When we look at a tree in summertime we only see one colour: green. And yet in the autumn these same leaves take on a whole variety of colour. The green colour in leaves is due to chlorophyll. There are other colours present in a leaf but we cannot normally see them. The pigment 'xanthopyll' makes yellow, 'carotin' orange and 'anthocyanin' is a bright red colour.

In the summer we only see the chlorophyll but as the weather starts turning colder the food that has been stored away in the leaf by the trees begins to flow out to the branches and trunks. Since no more food will be produced in the winter, the chlorophyll food factory closes down and disintegrates. As the chlorophyll disappears the other pigments that have been present all the time become visible. So the leaves take on all those beautiful colours which we enjoy seeing.

FACT FILE

A Bonsai is a decorative miniature tree that was first developed in Japan. Some bonsai trees can live for hundreds of years.

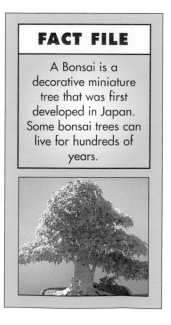

How is penicillin made?

Penicillin is one of nature's own miracles. It is the name we give to a powerful substance which fights bacteria and which is developed by certain moulds. It is an 'antibiotic', which means it is a substance produced by a living organism and acts upon other harmful organisms or bacteria.

Penicillin was discovered almost by accident, in 1928, by Sir Alexander Fleming, but it soon became the subject of intensive study. It was found that certain moulds produced this substance which had a powerful and destructive effect on many of the common bacteria which infect man, while it had no effect on many others.

Penicillin is very selective, so other antibiotics have been developed by scientists to fight other harmful bacteria. It can also be manufactured artificially for mass production.

FACT FILE

In 1347 a dreadful plague spread throughout London. Known as the 'Black Death', this epidemic was caused by rats. It was very infectious, and so spread rapidly, causing many thousands of deaths.

HOW DO BACTERIA AND VIRUSES DIFFER?

amoeba

bacteria

influenza virus

Bacteria are the simplest true living organism. Unlike other living cells, bacteria do not have a nucleus – their genes are scattered throughout their interior. Bacteria have a thick protective cell wall. There are thousands of bacteria in every single cubic metre of air that you breathe. Everything you touch is loaded with bacteria. They even live inside your body. Although bacteria can cause disease, the majority of them are completely harmless. They carry out the vital function of breaking down dead and waste materials. Bacteria in your gut, for example, help the body to digest food.

Viruses are even smaller than bacteria, but strictly speaking are not alive. To be 'alive' an organism must be able to grow and reproduce. Viruses cannot do this themselves and the only way they can reproduce is to enter a living cell and take control of it. This cell then becomes a living factory that can produce more viruses.

FACT FILE

Scientists are always looking for new cures for illnesses and diseases. Rainforests contain the bulk of the world's species of plants and trees. Each year new plants are discovered, and valuable plant chemicals are found. Hopefully one day these will become a valuable source of medicine.

How do plants and animals survive in deserts?

meat-eater
grazing animal
dung fertilizes the soil
nutrients are absorbed by the plant

The plants and animals living in hot deserts have all developed ways of conserving or storing water.

Cactuses and other succulent plants store water in swollen stems and leaves. Other desert plants have tiny leaves that reduce water loss with spines that protect the plant from grazing animals. Their roots may go down as far as 10 metres to reach water.

Reptiles are common inhabitants of deserts because they are cold-blooded and need heat if they are to remain active. Most other desert animals are either small burrowing rodents, or birds and animals that hide from the Sun among bushes or rocks at the hottest times of the day.

FACT FILE

Salt deserts form when shallow seas and lakes dry up, leaving a deposit of smooth salt in which no animals or plants can live.

How does life exist in the Arctic?

FACT FILE

There are about 40,000 polar bears living in the Arctic regions. Scarce food resources limit their numbers.

The Arctic is not continuously covered in snow and ice – in the south the marshy tundra can support herds of thousands of reindeer (caribou) in the summer.

In winter, however, conditions are far harsher, and the biting wind is the main problem. Animals have various ways of coping. Some, like reindeer, arctic terns and snow geese avoid it by migrating south. Some larger mammals, such as polar bears and arctic foxes have thick coats and develop a dense layer of insulating body fat in autumn to keep the winter wind out. Arctic hares, lemmings and other small mammals burrow under the snow in the worst weather. Surprisingly, very few mammals – apart from grizzly bears in the south hibernate.

A Siberian tiger

HOW DO MAMMALS DIFFER FROM OTHER ANIMALS?

Mammals are vertebrate animals that nourish their young with milk. All mammals are warm-blooded. At some stage in their development they will grow hair, although sometimes they are born without any at all.

True mammals all give birth to live young, which are smaller versions of the adult animal.

There is an unusual group of Australian mammals, called monotremes, who actually lay eggs. The echidnas, or spiny anteaters are monotremes and so is the duck-billed platypus.

Shrews are the smallest kind of mammal. The largest living land mammal is the African elephant.

FACT FILE

The duck-billed platypus has a leathery bill shaped like a duck's beak, a body similar to an otter and a tail very much like a beaver's. To make things even stranger, it has poisonous spurs on its legs too!

HOW ENDANGERED ARE PANDAS?

FACT FILE

Millions of African elephants have been hunted down and killed by poachers for their ivory tusks. These elephants are becoming an endangered species.

There were never any great numbers of pandas but farming has now destroyed much of their natural habitat in China. Due to shortage of food there are now less than 1,000 giant pandas remaining.

Humans have accelerated the extinction of many more animals by changing their environment so rapidly that the animals do not have time to adapt. One example is the destruction of the Indonesian rainforest which has left nowhere for the orangutan to live. Hunting is another reason for the reduced number of animals such as tigers, and the probable extinction of others.

HOW DO PARASITES LIVE?

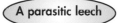

A parasitic leech

Parasites are animals that live at the expense of other animals. They rob the host animal of their food and can make them very sick.

The flea is a parasite that can be found on dogs, cats and most other warm-blooded animals, and lives by sucking their blood.

However, in other forms of relationship different animals can help one another. Some hermit crabs, for example, place sea anemones on their shells, hiding under their protective stinging tentacles. At the same time the sea anemone benefits because it shares the crab's food.

Similarly, the shrimp digs a burrow that it shares with the small goby fish. The fish benefits from being able to hide in the burrow, while acting as a lookout to warn the shrimp of approaching predators.

Most true parasites are very simple animals because they do not need complicated organs to digest their food. Indeed some parasites are simply a mass of reproductive organs.

FACT FILE

Cleaner fish are tiny fish living in coral reefs. They regularly clean parasites from much larger fish. Even large predatory fish queue up to be cleaned of skin parasites. The cleaner fish even swims into the predators's mouth without being eaten.

How are plagues of locusts formed?

For thousands of years locust swarms have devastated farmland throughout Asia and Africa. A swarm can be as large as 50 km long and contain more than 100,000 million locusts. A swarm of locusts can turn the sky totally black and wreak terrible damage on farmers' crops.

A locust is in fact a large grasshopper that normally lives a solitary and harmless existencc. When their population builds up to a high level they begin to mass together and migrate in search of food. These migrations can cover many thousands of kilometres.

FACT FILE

Other animals will pack themselves closely together and move in unison as a herd. This makes it difficult for a predator to catch an individual animal.

Science and Technology

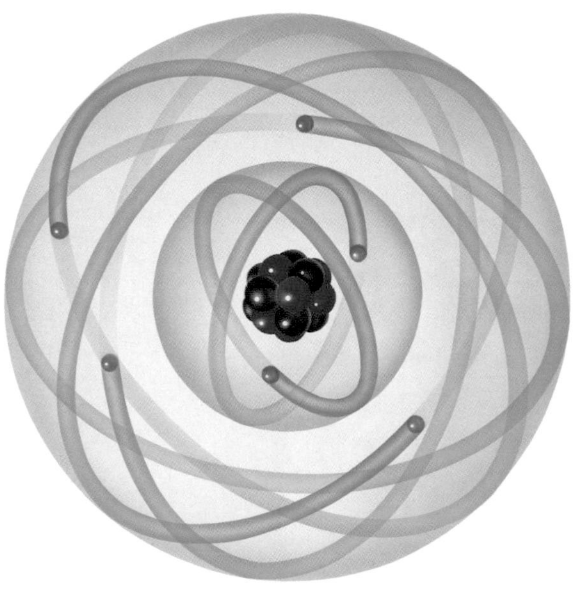

Contents

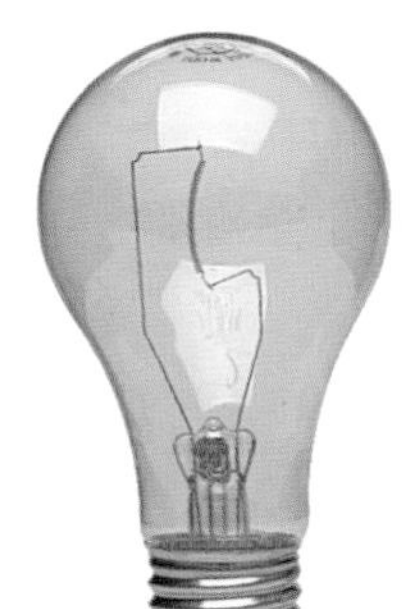

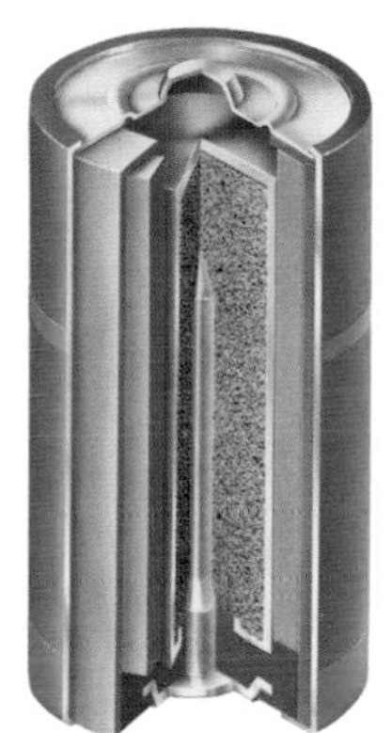

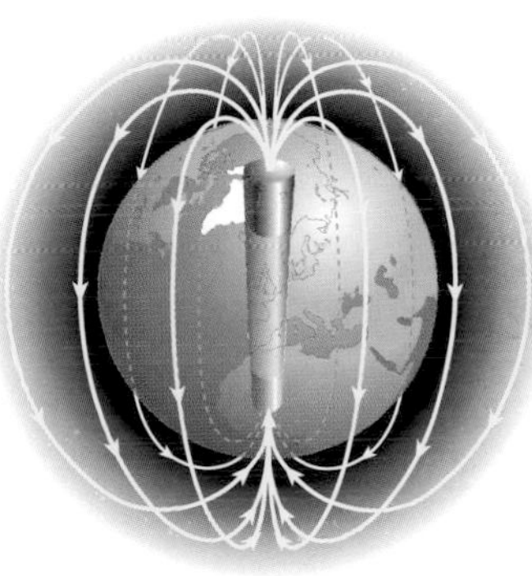

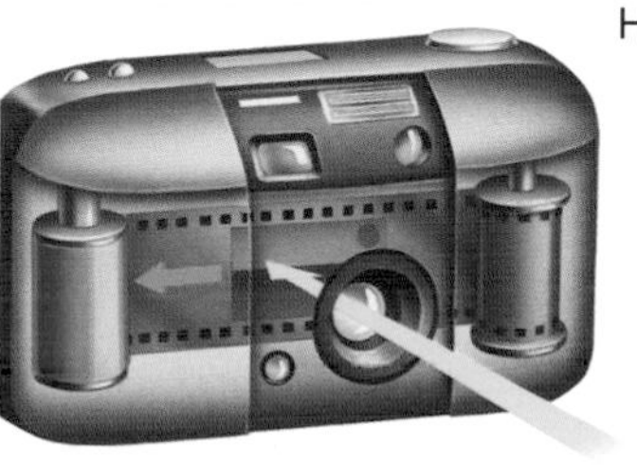

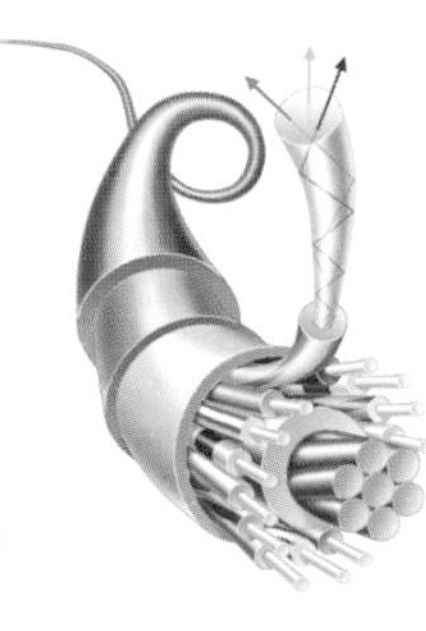

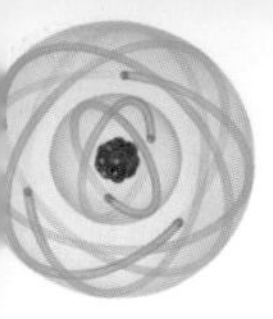

How many different elements are there?

There are 92 different elements that exist naturally, but it has been possible for scientists to create many more in the laboratory. These artificial elements are radioactive and they quickly decay or lose their radioactivity. Some may exist for only a few seconds or less.

Hydrogen is the lightest and uranium is the heaviest element.

New elements are created by bombarding other elements with radiation in an atomic reactor.

FACT FILE

At the centre of an atom is its nucleus, which has shells of electrons hurtling around it. The nucleus consists of protons, which are electrically charged particles, and neutrons, which have no electrical charge at all.

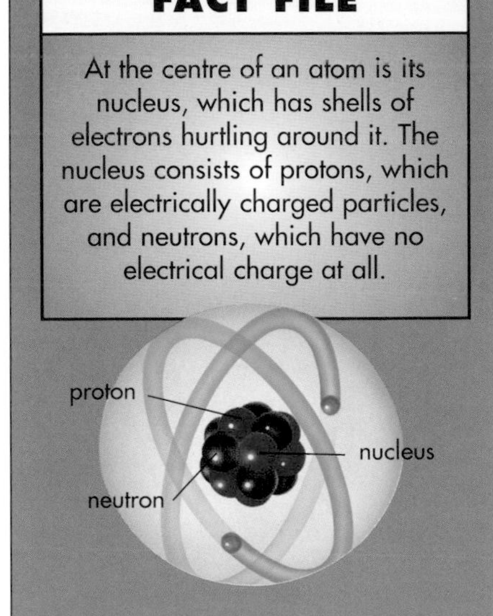

H hydrogen 1												
Li lithium 3	Be beryllium 4											B boro 5
Na sodium 11	Mg magnesium 12											Al alumin 13
K potassium 19	Ca calcium 20	Sc scandium 21	Ti titanium 22	V vanadium 23	Cr chromium 24	Mn manganese 25	Fe iron 26	Co cobalt 27	Ni nickel 28	Cu copper 29	Zn zinc 30	Ga galliu 31
Rb rubidium 37	Sr strontium 38	Y yttrium 39	Zr zirconium 40	Nb niobium 41	Mo molybdenum 42	Tc technetium 43	Ru ruthenium 44	Rh rhodium 45	Pd palladium 46	Ag silver 47	Cd cadmium 48	In indiu 4
Cs caesium 55	Ba barium 56	Lu lutetium 71	Hf hafnium 72	Ta tantalum 73	W tungsten 74	Re rhenium 75	Os osmium 76	Ir iridium 77	Pt platinum 78	Au gold 79	Hg mercury 80	Tl thali 8
Fr francium 87	Ra radium 88	Lr lawrencium 103	Rf rutherfordium 104	Db dubnium 105	Sg seaborgium 106	Bh bohrium 107	Hs hassium 108	Mt meitnerium 109	Uun ununnilium 110	Uuu unununium 111	Uub ununbium 112	
		La lanthanum 57	Ce cerium 58	Pr praseodymium 59	Nd neodymium 60	Pm promethium 61	Sm samarium 62	Eu europium 63	Gd gadolinium 64	Tb terbium 65	Dy dysprosium 66	H holm 6
		Ac actinium 89	Th thorium 90	Pa protactinium 91	U uranium 92	Np neptunium 93	Pu plutonium 94	Am americium 95	Cm curium 96	Bk berkelium 97	Cf californium 98	E einste 9

How does a periodic table work?

The periodic table is a list of all the elements, arranged in such a way that elements with similar properties are grouped together. Each element in the table is given a number, called an atomic number, which indicates the number of protons the atom has. (A single atom has the same number of protons as electrons.) Elements with the same number of electrons in their outer shells are grouped together in the table.

The groups are: Hydrogen, alkali and alkali earth metals, main metals; Transition and other metals; Non-metals and semi-metals; Noble gas non-metals; and finally Lanthanide and actinide series.

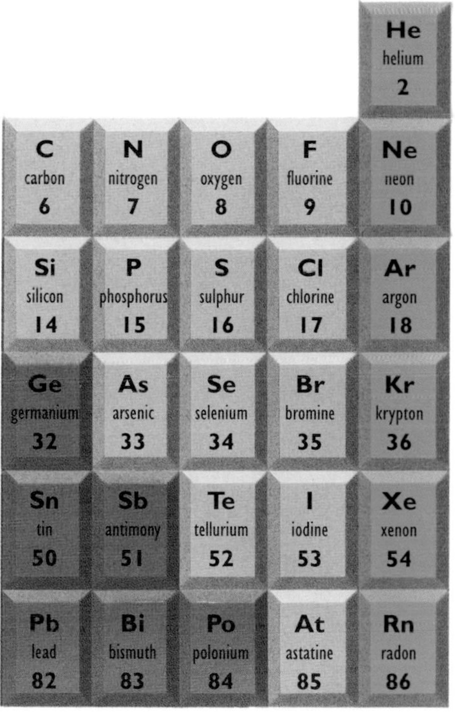

Er erbium 68	Tm thulium 69	Yb ytterbium 70
Fm fermium 100	Md mendelevium 101	No nobelium 102

FACT FILE

Many pure elements occur in different forms. Carbon can be a black powder like soot, but it can also be crystals, like the hard grey graphite used in pencil leads, or glassy crystals of diamonds. Organic compounds always contain the element carbon.

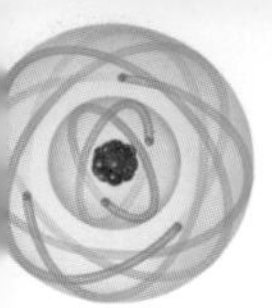

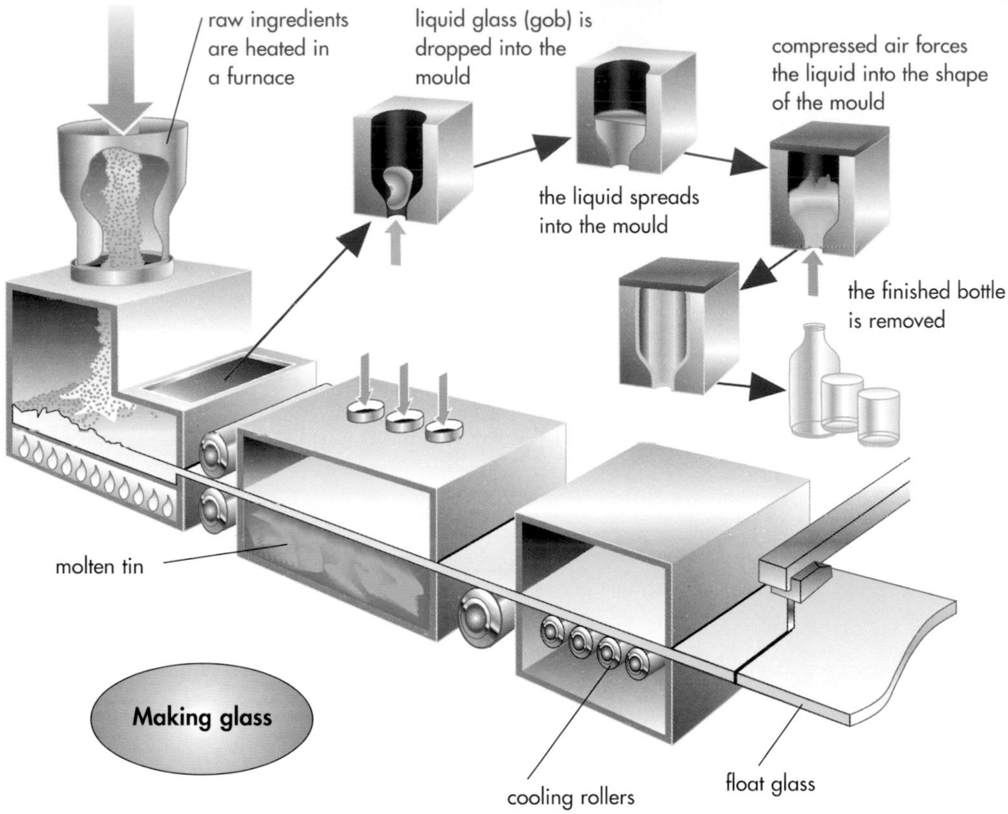

raw ingredients are heated in a furnace

liquid glass (gob) is dropped into the mould

the liquid spreads into the mould

compressed air forces the liquid into the shape of the mould

the finished bottle is removed

molten tin

cooling rollers

float glass

Making glass

HOW WAS GLASS DISCOVERED?

It was discovered that glass forms when melted solid materials are cooled quickly, so that they do not produce crystals. The main ingredients for making glass are sand, soda ash, or potash and lime, melted together at a very high temperature. Since these materials are found in abundance in many parts of the world, the secret of glassmaking could have been discovered in many countries.

The Romans were great glassmakers and used glass as a coating for walls. By the time of the Christian era glass was already being used for windowpanes.

FACT FILE

Mercury is the only metal that is a liquid at ordinary room temperature. It is a bright shiny colour and flows rapidly when poured out of a container, this is why it used to be called 'Quicksilver'. It is used today in thermometers and by dentists who mix it with silver to fill the cavities in your teeth.

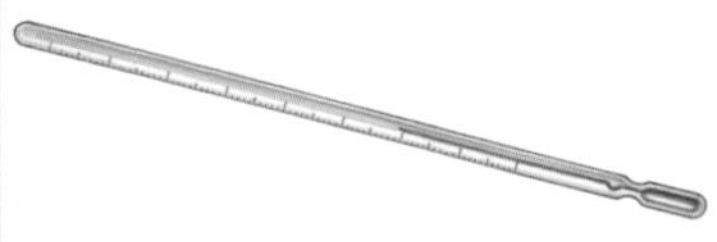

How are mirrors made?

FACT FILE

Mirrors are used in lighthouses to help reflect the light a long way to help ships out at sea. Some lighthouses have their own generators so that the light does not go out at any time.

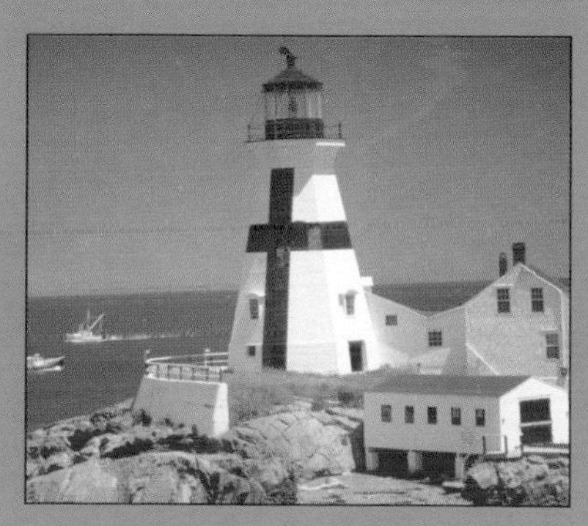

Mirrors are pieces of glass that have been coated with a reflective material on the back, so that when a beam of light strikes the surface none of it is absorbed. The beam of light is actually reflected away again.

The beam of light is reflected at exactly the same angle as it struck the mirror, but in the opposite direction. This can be visualized if you imagine a snooker ball striking the cushion of the table and bouncing back at an angle.

Mirrors are used in many ways for example in telescopes, flashlights, headlights of cars and lamps in lighthouses.

HOW DOES A BATTERY PRODUCE ELECTRICITY?

Electric current can be produced by battery cells. Dry cell batteries are being replaced, largely for environmental and economic reasons, with rechargeable batteries. These have a group of one or more secondary cells, so called because their electrochemical reactions are electrically reversible. A dry cell battery produces electricity by changing chemical energy into electrical energy. Part is changed into heat and part into an electric current. A battery contains two different electrodes separated by a conducting liquid or gel called the electrolyte. The substances react chemically with one another to produce an electrical current. A positive charge builds up at one electrode, flows through a conductor such as a wire to the other (negative) electrode.

FACT FILE

An alternative form of power has arrived with the development of wind farms. Huge windmills situated on exposed and windy areas drive dynamos to produce electricity.

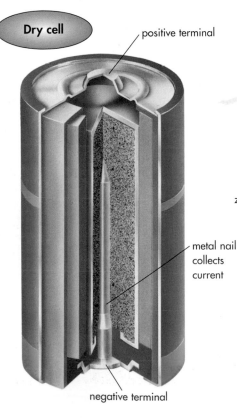

Dry cell

positive terminal

metal nail collects current

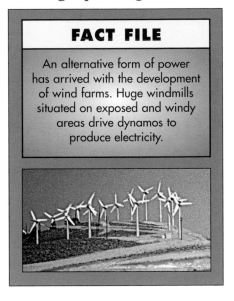

negative terminal

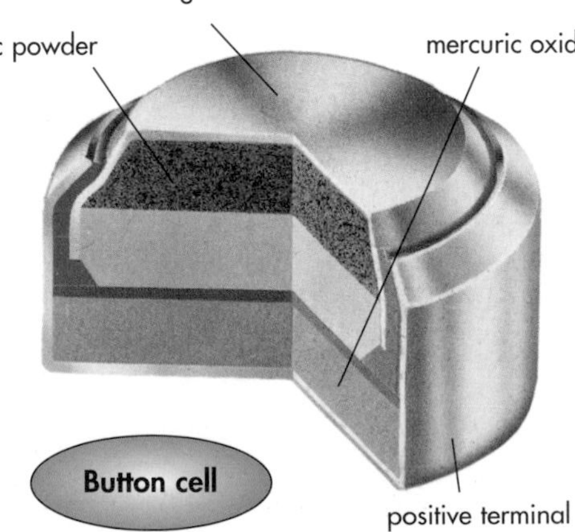

Button cell

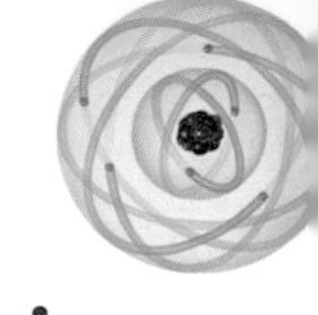

HOW DOES AN ELECTRIC LIGHT WORK?

sealed glass bulb

filament

metal contact through which current can flow

In 1800, Humphrey Davy connected wires to the ends of a weak battery and attached a piece of carbon to each of the free ends of the wires. By touching the two pieces of carbon together and drawing them slightly apart, he produced an 'electric arc', proving that electric light was possible, but the source of the electricity was not strong enough. In a modern light bulb, a current is passed through a very thin filament of metal with a high resistance to its flow, which becomes white-hot and produces light. The bulb contains an inert gas so the filament won't burn. The glass tubes in low energy bulbs are filled with mercury vapour and electronic ballast, through which electricity flows causing the mercury vapour to give off light in the ultraviolet range. This stimulates the phosphorous coating on the inside the glass tubes to produce visible light.

FACT FILE

Lightning is actually electricity. A huge electrical charge can be built up in certain weather conditions, and this leads to thunderstorms when a bolt of lightning leaps between the earth and a cloud. The air is heated to a tremendous temperature, causing the explosive noise of thunder as it suddenly expands.

How do lasers work?

Lasers are devices that produce a narrow beam of extremely strong light. Lasers amplify light by causing photons to be bounced back and forth in a substance (which can be solid, liquid or gas), which add extra energy. The result is that intense light is emitted in a very narrow beam. The intense beam of light produced by a laser can be used to produce images for publicity or entertainment purposes.

Lasers are also used to cut metal, and for precision cuts in operations. In CD players laser light is scanned across the CD's silvery surface, reading the tiny changes in light reflected back. They are also used in office printers and scanners. In engineering, the intense narrow beam of light is used to measure and align roads and tunnels.

FACT FILE

Lasers are used everyday in our shops and banks to scan banknotes to see whether they are forgeries. This is done by passing the note under an ultraviolet light scanner.

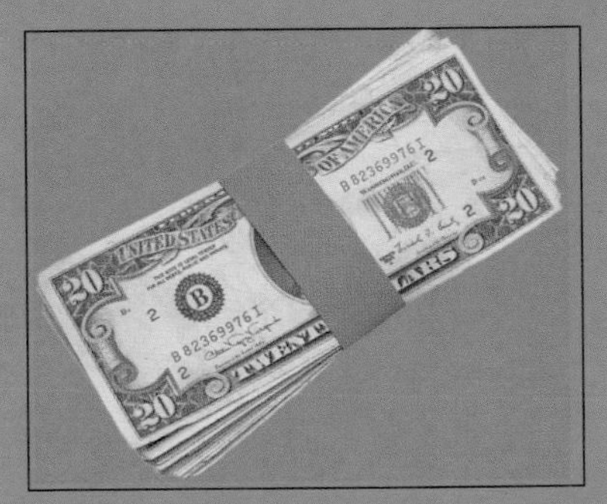

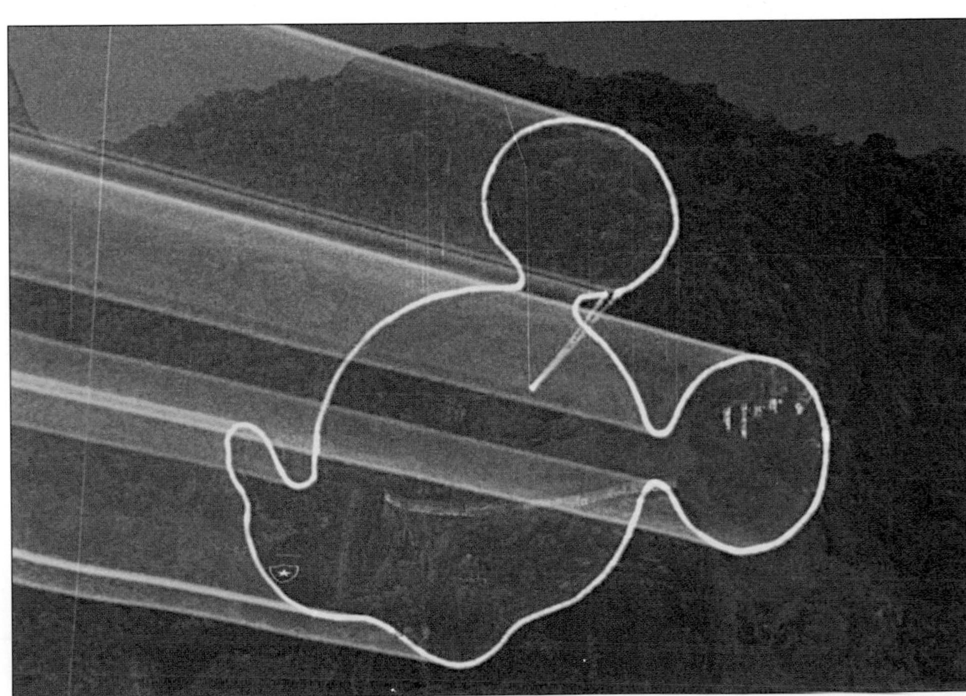

HOW DOES LIGHT TRAVEL?

Light is a form of electromagnetic radiation. It travels as waves that pass freely through space, even in the absence of air. Light waves have a wavelength and light is the visible part of these waves.

Nearly all of the light and energy reaching the Earth actually comes from the Sun, which is powered by a continuous thermonuclear reaction like a gigantic hydrogen bomb.

Although light only travels in straight lines, it can be made to bend around curves and angles using optical fibres. These are bundles of very thin strands of exceptionally clear glass. The fibres are treated so that their outer surface reflects light. When light is shone in one end of the bundle it passes along the fibres, reflecting from the sides as they curve and eventually emerging at the far end.

FACT FILE

As light is split by water droplets into a rainbow, colours are always produced in the same sequence: red, orange, yellow, green, blue, indigo and violet.

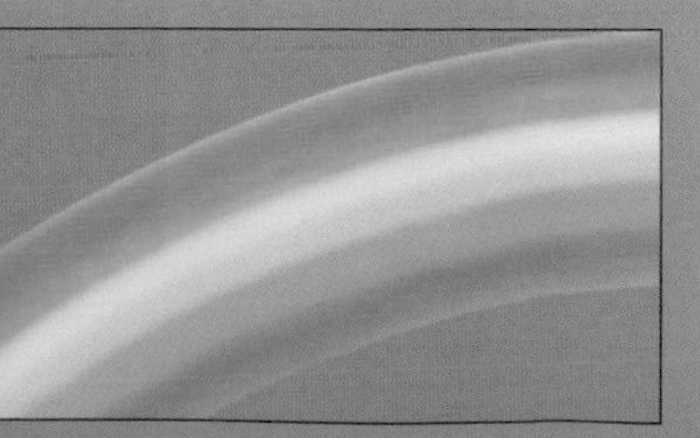

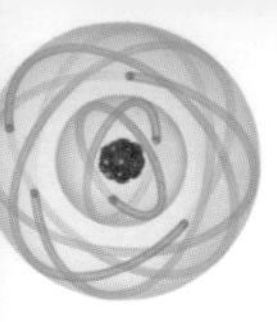

How does sonar work?

Sound waves travel extremely well through water. They are used to detect submarines, wrecks on the seabed, or by fishermen to find shoals of fish.

A sonar device under a ship sends out sound waves that travel down through the water. The sound waves are reflected back from any solid object they reach, such as shoals of fish or the seabed.

The echoes are received by the ship and can be used to 'draw' an image of the object, and its location, onto a computer screen.

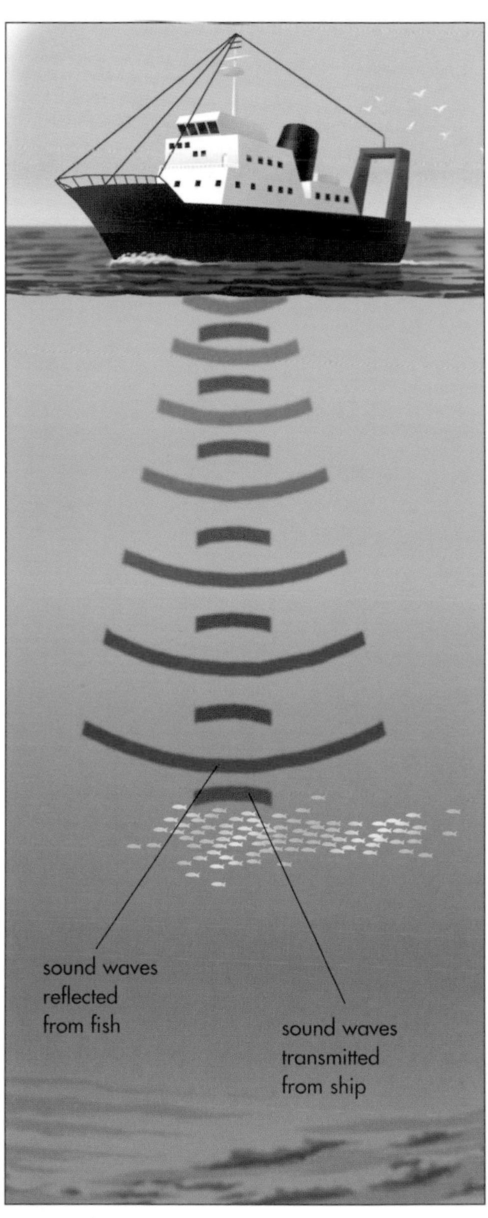

▲ Sonar, or echo sounding, is used by fishermen to detect shoals of fish. It can also be used to detect submarines or to find wrecks on the seabed.

FACT FILE

Concorde was an aircraft which actually broke the sound barrier and was the only supersonic airliner in regular use. When travelling at such very high speeds, an aircraft begins to build up a huge wave of compressed air in front of it causing a sonic 'boom'.

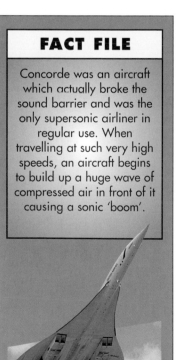

How do bats use sonar?

Bats also use sonar waves to navigate. Bats are nocturnal, which means they are active at night and sleep during the day. Since bats have to hunt for their food at night, you would imagine that they need exceptionally good eyesight. But this is not the case, as bats do not depend on their eyes for getting about. When bats fly, they utter a series of very high pitched sounds which are too high to be heard by the human ear.

The echoes from these sounds are thrown back to the bat when it is in flight, and it can tell whether the echo came from an obstacle nearby or far away. The bat can then change its course in flight to avoid hitting the obstacle!

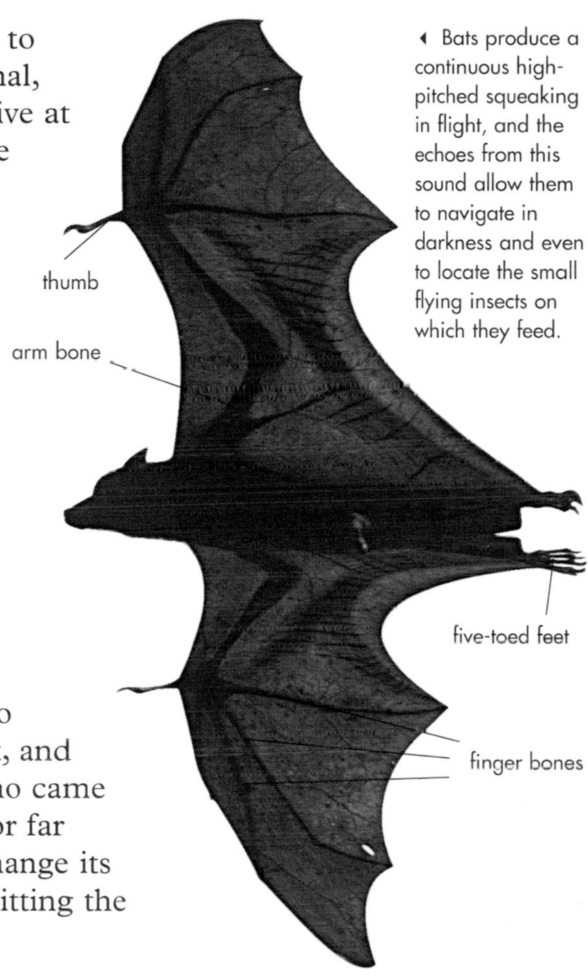

◂ Bats produce a continuous high-pitched squeaking in flight, and the echoes from this sound allow them to navigate in darkness and even to locate the small flying insects on which they feed.

FACT FILE

Musical instruments produce sounds in various different ways, but they all cause air to vibrate to carry the sound to your ears. Sounds travel as waves and it is the shape of the sound wave that determines the kind of sound that will be produced. The pitch of the sound (whether high or low) depends on the frequency of the sound waves.

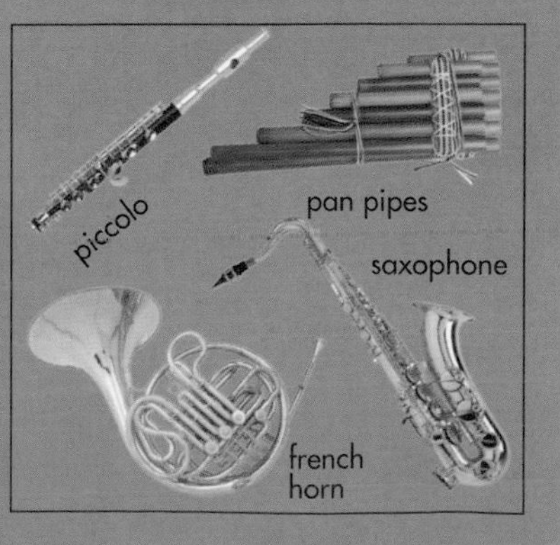

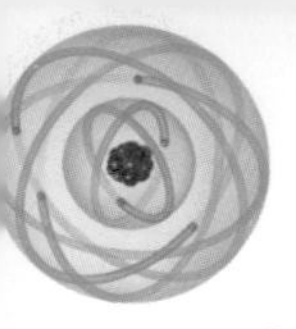

FACT FILE

Insects extraordinary eyes are made up of hundreds of tiny lenses. The images from all the lenses are made sense of by the insect's brain. Like us, insects can see in colour.

HOW DOES A CAMERA TAKE PICTURES?

The human eye is actually a form of camera. When you look around, your eyes actually 'take pictures' of the things that you see. The lens in your eye acts just like the lens in a camera. The retina of your eye acts like the film in your camera. In a camera light acts on a specially prepared sensitive surface of the film. If light didn't have any effect on certain chemically prepared substances, photography would be impossible.

When we open and close the shutter of a camera quickly, light comes in and strikes the film. When this happens, a chemical reaction takes place on the film. Certain tiny grains of silver bromide undergo a change. The film is taken out of the camera and treated with various chemicals to make the print visible and prevent further changes when exposed to light.

Digital cameras are a recent development. They convert the image they receive into electrical signals that are stored. These signals can then be read by a computer and used to produce a picture on the screen, which can then be printed out.

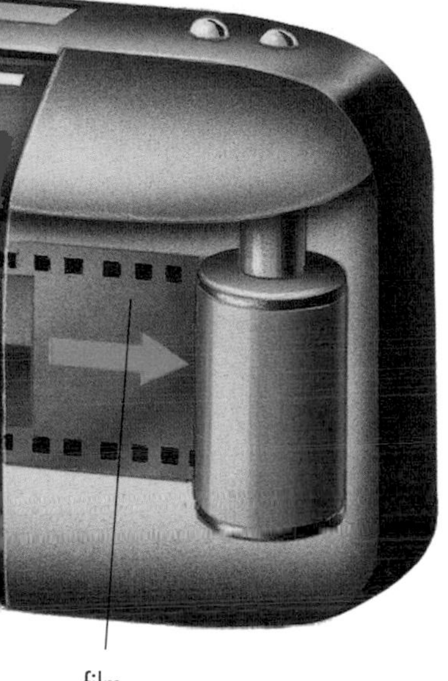

FACT FILE

Before photography we could only see a mirror image of ourselves or have a portrait painted by an artist. Now most people have a camera in the family.

HOW IS CAMERA FILM MADE?

The first step in making film for a camera is to mix gelatin with silver nitrate and potassium bromide in a warm, syrupy form. This has to be done in total darkness because the silver crystals are sensitive to light. The nitrate and potassium combine as potassium nitrate, and this is washed away. Silver bromide crystals are left in the gelatin. This is called the emulsion.

The film itself is made by first treating cotton fibres or wood pulp with acetic acid. This makes a white flaky product called cellulose acetate. This is then dissolved and the mixture forms clear, thick fluid known as 'dope'.

The dope is fed evenly onto chromium-plated wheels. As the wheels turn, heat drives off the solvents, and the dope becomes a thin, flexible, transparent sheet. Next, the film base is coated with the emulsion. The dry film is then slit into proper widths and wound into spools.

It is then ready to be placed into your camera and when you take a picture, light strikes the film and an image is formed.

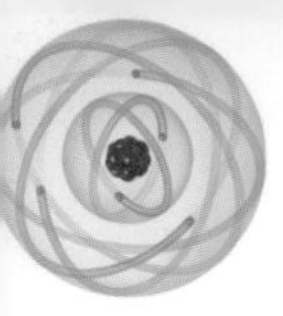

How does a telephone work?

FACT FILE

Light travels much faster than electricity and it is used in optical cables to carry communications for very long distances without electrical interference.

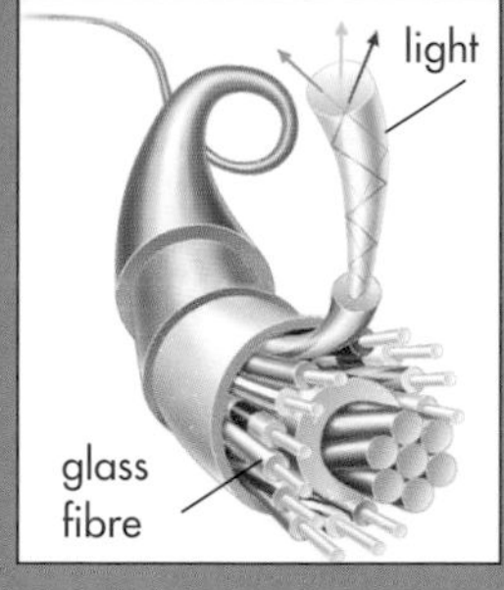

diaphragm

mouthpiece

earpiece

wire

Telephones transmit speech messages along wires by means of electrical signals. The handset is a loudspeaker and a very small microphone, which contains tiny grains of carbon. When you talk the sound waves cause a metal diaphragm to vibrate, pressing against the granules. The vibrations vary with the sound, and change the minute amount of current flowing along the wires to another receiver. When the current carrying the signal reaches another handset the same variations in the current run through an electromagnet, causing another diaphragm to vibrate and accurately reproduce the sound of your voice. Mobile phones are two-way radios that convert the sound to radio waves, which travel through the air until they reach a receiver at a nearby base station. The base station sends your call through the telephone network until it reaches the person you are calling. When you get a call, a nearby base station sends out radio waves that are detected by your mobile, where the signals are converted into voice or data.

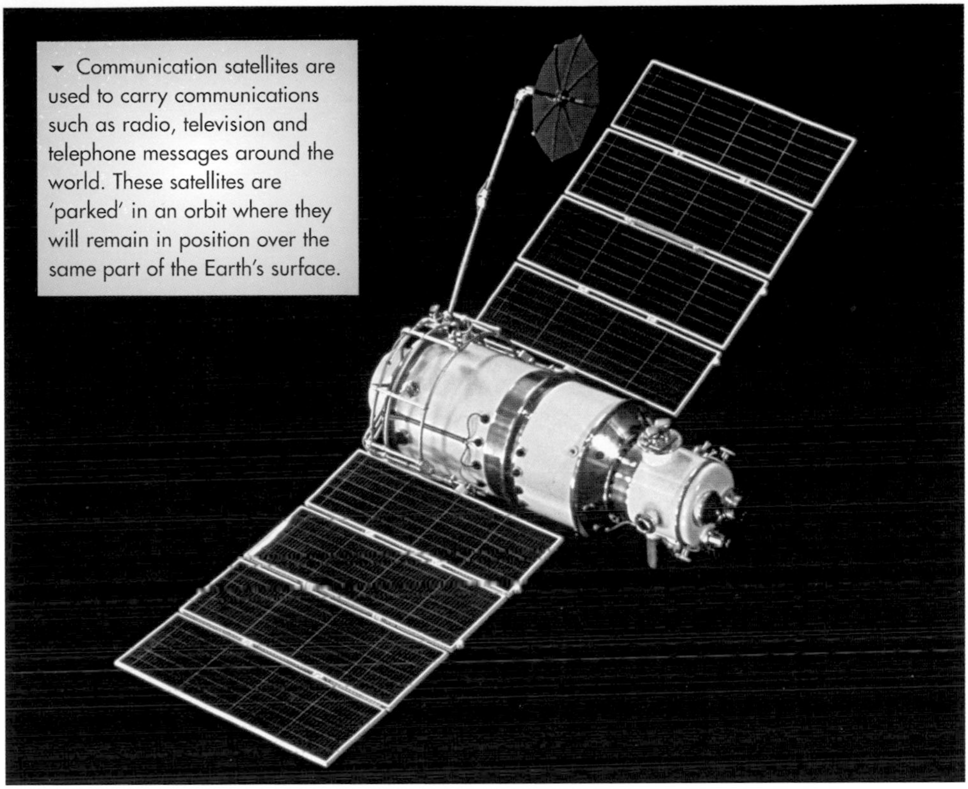

▾ Communication satellites are used to carry communications such as radio, television and telephone messages around the world. These satellites are 'parked' in an orbit where they will remain in position over the same part of the Earth's surface.

How do satellites aid communication?

FACT FILE

Satellites are not only used for communication purposes. Some satellites survey the Earth's surface so that we can give a more accurate weather forecast.

Satellites play a major part in today's communication. Radio, television and telephone communications are bounced off satellites to cover the greatest possible area of the world. Satellites orbiting the Earth must travel at high speed to escape being brought down by the Earth's gravity.

Geostationary satellites can be positioned right over the areas where they are needed. They can also be used as spy satellites, because they remain constantly over a region of interest.

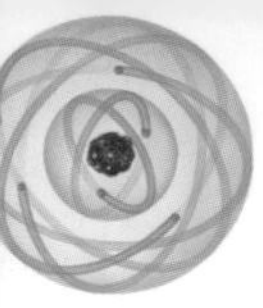

How do radios work?

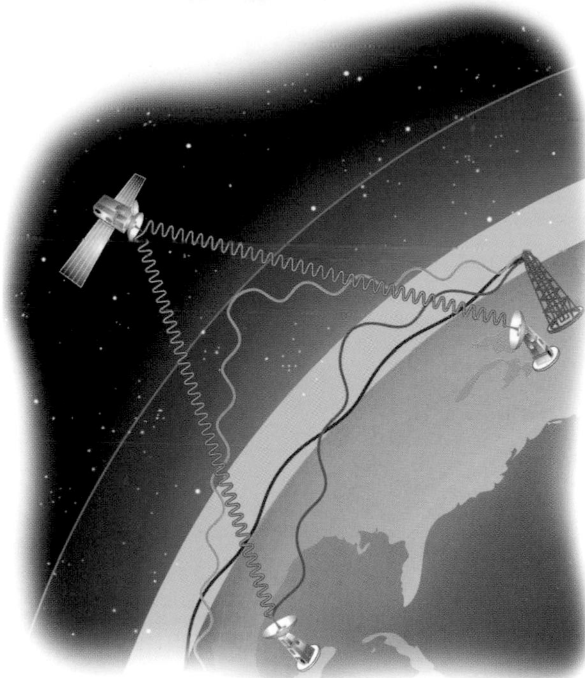

Radio signals are transmitted using a carrier wave. Radio waves form part of the electromagnetic spectrum. Those with the longest wavelengths are bounced very long distances off the ionosphere. A radio transmitter changes the radiowave to convey information. In AM radio, the height of the carrier wave is altered according to the sound picked up by a microphone. In FM radio, the frequency, or distance between the peaks of the radio wave is changed. The radio receiver picks up the signals, amplifies and decodes them. Digital radio works in the same way, but instead of sending out one analog signal, stations send out a bundled signal – both analog and digital. The digital signal layer is compressed. The combined analog and digital signals are transmitted and reach the digital radio receiver.

FACT FILE

Radios are used for many different purposes. This firefighter, for example, will need his radio to be in constant communication with his main control and also other firemen. Should he need assistance at any time all he has to do is use his radio which should speed up any rescue if this is necessary.

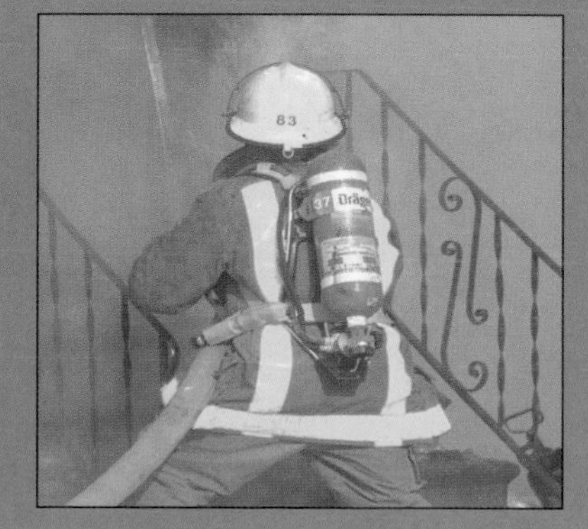

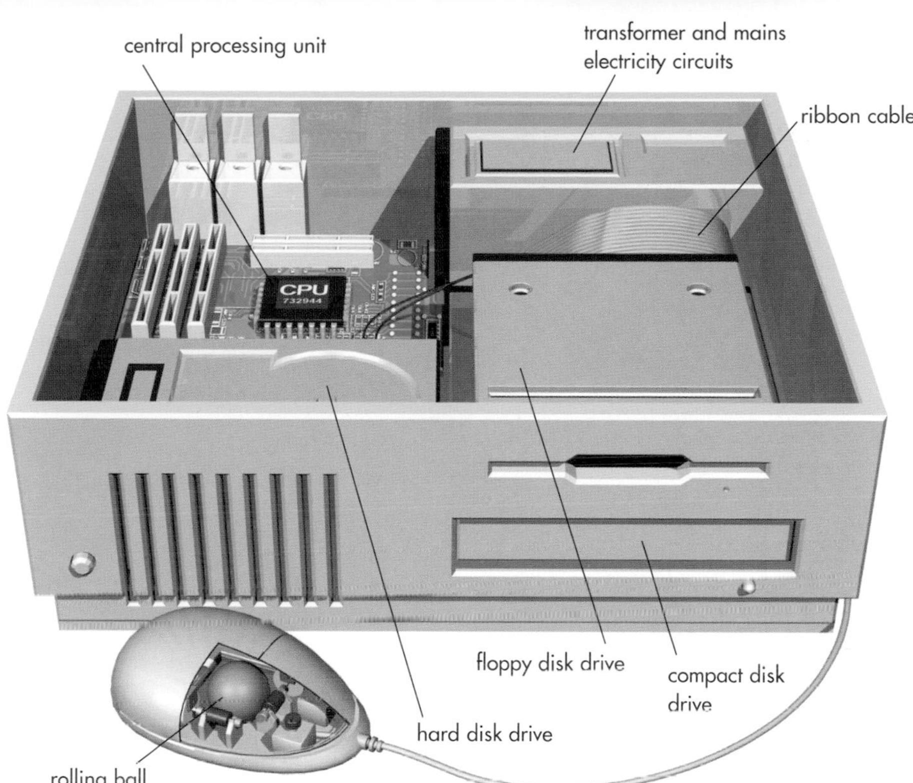

How do computers work?

FACT FILE

Any modern electrical device needs a huge number of connections to join together all the small components needed for it to work effectively. Printed circuits are complex electrical circuits that are literally photographed on to a layer of insulating material. This makes them light, compact and inexpensive.

A computer is a piece of equipment for processing information very rapidly and accurately. It processes words, pictures, sounds and numbers, and some computers can make billions of calculations per second.

The heart of a computer is a microprocessor which contains millions of tiny electronic devices on a silicon chip. Other chips form the computer's memory where information is stored until it is needed.

New data can be inputted from the keyboard or downloaded via a memory stick, dongle, CD or DVD drive, or from the Internet, wirelessly, along a telephone line.

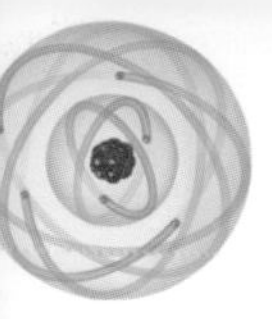

HOW IS MINING CARRIED OUT?

The earliest forms of mining involved following seams of metal in tunnels driven into the rock. This method is still in use today, usually in deep mines where other techniques would be impossible. Tunnels are made by using explosives and with automatic machines. Some of these mines go thousands of metres into the rock face, becoming very hot and dangerous.

Today we mine minerals, diamonds, metals, coal and rock for building material. Placer mining uses huge floating dredgers to extract metals. Strip mining is used to obtain coal and minerals that lie close to the surface. Open pit mining involves blasting into the rock to produce a huge quarry from which material is removed layer by layer.

FACT FILE

The metals that are used to make coins come from mines. Pure metals (those not mixed with other substances) are called noble metals and these include gold, silver, platinum and copper.

HOW IS COAL FORMED?

FACT FILE

Before we had central heating to warm our houses most people had coal fires, and matches were a quick and easy way to light them.

Coal is formed by the compressed remains of plants that lived in bogs 250–350 million years ago. This was during the Carboniferous Period when primitive animals first appeared on the land. Coal formed from the remains of tree ferns and other primitive trees which were covered with mud and sand and buried as new rock was laid down. Very gradually, over millions of years, this material turned into coal.

A similar process is taking place today in peat bogs, where the rotting remains of heather form peat. When the peat is dried it burns in a similar way to coal. In some parts of the world a soft shale, called brown coal, is mined. The hardest and purest form of coal is called anthracite.

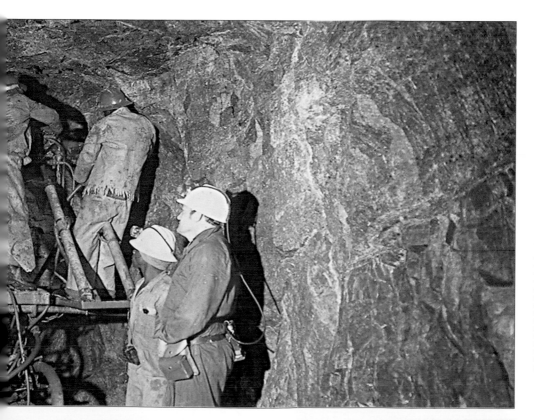

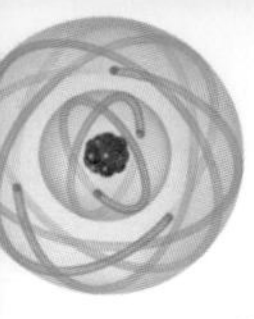

How does a compass work?

▼ The magnetized needle on a compass tries to align itself with the Earth's field of magnetic force.

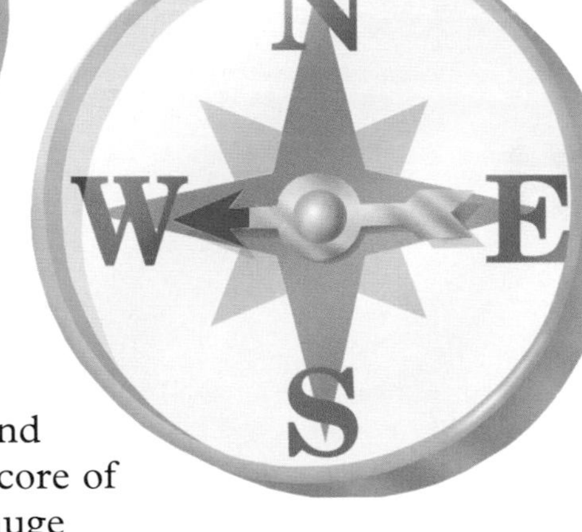

Electrical currents are able to influence other electrical currents and this force is called magnetism. The core of the Earth actually functions like a huge magnet. On a compass the magnetized needle tries to align itself towards the Earth's field of magnetic force. The needle is balanced on a pointed pin or floats on oil to allow it to rotate freely and to reduce any friction.

A compass needs to be used with care, because if it is near any object that can distort the Earth's magnetic field it will give a false reading. An object made of iron or steel that is nearby will cause the compass needle to swing wildly.

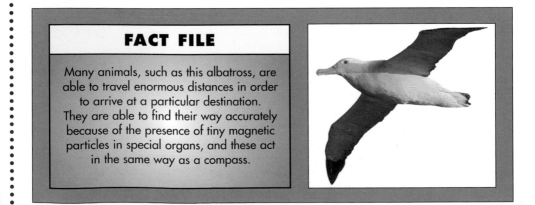

FACT FILE

Many animals, such as this albatross, are able to travel enormous distances in order to arrive at a particular destination. They are able to find their way accurately because of the presence of tiny magnetic particles in special organs, and these act in the same way as a compass.

How is an electromagnet made?

FACT FILE

One of the most important uses of magnets is in electric motors which power many machines, ranging from small toys to enormous railway engines. Video and audio tapes also depend on magnetism.

Electromagnets can only produce magnetism when an electrical current passes through them. They usually consist of a metal core made of iron or similar material, around which are wrapped many coils of thin insulated wire. The metal core becomes magnetized when an electric current passes through the wire coil, but the effect disappears immediately the current is shut off. Very powerful electromagnets can be made by using many coils and strong electrical currents.

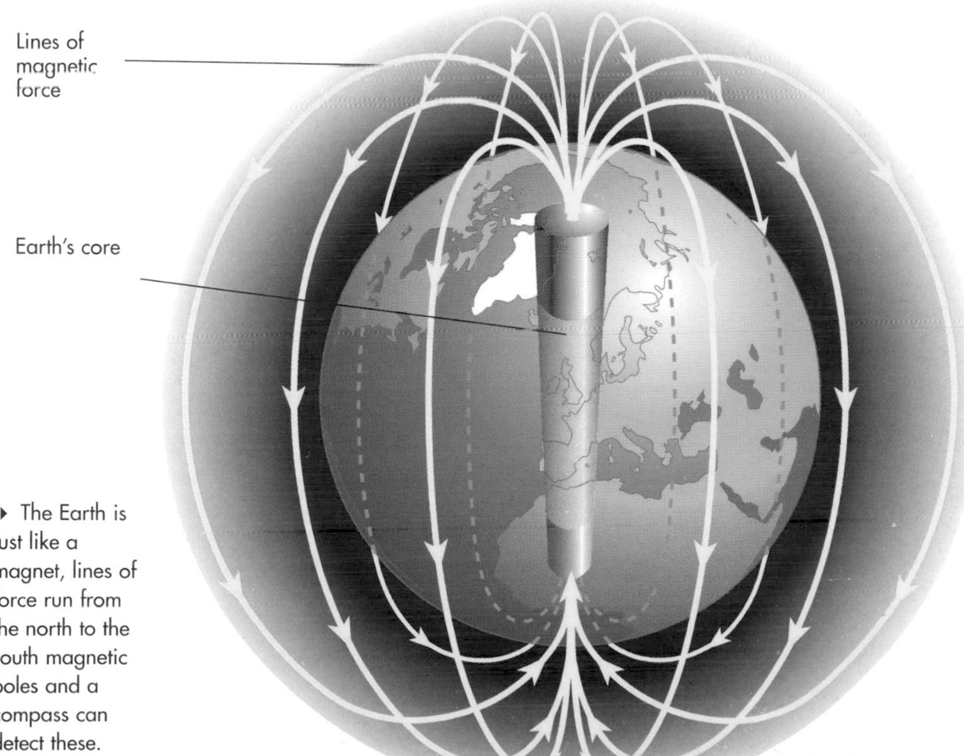

▸ The Earth is just like a magnet, lines of force run from the north to the south magnetic poles and a compass can detect these.

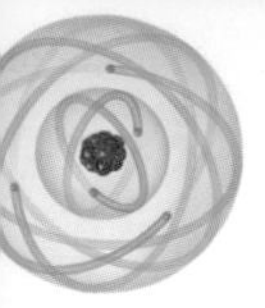

How does a boat float?

The reason a boat, whatever size, can float on the surface of water is because it is the fluid itself which holds it up. The water offsets the force of gravity which tries to pull everything to the centre of the Earth.

The upward push on a floating object is called 'buoyant force' or simply 'buoyancy'. If you want to feel this force just take a blown-up beach ball into the water. You will feel that the water seems to push up on the ball. When a solid body is placed in a liquid it pushes some of the fluid aside. If the solid is less dense than the fluid, it will float. A boat contains large quantities of air and is less dense than water. It weighs less than the water it pushes aside, so it floats.

FACT FILE

Helicopters are lifted into the air by their large rotating propellers or rotors. These work like narrow wings generating lift as they spin.

▾ The hovercraft is very useful as a means of transport in shallow waters where a conventional boat would run aground. Because they are flat, hovercraft can hold a large number of vehicles and are used as car ferries.

▾ Air pushing over the upper surface of an aircraft's wing reduces in pressure, allowing higher-pressure air underneath the wing to exert an upward force, thus enabling the aeroplane to fly.

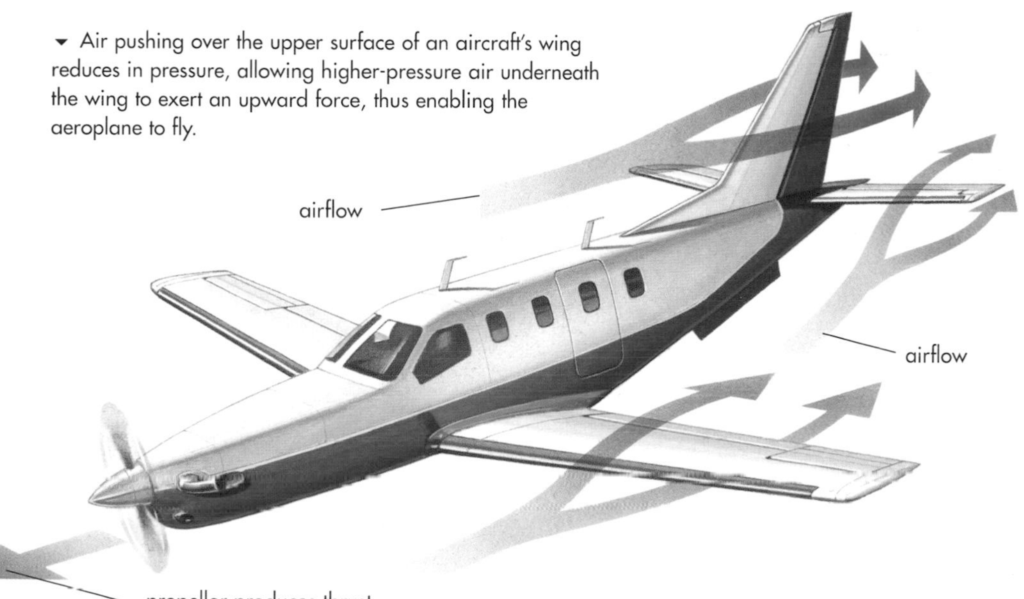

HOW DO AEROPLANES FLY?

As an aeroplane moves through the air, the air passes over the surface of its wings. These wings are shaped with a curved top surface and a flatter lower surface, which means that air passing over the top of the wing has to travel a little faster than that below the wing. This causes the pressure to lower above the wing, while the air pressure below pushes up. The end result is the lift that keeps the aeroplane in the air.

The tail surfaces of the aeroplane keep the wing at the proper angle to provide the right amount of lift. The power to propel the aeroplane along can come either from the engine, or, in the case of gliders, from rising air currents.

Jet engines propel a plane just like a rocket, with a stream of hot gases.

FACT FILE

Leonardo da Vinci (1452–1519) drew his plans for a helicopter hundreds of years before flying machines were even invented.

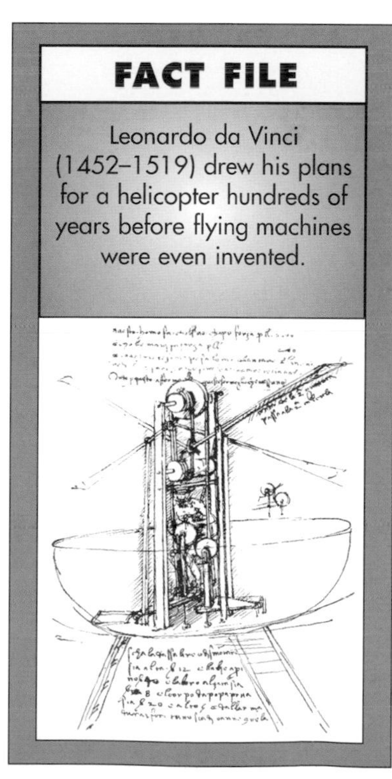

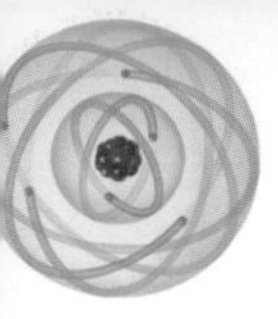

How is nuclear energy produced?

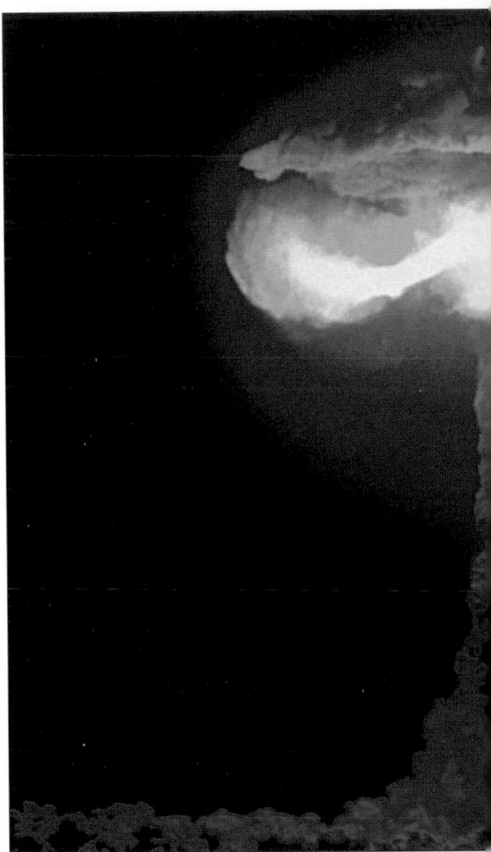

Nuclear energy is produced by changes in the nucleus of an atom of a radioactive element such as uranium or plutonium. This process is called nuclear fission.

The nucleus is split by bombarding the atom with a neutron particle. Each time the uranium atom is split in this way, it releases energy. It also produces three more neutrons, which then go on to split other uranium atoms. This is called a chain reaction because, once started, it will continue the process of nuclear fission while releasing very large quantities of energy.

In a nuclear power station this chain reaction has to be controlled. The reactor's core of uranium is surrounded with a substance that slows down and absorbs the escaping neutrons causing the material to become hot. Steam generated by this heat is used to drive turbines to produce electricity.

FACT FILE

A nuclear power station produces electricity by using a nuclear reactor which has a core of uranium, a highly radioactive material. Safety concerns have limited the use of power stations.

How do nuclear weapons work?

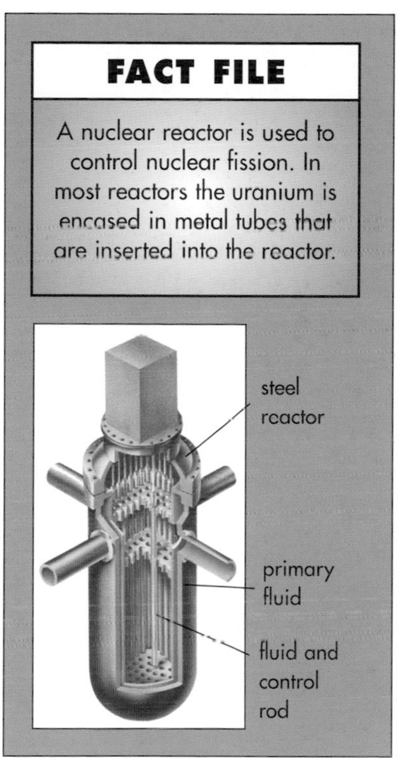

FACT FILE
A nuclear reactor is used to control nuclear fission. In most reactors the uranium is encased in metal tubes that are inserted into the reactor.
steel reactor
primary fluid
fluid and control rod

An atom bomb is a form of uncontrolled nuclear fission. When a large enough mass of uranium is put together, a fission reaction starts. The flood of neutrons emitted becomes so enormous that a vast amount of energy is released in a very short time, producing an atomic blast.

Hydrogen bombs have an atomic bomb at their core, but it is surrounded by a layer of light material. Using the power released from the fission of the uranium or plutonium core, this layer of material causes a fusion reaction like the one in the centre of the Sun. This nuclear fusion releases more heat energy than a fission explosion, as well as huge amounts of radioactivity.

How do geysers get so hot?

A geyser is really a hole in the ground which is filled with hot water. There is a tube that leads from the surface to underground reservoirs which serve as storage basins for the water. Most of the water comes from rain and snow.

Deeper in the Earth the rock is very hot. Gases from these hot rocks, mostly steam, rise through cracks in the rock and reach the underground reservoirs. They heat the water there to above boiling temperatures.

If the steam and water can rise freely from below, the result is a steadily-boiling hot spring. However, because the passageway from the water is not straight, the geyser erupts as the trapped water suddenly turns to steam. Steam requires more room than water, so it pushes up the column of water above it. Instead of just an overflow at the surface, there is a violent eruption as a result of the steam bursting upward. This produces the spectacle of a geyser!

FACT FILE

This hotel heats water for leisure purposes. The pool is a luxury attraction and people have always found pleasure swimming in warm water.

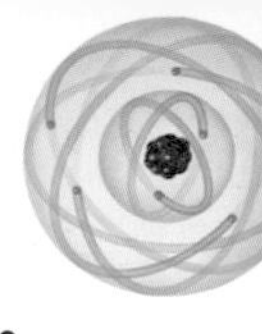

How does water boil?

When a liquid is heated, at a certain point it begins to change to a gas, or vapour, called steam. This happens because at high temperatures the molecules in the liquid move faster, until they escape into the air. Light molecules escape more easily than heavy molecules, which means that heavy, thick liquids only boil at extremely high temperatures.

The boiling point of a liquid depends on the air pressure. The pressure becomes lower at altitude, so high up on a mountain slope, water boils at a much lower temperature than normal. Water boils at 100°C at sea level, but at only 72°C at an altitude of 3,048 metres.

When water boils the steam it produces is not visible while the water remains at boiling point. However, as the steam cools it forms tiny droplets of water, making it look cloudy. This is what you can see when your breath 'steams' in very cold weather.

FACT FILE

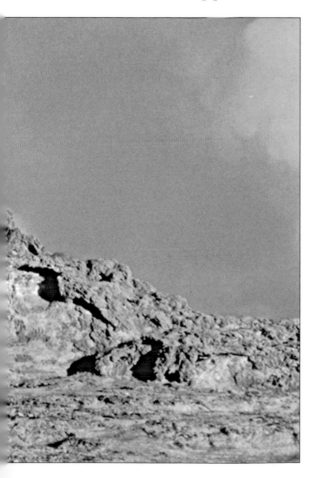

Water even exists in the driest places in the world, such as a desert. It is stored in porous rock and sand. Sometimes the edges of these water deposits are exposed and an oasis is formed where plants will grow and animals can live.

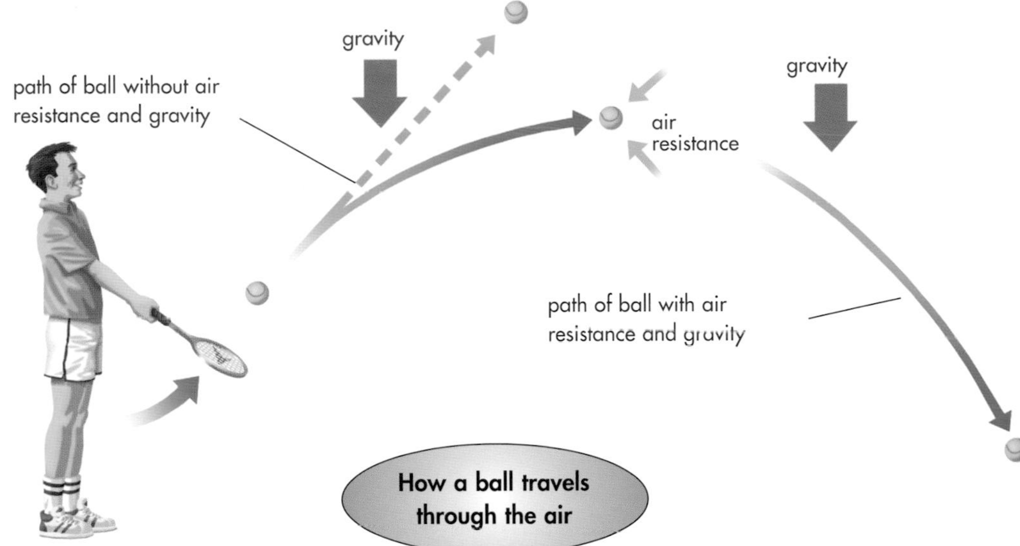

HOW DOES GRAVITY WORK?

Gravity is the force that pulls towards the centre of the Earth. It doesn't matter where you stand on the Earth's surface, the ground is always 'down'.

The force of gravity depends on the mass, or amount of material, of an object. Objects only feel heavy because of their mass.

Newton realised that gravity not only affects the Earth, but it also controls the movement of the planets and the stars, as well as the orbit of the Moon around the Earth.

When you whirl something around your head on the end of a piece of string it flies outwards and appears to defy the force of gravity. This is called centrifugal force. When you let go of the string the centrifugal force makes the object fly away in a straight line.

FACT FILE

Sir Isaac Newton (1643–1727) was the first scientist to develop the laws of gravity. He supposedly was inspired by seeing an apple fall from a tree.

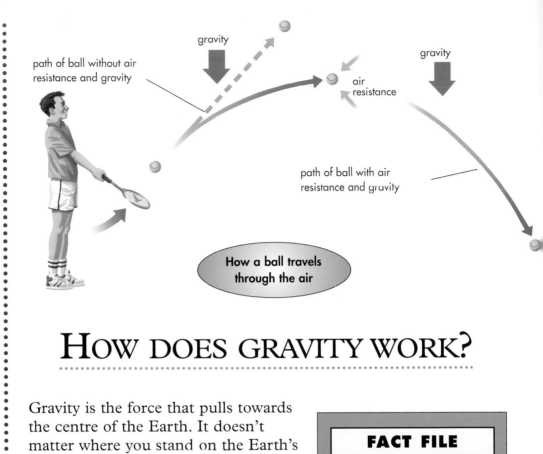

How can levers be useful?

For thousands of years people have used levers as a way of transferring a force from one place to another, and to change the amount of movement that results. Levers are really useful when you need to move a heavy object without the use of machinery.

To move a heavy object, a long lever can help. The lever is free to move about a point called the fulcrum. The shorter end of the lever is placed under the object, and force is applied to the longer end. This will cause the object to be lifted, but the long end of the lever will have to be pushed down a long way to lift the object only a short distance.

For example, with a long-enough lever you could lift a car for a short distance.

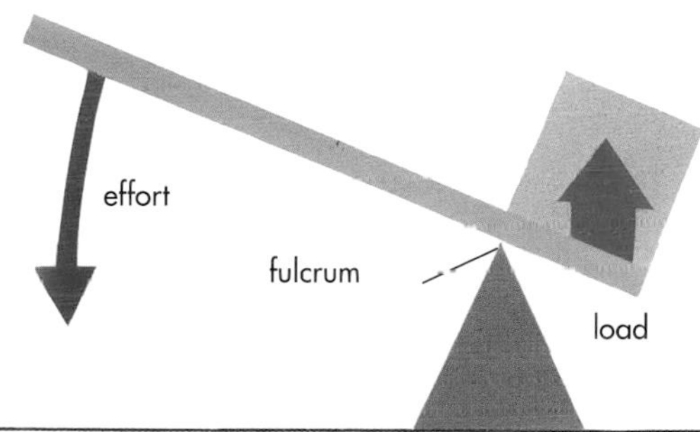

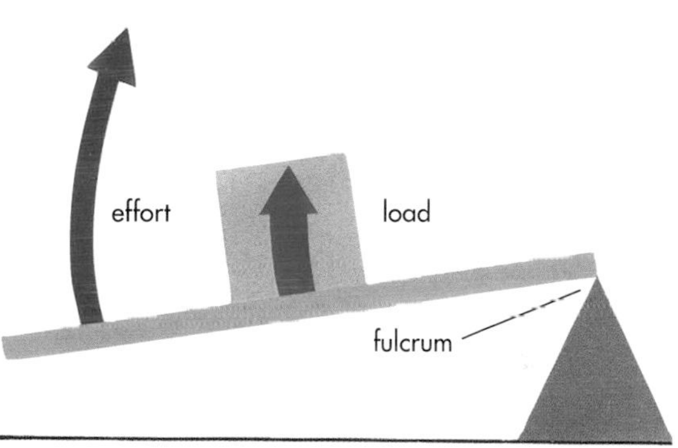

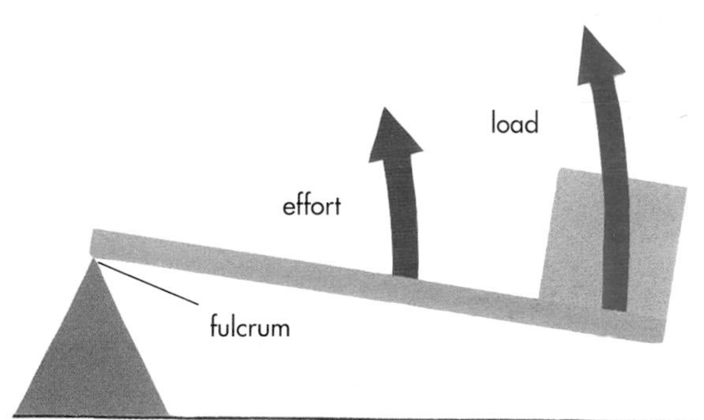

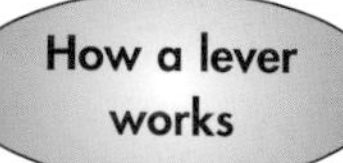

FACT FILE

Scissors work with a lever action. The cutting blades are worked by putting your forefinger and thumb into the handles and pushing together.

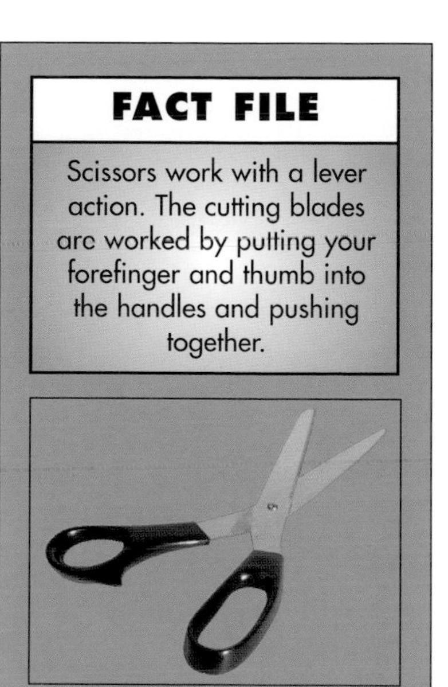

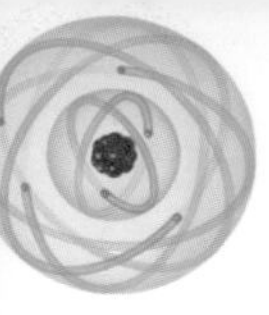

How are plastics made?

The word plastic literally means 'capable of being moulded or modelled'. When heated, plastics are somewhat like modelling clay. This is what gives them their name.

The starting point in making a plastic is the molecule. It is the smallest division of matter that still acts like the whole material from which it comes.

The chemist causes the molecules of certain materials to form a long chain, the links being the molecules. The new 'long-chain' molecule acts differently from the single molecule. It creates materials with new properties. When molecules link in this way we say they 'polymerize'.

A 'polymer', or material made from long-chain molecules, is the beginning of a plastic. It has to be changed to be suitable for moulding. At this stage it is ground into fine powder or made into pellets. Colours are added to this and chemicals are worked in to make it flexible. Some plasticizers are also added. These are chemicals which change a plastic that is stiff as a board into a material flexible enough for a raincoat.

A polymer of soft plastic

Each kind of plastic is derived from different materials. Some may come from coal, some from salt, some from wood or cotton fibres and so on. But in each case the molecules have to be rearranged in the right way and chemicals must be added.

FACT FILE

Buttons are a very good example of all the different sizes, colours and shapes that can be made from plastic. It is an adaptable material which can be drilled and moulded easily.

HOW CAN PLASTIC BE SO IMPORTANT?

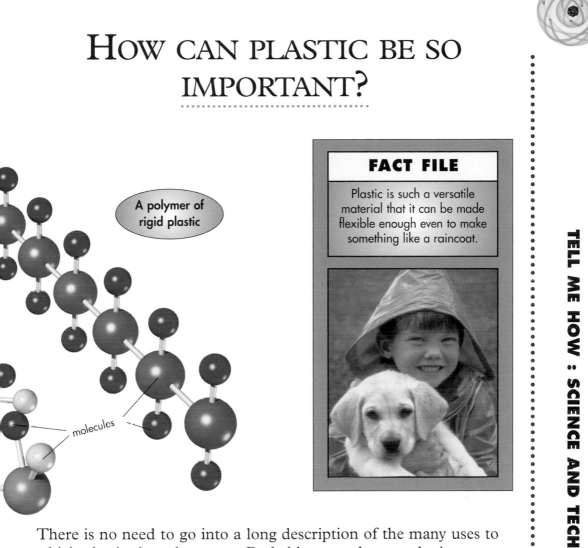

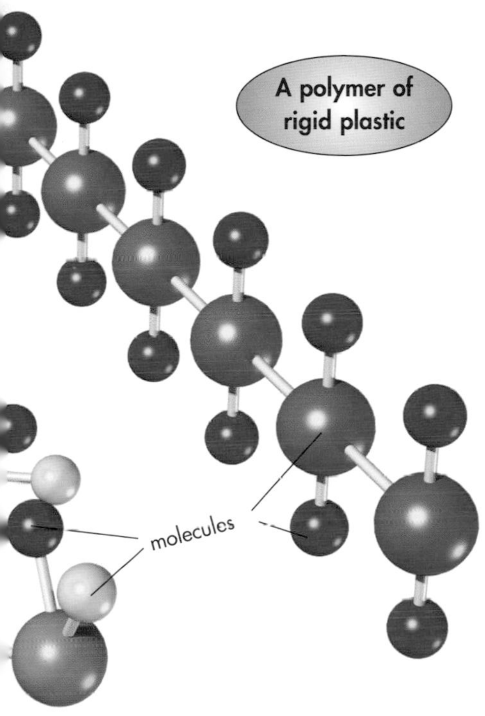

FACT FILE

Plastic is such a versatile material that it can be made flexible enough even to make something like a raincoat.

There is no need to go into a long description of the many uses to which plastics have been put. Probably not a day goes by in our life when we don't use or touch a plastic product.

Plastics have many unique properties which make them very useful for special purposes. They resist the flow of electricity, they insulate against heat, they are light in weight and wear extremely well. It is also possible to make them unbreakable.

Plastic is such a good insulator that it is used to cover copper wires in everyday household wiring. Tools such as screwdrivers, which may be used on electrical appliances, have plastic handles to provide insulation for the electrician in case the current is accidentally switched on.

Plastics made from organic compounds such as ethene can be incredibly strong. The bodies of racing cars are made from plastic that has been reinforced with glass fibre.

How does an electric motor work?

Most powered devices in the home contain an electric motor, which turns electric energy into movement. When an electric current passes along a wire in the field of a magnet, it exerts a force to move the wire. Usually the magnet is still, while the coil carrying the current spins round inside it. Domestic motors run on alternating current, and the current in the coil is rapidly reversed so the magnet's poles change direction, forcing the coil to make another half-turn. This process is repeated very rapidly as the motor turns.

When a motor runs from a direct current, which flows in only one direction, a device called a commutator reverses the current and causes the coil to rotate.

It is this motion that can be used to drive a huge number of machines, such as washing machines, hairdriers and food processors to name but a few.

FACT FILE

A voltmeter measures voltage. An electrical current flows from an area with high to low electrical potential, as in one battery terminal to another. The difference between the two is then measured in volts (V).

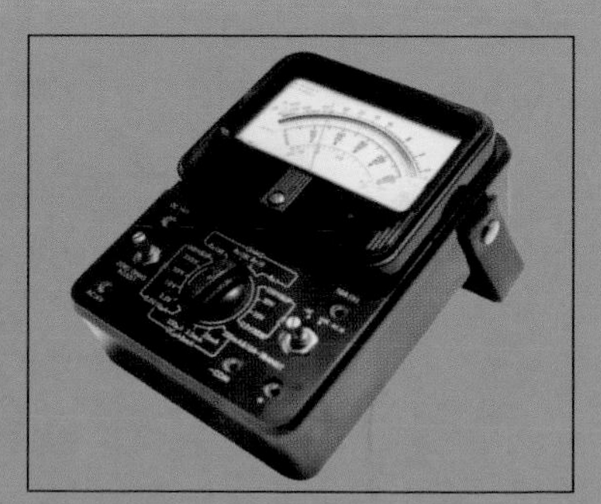

How can vehicles be powered by electricity?

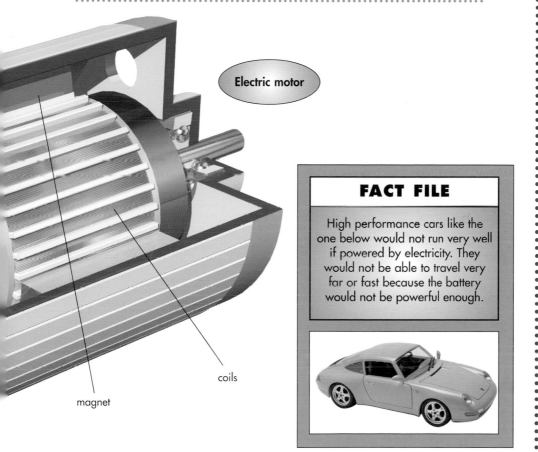

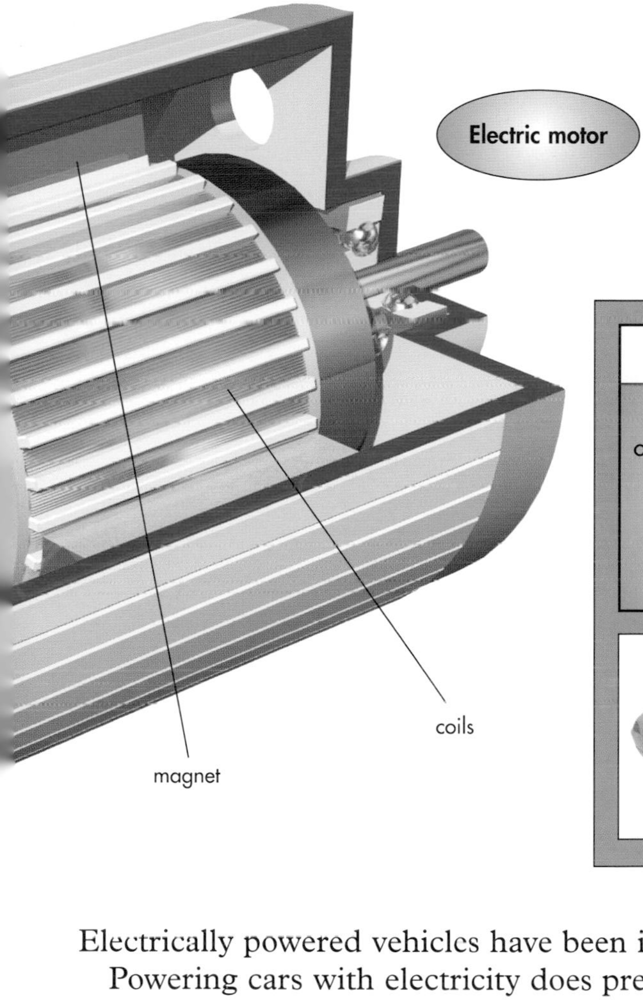

FACT FILE

High performance cars like the one below would not run very well if powered by electricity. They would not be able to travel very far or fast because the battery would not be powerful enough.

Electrically powered vehicles have been in use for many years.

Powering cars with electricity does present certain problems, however, as the batteries are heavy and a car's energy requirement is high. This means that the distance an electric car can travel before it is recharged may be too low for many uses.

Where vehicles can obtain electrical energy from a fixed wire or track, there is no problem about the electrical supply. Electrically powered trains, such as ones used in France, are the fastest in the world.

Specially designed electrically powered wheelchairs and vehicles enable disabled people to move about at the same speed as a pedestrian. These are powered by rechargeable batteries.

Earth and Space

CONTENTS

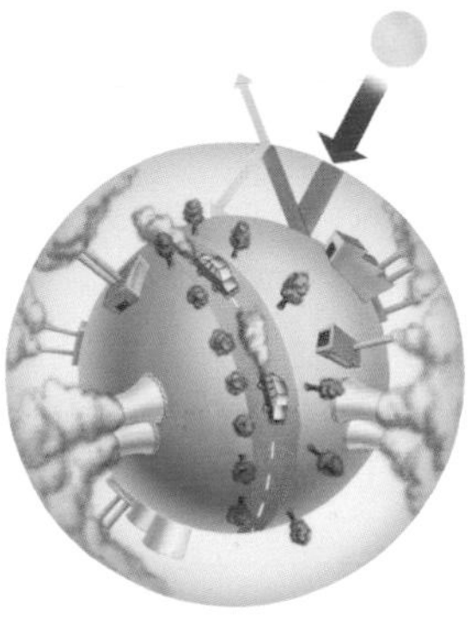

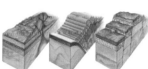

FACT FILE

When people travel long distances by fast jet plane they often get a feeling of confusion which is known as jet lag. The reason for this is because modern aircraft travel so fast that they may cross several time zones in a short time during a flight. It may take a couple of days for your brain to adjust.

12 1 am 2 3 4 5 6 7 8 9 10

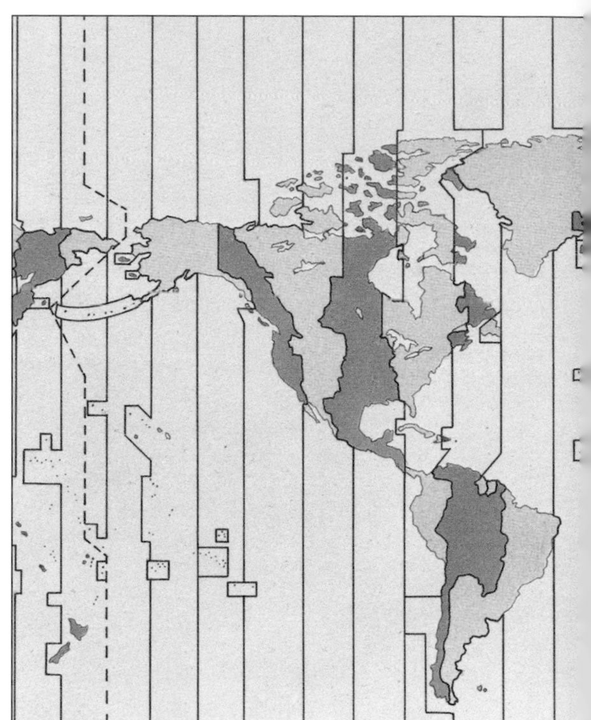

HOW DOES TIME DIFFER AROUND THE WORLD?

So that it gets light and dark at approximately the same time all over the world, it is necessary to adjust the clocks. If we did not do this, you might find that dawn was at 10 o'clock in the evening.

In the year 1884 time zones were set up around the world, measured from Greenwich in London. Each time zone on the east or west of Greenwich has a different time.

Each zone is either one hour ahead or one hour behind its neighbouring zone – it is one hour earlier to the west of each zone, and one hour later to the east.

One example of the time difference is, when it is 12 noon in Britain it is 10 o'clock at night in Sydney, Australia.

1 pm 2 3 4 5 6 7 8 9 10 11 12

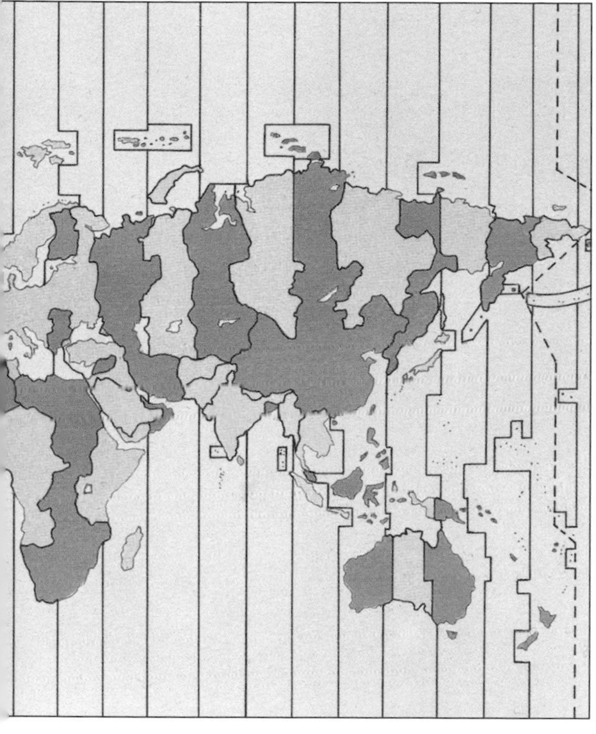

FACT FILE

Mapmakers puzzled for many years how to draw the curved surface of the globe accurately onto a sheet of paper. In 1569, Gerardus Mercator showed how to convert the rounded shape of the world into a cylindrical shape. By dividing the Earth into 'orange peel' segments it gave a truer image of the size of the countries.

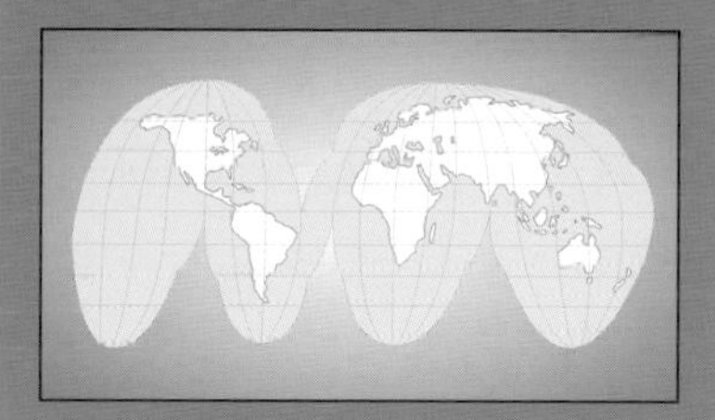

HOW FAST DOES THE EARTH MOVE?

The Earth orbits the Sun every 365¼ days. The Earth's orbit is not quite circular and when it is closest to the Sun, it moves at 18.2 miles per second and when it is farthest away from the Sun it travels at 18.8 miles per second.

The Earth also rotates about its own axis once every 23 hours, 56 minutes and 4.091 seconds. This means that the stars rise just under four minutes earlier each day. In four years this adds up to a whole day, which is why a day is added to the calendar at the end of February every fourth year, or 'leap year'.

In addition to the Earth's own movement, our solar system is orbiting the Milky Way galaxy at 160 miles per second, and the galaxy is travelling through space at about 390 miles per second.

HOW ARE WAVES CAUSED?

FACT FILE

The depth of the ocean varies widely, but the deepest part found so far is called the Marianas Trench, in the Pacific Ocean. It is an amazing depth of 11,034 m (36,200 ft).

It is noticeable that on a calm day there are very few waves, but on a stormy or windy day there are many waves. This is a result of a combination of the wind and the shape of the seabed. The wind blows the surface layers of the sea, gradually forming a rolling movement of the water. A wave is, in fact, an up-and-down movement of water particles. As the bottom of a wave strikes the ground, at a short distance from the shore, it slows down because of the friction. The top continues, and then topples over, and this is what forms a 'breaker'.

How dangerous are whirlpools?

Whirlpools occur when two opposing currents meet. They cause the water to spin round and round very rapidly. Huge whirlpools at sea are normally caused by powerful tides.

The most famous whirlpool is the Maelstrom, which appears between two islands off the coast of Norway. Sometimes this whirlpool is even strong enough to destroy small ships.

The ancient Greeks believed that the Charybdis whirlpool in the Mediterranean was caused by a monster.

FACT FILE

Flooding usually occurs when water cannot drain away fast enough in the rivers after heavy rainfall, causing them to burst their banks. Huge dams and sluice gates are often installed to reduce the risk of flooding.

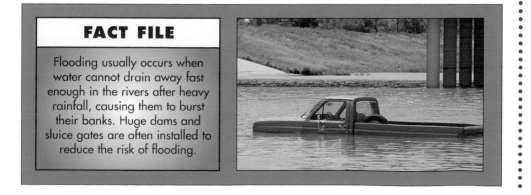

How are rivers formed?

Rivers are formed over thousands of years, as excess rain and melted snow or ice from glaciers makes its way from the land to the sea. Water drains through the ground into small streams, which join up with others as they flow downhill, eventually forming a river in the bottom of a valley.

Over thousands and thousands of years the water erodes a channel for itself. Because the flow of water is not even, the river bed can be carved into curves as one side is eroded more than the other and the position of the riverbed can change.

The power of erosion by glaciers, snow and rivers is enormous and over millions of years they grind down entire mountain chains.

FACT FILE

Usually water flows down a river, but near the coast the flow is reversed as the tide comes in. In a few large rivers very high tides force water far up the river valley and as the valley narrows, the water builds up and eventually a wave called a tidal bore passes back up the river.

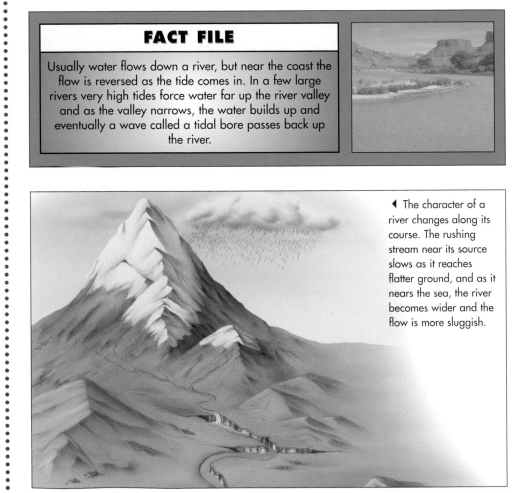

◀ The character of a river changes along its course. The rushing stream near its source slows as it reaches flatter ground, and as it nears the sea, the river becomes wider and the flow is more sluggish.

HOW ARE WATERFALLS MADE?

Small waterfalls can occur anywhere that water travels down a steep slope. But what makes large waterfalls? Water erodes soft rock, such as sandstone or shale much more easily than hard rock such as granite, so where the course of a river goes over both types, the upper layers of soft rock will be worn away more quickly, and the water (which always flows downwards) will drop down from the harder rock above, causing further erosion.

Waterfalls can be seen at the head of glacial valleys in mountains. Yosemite Falls, in Yosemite National Park, Wyoming, occurs as meltwater from a hanging valley made by a small glacier drops down to the floor of a deeper valley made by a far bigger glacier.

FACT FILE

For many centuries icebergs have been a hazard to shipping. The famous *Titanic* sunk after hitting an iceberg. Ice floats because it is lighter than water, but nine-tenths of the iceberg still lies under the water. Aircraft and space satellites now plot the path of floating icebergs, so that ships can be warned.

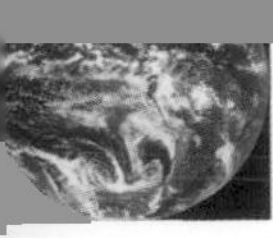

How are mountains formed?

All mountains are formed as the result of violent changes in the Earth's surface, most of which happened millions of years ago.

Folded mountains were made of rock layers that had been squeezed by great pressure into large folds.

In dome mountains, the rock layers were forced up to make greater blister-like domes on the surface of the Earth. In other cases it was molten lava, coming with great pressure from the centre of the Earth, which lifted these rock layers.

Volcanic mountains are made up of lava, ash and cinders which poured out from the Earth's core.

Block mountains are the result of breaks, or faults, in the Earth's crust. Huge parts of the surface, including entire 'blocks' of rocks, were raised up or tilted at one time.

So now you can see that mountains can be formed in many ways.

FACT FILE

Glaciers are large massses of ice that form on land and move slowly under their own weight. Glaciers have shaped most of the world's highest mountains, carving out huge valleys.

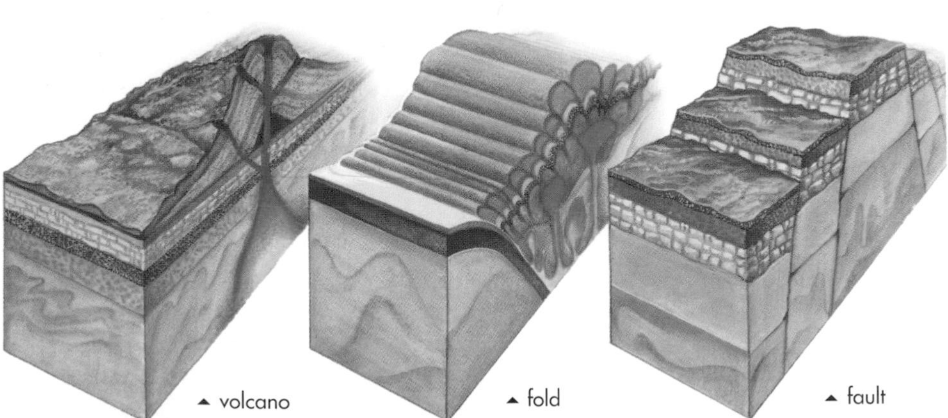

▲ volcano ▲ fold ▲ fault

HOW DOES RAIN CAUSE ROCKSLIDES?

The reason we get rockslides after heavy rain is because the rainwater enters cracks in the rock where as it freezes, it expands and opens the crack wider. As the thaw starts, the pieces of rock splinter and separate from the main rock. Loose rock is continuously building up on a mountainside, but it is normally only the small pieces that slide down. This loose, broken rock is called scree. A rockslide will take place when a mass of this broken rock slides down the side of a mountain mixed with a torrent of mud.

FACT FILE

As water vapour builds up in the winds blown towards mountains, they are forced to rise and the temperature drops. The water condenses into clouds at these higher altitudes. This is why mountain peaks are often seen to be surrounded by layers of cloud.

HOW ARE VOLCANOES FORMED?

FACT FILE

Boiling water is blasted out of the ground by a geyser. When the hot water emerges, it forms a hot spring. In some countries they use these springs for heating purposes.

The reason volcanoes are formed is because the temperature under the surface of the Earth becomes hotter and hotter the deeper down you go. At a depth of about twenty miles, it is hot enough to melt most rocks.

When rock melts, it expands and needs a lot more space. In some areas of the world mountains are being uplifted. The pressure is not so great under these rising mountain ranges, and so a reservoir of melted rock known as 'magma' may form underneath them.

This molten rock rises along cracks formed up the uplift. When the pressure in the reservoir becomes greater than the roof of rock over it, it bursts out as a volcano.

During the eruption, hot gaseous liquid, or solid material is actually blown out. The material piles up around the opening and a cone-shaped mound is formed. The cone is the result of a volcano.

In February, 1943, in the middle of a cornfield in Mexico, people saw a rare and amazing thing take place. A volcano was being born! In three months it had formed a cone about 1,000 feet high.

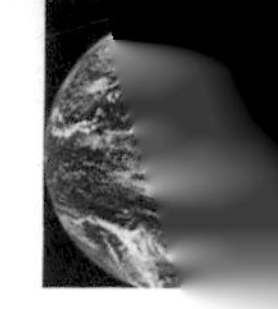

How do volcanoes erupt?

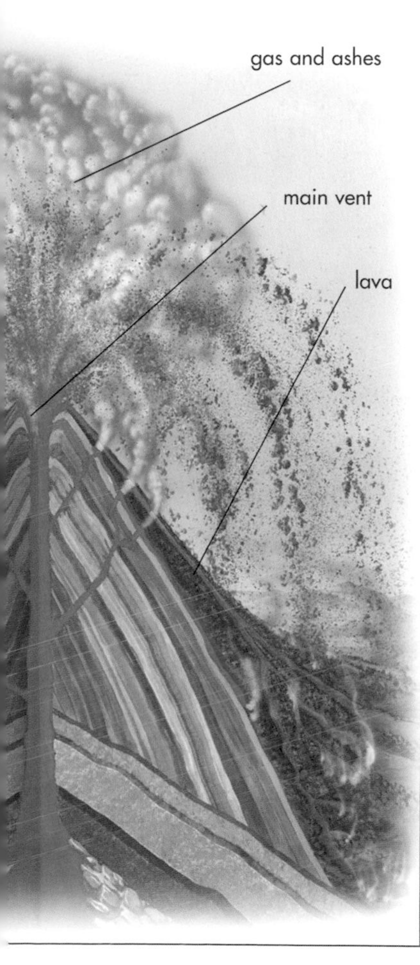

FACT FILE

The edges of the Pacific plate are surrounded by volcanic activity. Earthquakes and hot springs, caused by the shifting of the crust, and hot lava rising near the surface. There is even a volcano in the cold wastes of the Antarctic.

In the centre of a volcano is a mass of molten rock, which when it reaches the surface is known as lava. Its temperature can be as high as 1,200°C. Lava can be as runny as water or so thick that it scarcely moves at all. When the pressure in the centre of the volcano becomes too great it simply erupts.

When a volcano erupts it hurls out masses of dust and rocks, ash, steam and sulphurous gases. Lava may escape from the crater in the centre or find its way out through vents in the side of the volcano, solidifying as it cools in the air. A major volcanic eruption can hurl boulders high into the air. These boulders, called volcanic bombs, can be very large in size.

Pompeii and Herculaneum were both Roman towns that were buried under volcanic debris when Mount Vesuvius erupted in AD79. Many people were overcome while trying to escape and the two towns are still being excavated today.

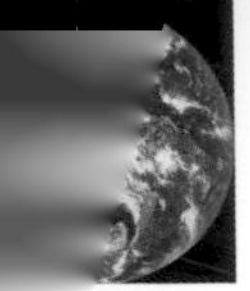

How does rain fall?

There is always water vapour in the air and during the summer there is more because the temperature is higher. When there is so much vapour in the air it only takes a tiny drop in temperature to make the vapour condense and form tiny droplets of water, and we say the air is saturated.

FACT FILE
A rainbow is one of the most beautiful sights. It is quite simply a great curved spectrum, or band of colours, caused by the breaking up of light which has passed through raindrops

So what happens when all these water droplets in a cloud meet a mass of cooler air? If the air is very moist the droplets cannot evaporate. Instead they get bigger and bigger as more and more condensation takes place. Soon, each tiny droplet has become a drop and it starts to fall downward and we have rain!

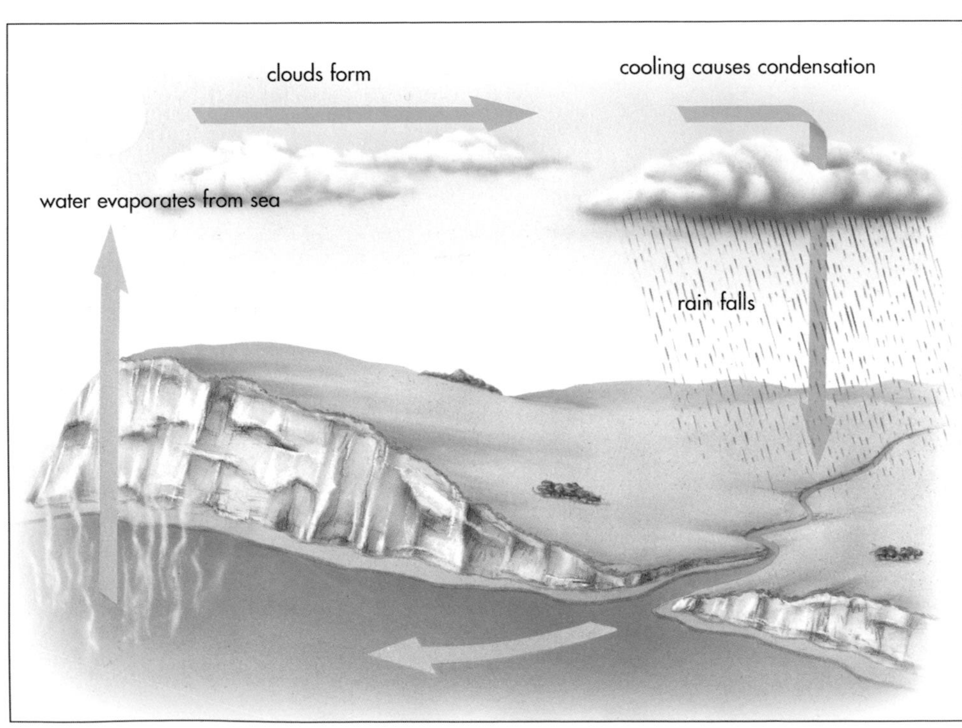

HOW DOES PRESSURE AFFECT OUR WEATHER?

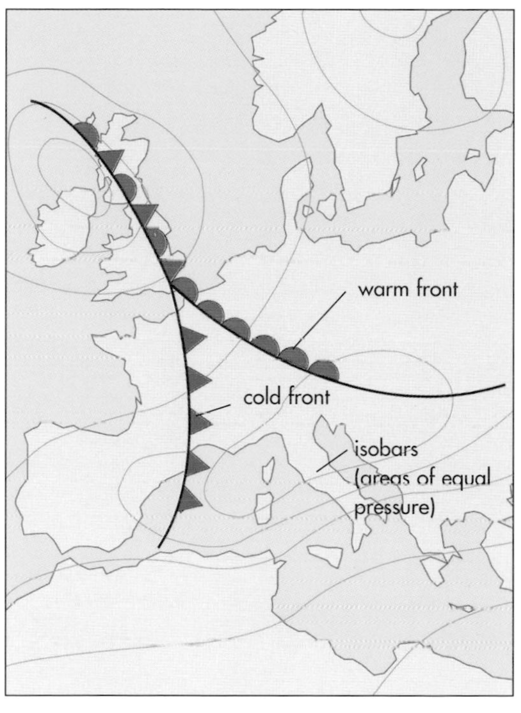

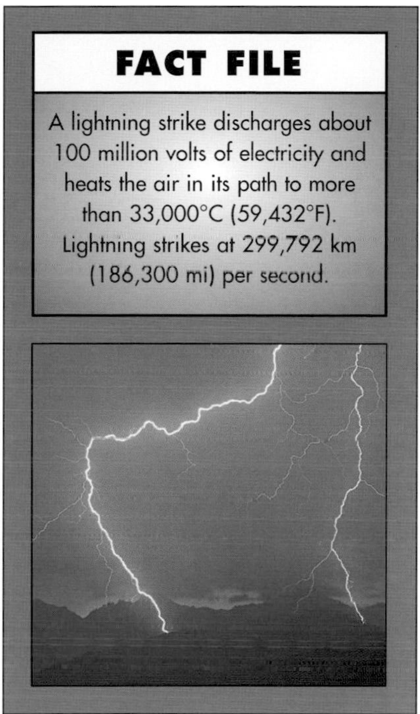

Weather is simply what the air or atmosphere is like at that time. No matter what the air is – cold, cool, warm, hot, calm, breezy, windy, dry, moist, or wet – that is still weather.

Air pressure differs across all parts of the Earth's surface, and this difference causes winds. Air will move from an area of high pressure, or an anticyclone, to an area of low pressure, or a depression.

Depressions are usually associated with bad weather conditions and rain. These changes in air pressure can be measured by an instrument called a barometer.

When meteorologists talk about a weather front, they are referring to the boundary between two masses of air at different temperatures and pressures. Increasingly accurate forecasting is now possible with the aid of satellites and computer technology.

HOW DOES AIR BECOME POLLUTED?

Air pollution is mostly caused by human activities. Exhaust fumes from motor vehicles are one of the main pollutants. They contain greenhouse gases which are thought to contribute to global warming. They also contain substances such as sulphur and nitrogen oxides that can cause damage to our lungs.

Very large amounts of pollution are produced as a result of more and more industry. In many countries industrial pollution is now controlled, but it still causes a large amount of damage to our health and the environment in many developing countries.

Another recent form of pollution came from parts of Asia where they were burning down the rainforest to clear the land for farming.

FACT FILE

Deforestation can have a terrible effect on the ecology of a region.

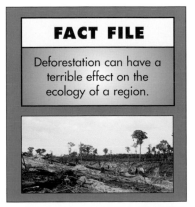

How can aerosols damage the Earth?

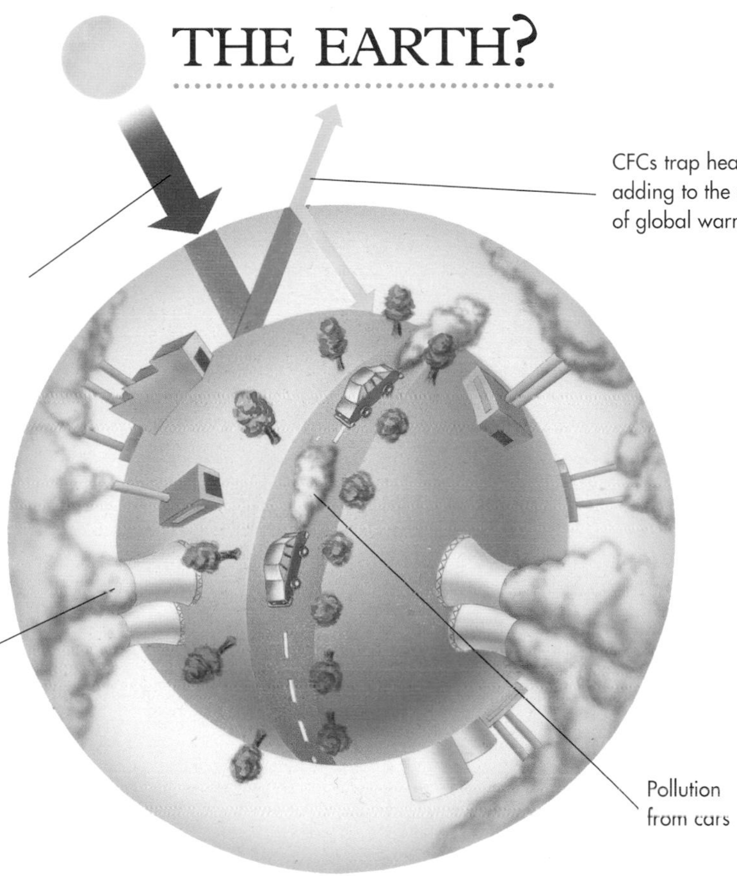

Heat from the Sun hits the Earth

CFCs trap heat adding to the effects of global warming

Pollution from factories

Pollution from cars

Mammoths lived in an area with a cool climate, but gradually the weather began to get warmer. Unable to adapt, the mammoth became extinct.

Scientists have discovered a gap in the protective ozone layer around the Earth. Ozone, a form of oxygen, filters out more than 90 per cent of the Sun's harmful rays.

The hole in the ozone layer has been blamed on our use of chemicals called chlorofluorocarbons (or CFCs). They were widely used in refrigerators, freezers and aerosol cans.

The use of CFCs has now been heavily restricted, but it may take many many years before the ozone layer actually repairs itself.

HOW DOES AN EARTHQUAKE BEGIN?

200 million years ago

100 million years ago

Pangaea

Laurasia

Gondwanaland

The Earth's crust is made up of about 30 huge plates, called tectonic plates, that float on the semi-liquid mantle surrounding the Earth's core. There are currents and movements in the mantle, so these plates move very slowly in relation to each other.

Earthquakes are evidence of this movement. Most of the areas where earthquakes take place are along the edges of these plates. Friction holds the plate edges together for a while, but continuing movement means that huge stresses build up. The tension is suddenly released when the plates shift sharply, but this causes an earthquake. There are other causes of earthquakes, but they all involve sudden movement of the crust along a fault or crack.

FACT FILE

Primeval Earth was a violent and poisonous place. The mass of seething chemicals gave rise to primitive life. It was the presence of these life forms that eventually produced the Earth we know.

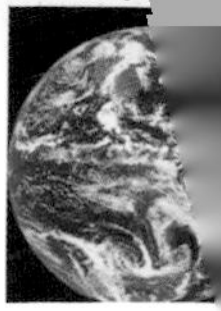

Tornadoes are a regular meteorological event in the southern states of the USA. They cause huge damage in a narrow strip as they pass over the land.

HOW DOES A TORNADO START?

A tornado is formed when huge masses of clouds moving in different directions meet. The air starts to spin in a spiral and a funnel of twisting air reaches out towards the ground. The low pressure inside the funnel sucks up soil, dust and anything else it touches.

Tornadoes are violent destructive whirlwinds whose force is concentrated into a much smaller area than a hurricane. They travel across land at very high speeds and the roaring noise they make can be heard 40 km away.

FACT FILE
Enormous hurricanes sweep across the tropical oceans and cause floods and devastation.

How big are asteroids?

Asteroids are small rocky or icy bodies that orbit the Sun. There are over 100,000 in orbit and some measure less than 1 km across, while the largest is 1,003 km. They are sometimes called minor planets. Most asteroids are found in an orbit between Mars and Jupiter, and more than 7,000 of them have been identified.

Asteroids are actually smaller than any of the planets, and only a few of them have a diameter of more than 30 km.

The term asteroid is usually applied to objects larger than 1.6 km in diameter.

One asteroid, called Ida, has a tiny moon of its own and this is the smallest known satellite in the Solar System. Asteroids were probably formed at the same time as the planets.

The 'asteroid belt' lies between the orbits of Mars and Jupiter. It is thought that this may have been the shattered remains of a planet destroyed by Jupiter's enormous gravity.

FACT FILE

Many asteroids have struck the Earth already, and many scientists believe that such an impact resulted in the extinction of the dinosaurs about 65 million years ago.

How are meteorites formed?

Meteorites are made of rock or metal. They enter the Earth's atmosphere at speeds of at least 11 km per second, which makes them glow brightly. Several thousand meteorites enter the Earth's atmosphere every year, but very few of them reach the ground.

The largest known meteorite is made of iron and weighs 66 tonnes. It probably fell to the Earth in prehistoric times in what is now called Namibia, southwest Africa.

It is very hard to find meteorites. Recently, researchers have been finding them on the ice sheets in the Arctic and the Antarctic, where they are easier to locate.

On planets and moons with no atmosphere, huge numbers of meteorites strike with enormous power. Our own Moon is estimated to have 3,000,000 meteorite craters measuring 1 m or more in diameter.

However, meteorite craters are rare on Earth because the atmosphere slows the meteorite and usually burns it up. Many ancient meteorite craters have been worn away by water and weather over thousands of years.

The Asteroid Belt

FACT FILE

An enormous meteorite caused this huge impact crater at Wolf Creek in Australia. The amount of energy the impact released would have been equivalent to hundreds of nuclear weapons.

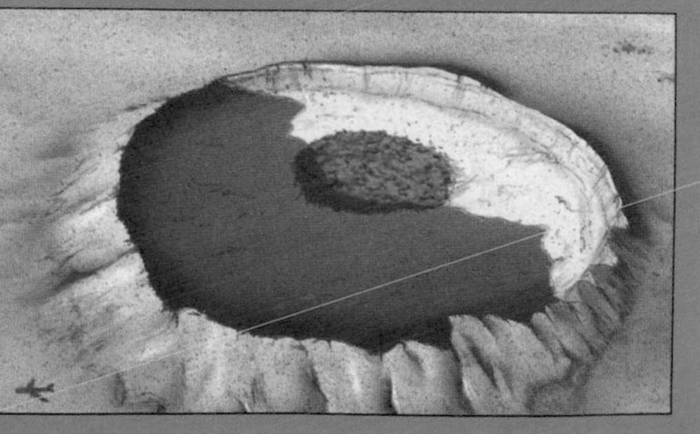

HOW DO STARS FALL?

For thousands of years men have looked up at 'falling stars' and wondered what they were and where they came from. Today, however, we know that they are not 'stars', but 'meteors'. Meteors are small solid bodies which travel through space and may also pass through the Earth's atmosphere.

When meteors come into our atmosphere we can see them because they leave a fiery train of light which is caused by the heat made by the rubbing of air upon their surfaces. Thousands of meteors fall to Earth each day but, as most of the Earth's surface is covered by water, they usually fall into the oceans or lakes.

Meteors may appear in the sky singly, which is why they are often mistaken for a 'falling star'. Astronomers now believe that meteors are the broken fragments of comets. They move through space as a meteor swarm or stream, and move in regular orbits, or paths, through space.

FACT FILE

Sometimes it is very difficult to see stars. The stars are still there but it may be that clouds are covering the night sky. Also there are so many artificial lights from our homes and street lighting, that it is often not dark enough to see the stars.

How do stars make pictures?

Have you ever looked at the stars and made squares, letters or other pictures out of them? For many years people have done the same thing and have given names to the groups of stars they observed. Such a group is called a 'constellation' which comes from the Latin word meaning 'star' (*stella*) and 'together'.

The names in use today have been handed down to us from the Romans and Greeks. What the Greeks knew about the stars came partly from the Babylonians. The Babylonians named some of their star 'pictures' after animals and others after kings and queens. Later, the Greeks changed many of these names to those of their own heroes such as Hercules, Orion and Perseus.

The Milky Way

The Romans made further changes and these names are still used today. For example, *Aquila* is the eagle, *Canis Major* and *Canis Minor* are big and little dogs and *Libra* is the scales. Later on astronomers added more constellations, and today they recognize 88 constellations in the sky.

FACT FILE

Halley's Comet returns to Earth every 76 years after having travelled out close to the orbit of Pluto. Its last visit to Earth was in 1986.

HOW MUCH DOES THE ATMOSPHERE WEIGH?

The Earth is surrounded by a thick blanket of air, called the atmosphere, which is made up of about 20 gases. The two main gases are oxygen and nitrogen. It also contains water vapour and dust particles.

Air is matter and, like all matter, it has weight. Weight is the measure of the pull of gravity on matter. If you place a stone on a pair of scales and it weighs 5 kilograms, it means that gravity is pulling the stone with a force of 5 kilograms.

Earth's gravity pulls on each particle of gas and dust in the atmosphere. If it was possible to place this on a pair of scales it would weigh about 5,700,000,000,000,000 (quadrillion) tonnes!

The air presses down on us and against us from all sides. Something like a ton of air is pressing against you at this very moment, and yet you are not aware of this because your body is made to live with this pressure.

The Earth's atmosphere is one of the things that makes it a planet of life. It is the air we breathe, it shields us from certain rays of the sun, it protects the Earth from extremes of hot and cold and serves us in many other ways.

FACT FILE

Beneath the land and water that cover the Earth's surface lie layers of rock and metal at very high temperatures. The deepest mines ever dug have not reached the bottom of the outer layer, called the crust. Under the crust is a layer of partly solid and partly molten rock.

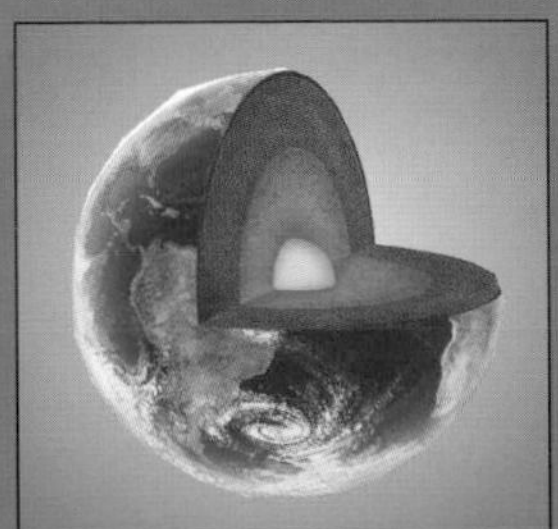

HOW OLD IS THE EARTH?

The Earth began to be formed over 4.5 billion years ago, but for millions of years nothing could live here. Gradually, the Earth's crust and the atmosphere formed.

As soon as it was proved that the Earth revolved around the Sun (meaning that it was part of the solar system), then scientists knew where to start. To find the age of the Earth it was necessary to find out how the Sun and all the planets came into being.

There are two theories: the nebular hypothesis theory whereby a mass of white-hot gas whirled about in space getting smaller and hotter all the time, eventually throwing off rings of gas which condensed to form a planet. And secondly, the planetisimal theory: a great star pulled on the sun and caused parts of it to break away attracting tiny planetisimals (planetisimals are a huge mass of small, solid bodies). Whichever theory is right, astronomers have worked out that the Earth is probably 5,500,000,000 years old.

The surface of the Earth is changing all the time. Over millions of years, an original, single land mass broke up and moved to become the continents we recognize today.

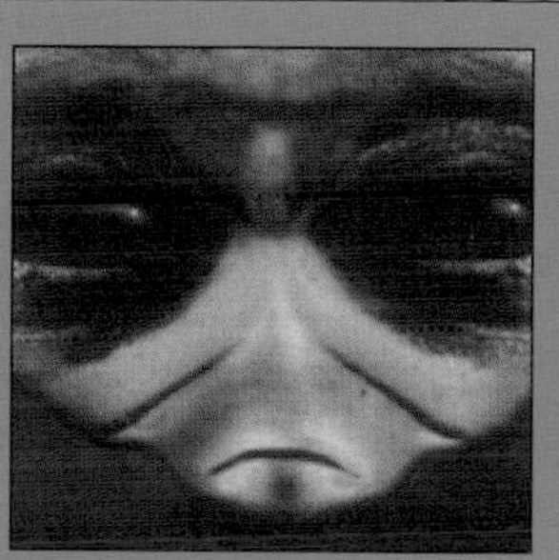

FACT FILE

No one has ever proved that life exists on other planets. However, as there are billions of stars, some with planets, it seems unlikely that Earth is the only place with the right conditions for life. Astronomers use radio telescopes to search for messages from other civilizations.

How could planets collide?

Look up into the sky and see all the stars and planets and you might wonder if there might be a collision some day. But luckily this is not likely to happen.

What we fail to realize is how much further away certain stars and planets are from the Earth than others. To get a better idea of this, let's consider our solar system and its planets.

Let's imagine your head is the Sun in both size and location in the solar system. Your head is then in the centre of a number of rings of different sizes. These rings are the orbits which the planets travel around the Sun.

With your head as the centre, Mercury is the nearest (about 6 metres away from you), Venus moves around in the second ring (12 metres away), in the third ring is Earth (16 metres from your head), in the fourth ring is Mars, smaller than Earth, and 25 metres away. Next is Jupiter, the largest of all the planets, in the sixth ring is Saturn, nearly a city street away, Uranus is nearly two streets away and finally, Pluto, which is nearly four streets away.

Since each of them goes around you in its orbit without ever changing, you can now see why they are not likely to bump into one another!

FACT FILE

Mars is known as the 'Red Planet' because it is covered by a stony desert that contains lots of iron oxide, making it appear a rusty-red colour. At one time Mars had an atmosphere containing oxygen, and valleys through which water may have flowed.

Saturn

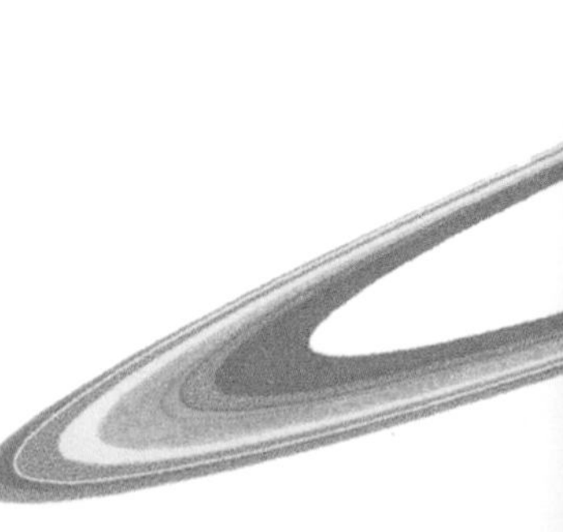

How was the light year discovered?

crescent phase

FACT FILE

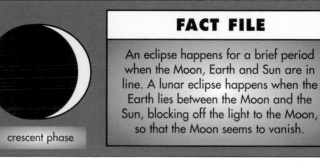

An eclipse happens for a brief period when the Moon, Earth and Sun are in line. A lunar eclipse happens when the Earth lies between the Moon and the Sun, blocking off the light to the Moon, so that the Moon seems to vanish.

Neptune

The time that it takes for a beam of light to travel between stars in a vacuum is determined and measured in light years using the 'constant' that is the speed of light. This is the 'c' in Einstein's famous equation $E=mc^2$. The finite speed of light was the really important determination, made first by a Danish Astronomer called Olaus Roemer, in 1676, when he was studying the motion of Jupiter. In our own time Professor Albert Michelson spent years trying to determine the exact speed of light. He arrived at a speed of 300 km (186,284 mi) per second, and this is now considered to be quite accurate. If we multiply this by the number of seconds in a year, we would find that light travels at a speed of 5,880,000,000,000 miles in a year – and this is called a light year.

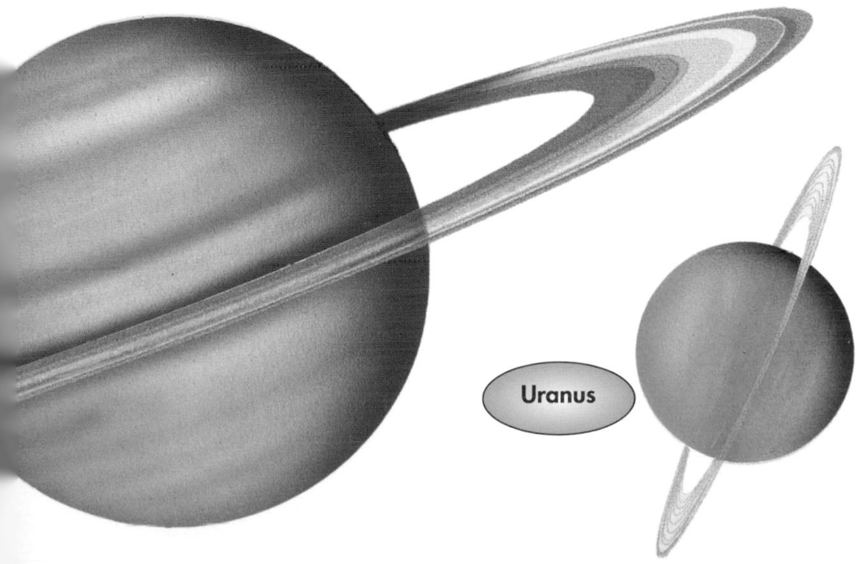

Uranus

HOW FAR DOES OUTER SPACE GO?

Most astronomers believe that the universe we see is only part of the whole universe. They picture the whole universe as extending much further into space. But how far does it really extend and does it go on forever? Perhaps there is an end to it and, if there is an end, what lies beyond it?

The answer may lay in the nature of space itself and the fact that space curves around on itself. This means that you can never get 'outside' space because your path will always curve around and lead you back again.

So, just as it is possible to fly around the earth indefinitely without leaving it, you could also travel out in space for as long as you wished – but NEVER outside it.

FACT FILE

The first person to travel in space was a Russian cosmonaut named Yuri Alekseyevich Gagarin. His spaceship was called Vostok I and he went on 12 April 1961.

A Black Hole space tunnel

How fast does the Earth move?

The Earth has two motions – it spins on its axis and it moves in an orbit around the Sun.

The period of rotation through 360 degrees (that is one complete turn of the Earth) takes 23 hours, 56 minutes and 4.091 seconds.

It was believed that the speed of the rotation never changed, but it has been found that there are tiny variations. Because of the friction of ocean tides and changes in the Earth's crust, our day may be getting longer at the rate of about one-thousandth of a second per century.

A planet moves faster when it is closer to the Sun and since the Sun does not stay the same at all times, the orbital speed is constantly changing.

FACT FILE

Humans have a built-in body clock and normally have a good idea of the time even without the use of clocks, because our body is aware of the amount of time that has passed since daybreak.

How big is the universe?

Not only do we not know how big the universe is, but it is also impossible for the human mind to imagine how big it might be.

The reason for this is that Earth is only a a very tiny part of the solar system which consists of the Sun, the planets that revolve around it, the asteroids, which are tiny planets, and the meteors.

Again this solar system is only a tiny part of another much larger system called 'a galaxy', which is made up of many millions of stars, and they may also have solar systems of their own.

There are probably millions of galaxies and perhaps all these galaxies put together are still only a part of some larger system!

FACT FILE

More than two-thirds of the Earth's surface is covered by seas and oceans. About 72 per cent of the Earth's surface is water. This water is either in the oceans, locked away as ice at the poles, or held as water vapour in the atmosphere. All the Earth's water is known as the hydrosphere.

What is the Earth made of ?

The Earth is a big ball, or sphere, made mostly of rock. The inside is molten rock, but the outside cover is hard rock.

The outside of the Earth is a crust of rock, called the lithosphere, about 16 to 48 km (10 to 30 mi) thick. The high parts of this crust are the continents, and the low parts of it hold the waters of the oceans, seas and lakes. All the water on the surface is called the hydrosphere. The crust of the Earth has two layers: the upper layer, made of granite, and a thicker, lower layer made of basalt. Between the central ball and the rocky crust is a shell about 3,219 km (2,000 mi) thick called the mantle.

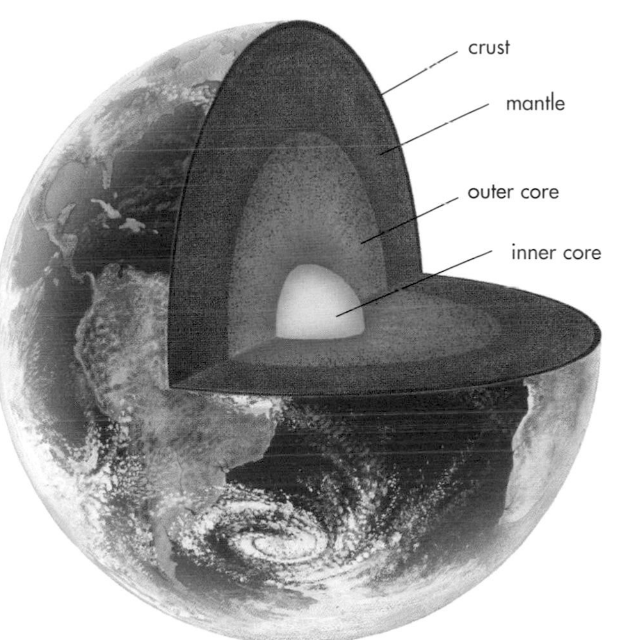

In drilling wells and mines, it has been found that the deeper the hole is made, the higher the temperature becomes. At 3.2 km (2 mi) below the surface of the Earth, the temperature is high enough to boil water. At the core, the temperature is believed to be as high as 5537.7°C (10,000°F).

FACT FILE

Volcanoes are openings in the Earth's crust through which molten lava, red-hot rocks, steam and fumes pour out. Most volcanoes have a single central pipe through which lava reaches the surface, building up into a cone as it cools. This consists of layers of lava and volcanic ash with a crater at the centre. Active volcanoes smoke and spit out pieces of lava.

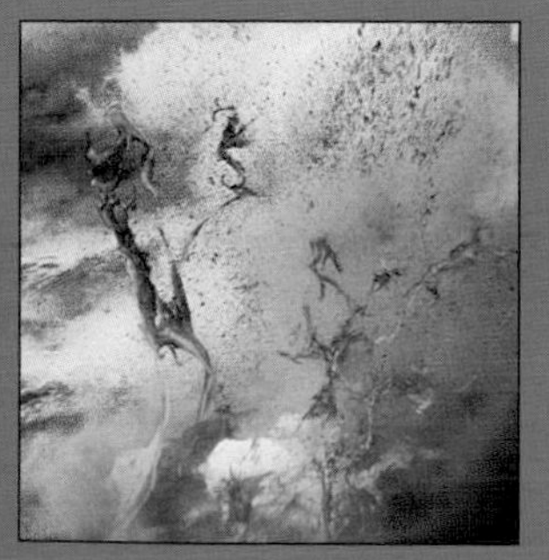

How are stars formed?

A star is a huge ball of bright, hot gases. Stars contain a great deal of hydrogen which is their main source of energy. They also contain many different chemical elements such as helium, nitrogen, oxygen, iron, nickel and zinc.

Stars come into existence in the vast clouds of dust and gas that move through space. They begin to form when a large number of gas particles whirl together within such a cloud. These particles attract more particles, and as the group gradually gets larger and larger, its gravitational pull gets stronger and they form a giant ball of gas.

As this ball grows, the particles inside press down on those below them and pressure builds up inside the ball. Eventually the pressure becomes strong enough to raise the temperature of the gases and they begin to glow. When the pressure and temperature inside the ball become very high, nuclear reactions take place and these gases become a star. This process will take a few million years!

Our Sun is actually a star and it is about 109 times the diameter of Earth.

FACT FILE

A nebula is an enormous mass of gas and solid material that appears to be solid. However, it is mostly composed of dust and gas which slowly condenses into stars.

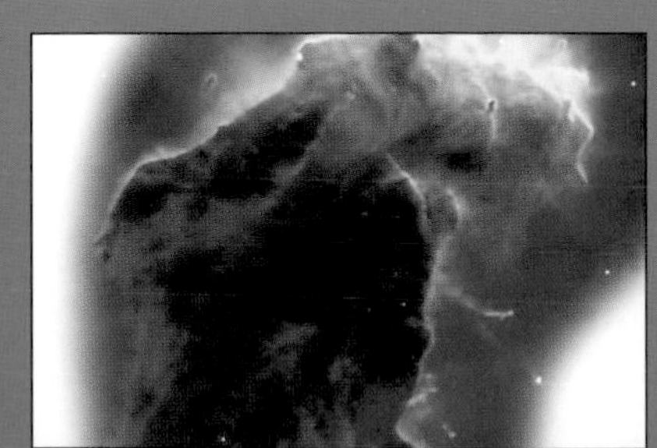

How far away are the stars?

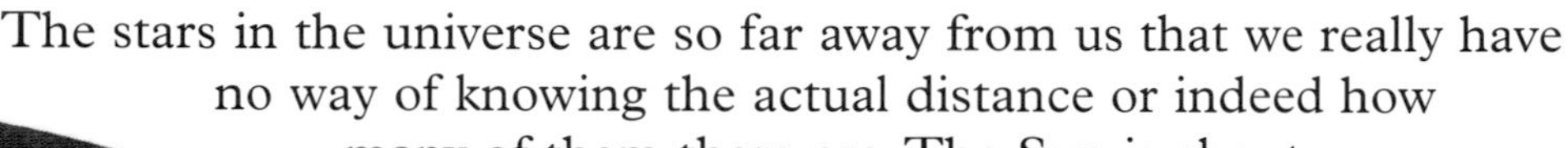

The stars in the universe are so far away from us that we really have no way of knowing the actual distance or indeed how many of them there are. The Sun is about 93,000,000 miles from Earth and as light travels at the rate of 186,000 miles a second it would take eight minutes for the light from the Sun to reach us. The closest stars to Earth are Proxima Centauri and Alpha Centauri. Their distance from the Earth is 270,000 times greater than the distance from the Sun to the Earth, making their distance from us 270,000 times 93,000,000 miles! This means that it would take their light four and a half years to reach the Earth.

The distances involved are so great that a unit for measuring this distance was worked out and this is called the light year. A light year is the distance that light travels in one year. Of the numerous stars in the sky you can only see about 6,000 without a telescope. If you were looking up and counting the stars, the most you would be able to count at any one time would be little over one thousand stars.

FACT FILE

The large Hadron Collider, successfully tested in 2010 will teach us more about particle acceleration and the birth of stars and the deepest laws of nature.

HOW DOES A SPACE SHUTTLE REACH SPACE?

The space shuttle is the first reusable spacecraft. It was developed to provide a reusable, and therefore cheaper, vehicle for launching satellites and for other work in space.

The shuttle itself is a bulky delta-winged aircraft with extremely powerful rocket motors.

When it is launched, two solid-fuel booster rockets are strapped to its sides and a giant fuel tank is fixed to its belly. The rockets and fuel tank both fall away after the launch, and the rockets are recovered and then reused. At takeoff the space shuttle weighs 2,000 tonnes. It burns almost all of its fuel in the first few minutes after launch, then continues to coast into its orbit 300 km above the surface of the Earth.

When it is in orbit the shuttle's cargo bay opens to release satellites or allow the crew to work in space. The shuttle lands on a runway just like a conventional aeroplane.

FACT FILE

You cannot breathe in space because there is no air. Oxygen is the gas we need to stay alive so all space missions carry their own air supply. When astronauts go on a 'space walk' they wear a space suit that provides them with the correct air and pressure.

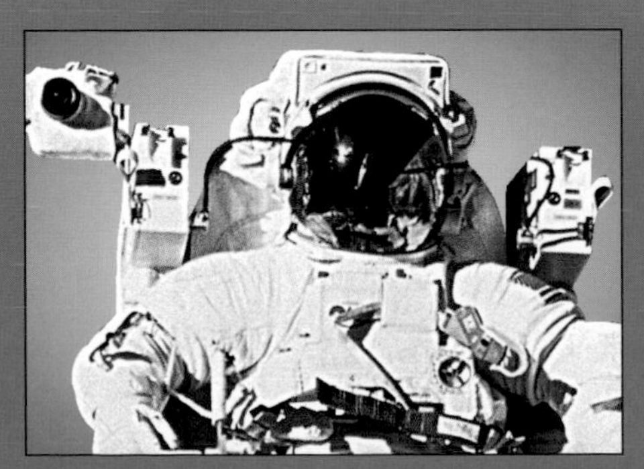

HOW ARE ROCKETS AND SHUTTLES POWERED?

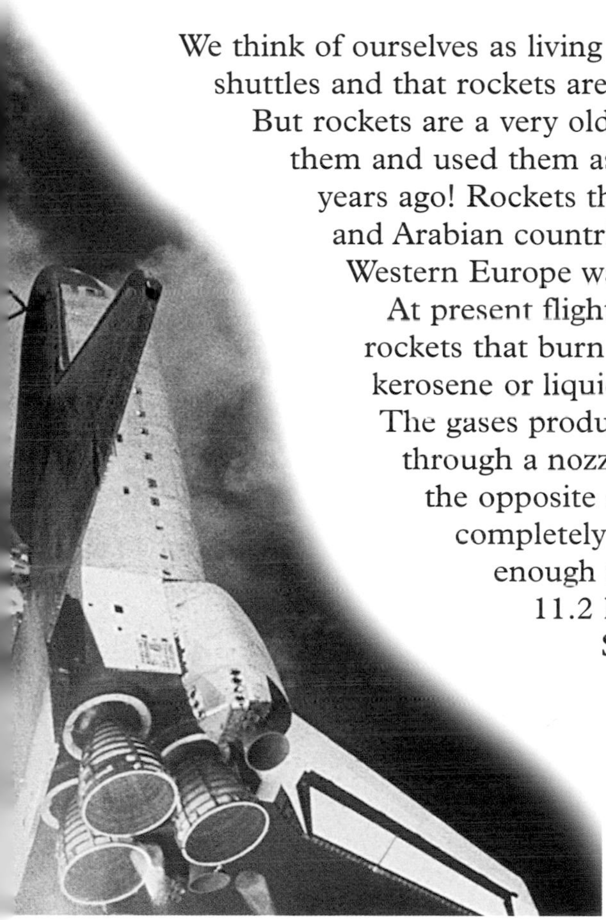

We think of ourselves as living in the age of rockets and shuttles and that rockets are rather a modern invention. But rockets are a very old idea. The Chinese invented them and used them as fireworks more than 800 years ago! Rockets then became known in Indian and Arabian countries. The first record of them in Western Europe was in CE 1256.

At present flights into space are powered by rockets that burn liquid oxygen with either kerosene or liquid hydrogen, or by solid fuel. The gases produced are forced downwards through a nozzle, which forces the rocket in the opposite direction. To escape completely from the Earth, rockets have enough thrust to reach a speed of 11.2 km (7 mi) per second.

Space agencies are trying different forms of fuel for craft once they are beyond the Earth's influence, such as nuclear power, ion drives or even sailing on the solar wind.

FACT FILE

Space stations are constructed from modules small enough to be carried into space by rockets or the space shuttle. They are assembled once they are in orbit. Space stations allow the crew to work in space for long periods in conditions of zero gravity.

The Prehistoric World

CONTENTS

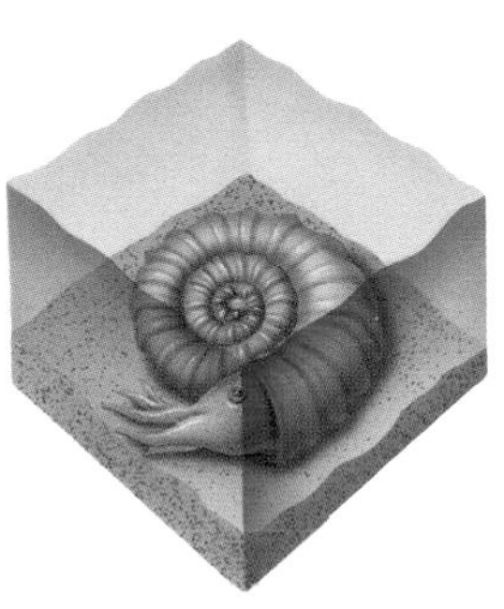

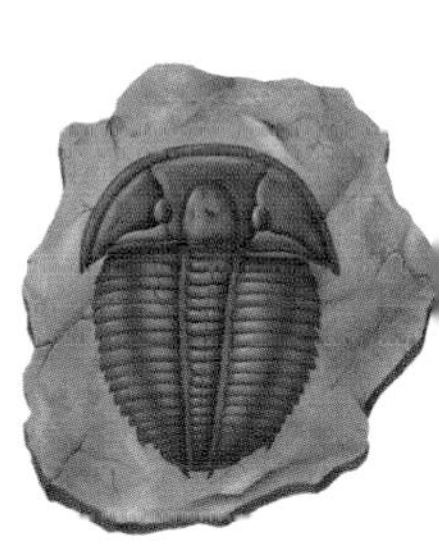

HOW ARE PREHISTORIC TIMES CATEGORIZED?

Geological time covers many millions of years and it has been divided up into eras, which are periods of time identified by the fossilized forms of life from that period.

The oldest era, called the Palaeozoic, contains fossils ranging from many primitive life forms up to some of the earliest land-dwelling animals. During this era fishes, amphibians and early reptiles appeared.

The Mesozoic era was the age of giant reptiles, when dinosaurs stalked the world.

The Cenozoic era in which we still live is the age of mammals and birds. All fossils can be placed in these eras, which are subdivided further into smaller periods as shown on the chart here.

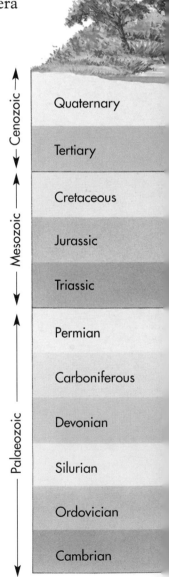

Era	Period
Cenozoic	Quaternary
	Tertiary
Mesozoic	Cretaceous
	Jurassic
	Triassic
Palaeozoic	Permian
	Carboniferous
	Devonian
	Silurian
	Ordovician
	Cambrian

FACT FILE

Now the habits of dinosaurs are becoming better understood, museums are able to mount their fossilized remains in realistic poses that show people how they lived.

How have we learnt from prehistory?

Almost everything that we know about the living things on Earth before humans evolved has been learnt from fossils. Fossils are the remains of dead animals and plants that have been turned to stone over millions of years.

By studying these remains scientists have been able to come up with the type of animals that existed both on land and in water and also details of the type of food they needed to exist.

Records of prehistory and examples of fossils can be found in many of our modern museums.

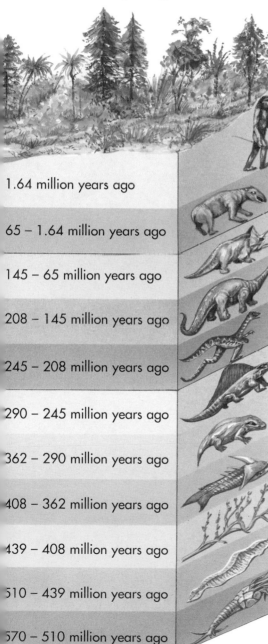

1.64 million years ago

65 – 1.64 million years ago

145 – 65 million years ago

208 – 145 million years ago

245 – 208 million years ago

290 – 245 million years ago

362 – 290 million years ago

408 – 362 million years ago

439 – 408 million years ago

510 – 439 million years ago

570 – 510 million years ago

FACT FILE

This shark, called *Carcharocles*, lived about 15 million years ago, and was about the size of a bus. Only its huge teeth have survived and so scientists were only able to estimate its actual size.

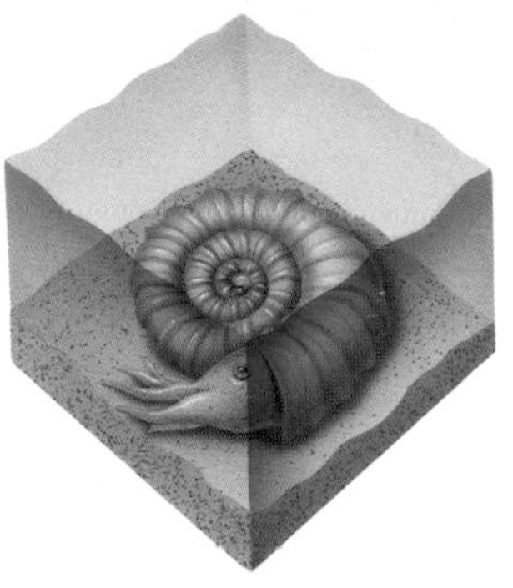

When an organism dies, the soft parts rot away.

The hard shell is covered with a layer of silt.

A hard mineral fossil is gradually formed.

HOW ARE FOSSILS FORMED?

Fossils result from the death of an animal that took place millions of years ago. The soft parts of the animal rot quickly, and the bones or shell are scattered by scavenging animals.

Some of these remains are buried in mud or sand. If they are not disturbed in any way, more mud is deposited until the remains are deeply buried. Under great pressure from deposits above, the mud eventually compacts into sedimentary rock.

Sometimes a fossil will retain the shape and structure of the hard parts of an animal, such as fossilized dinosaur bones. These are not the original bones because minerals have replaced them over the years, but they retain the same shape. Other fossils are just the impression of an animal or plant created when it was buried.

FACT FILE

Trilobites were once among the most abundant animals on Earth. They lived only in the sea and survived for millions of years, evolving into some strangely shaped forms before they suddenly became extinct.

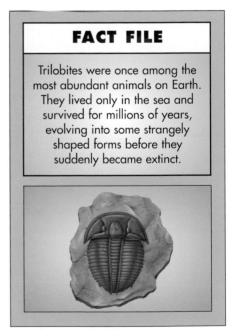

How are fossils found?

Each year fossils are unearthed and they add to our knowledge of prehistoric life. Sometimes they are discovered by ordinary people walking in the countryside, most frequently in rocky places, where the soil is being washed away constantly by water, such as at the bottom of cliffs. Fossils have also been found by people working in mines or quarries and sometimes they are exposed by erosion and can be seen sticking out of cliff faces. Expert geologists and palaeontologists are able to identify those rock formations that are most likely to contain fossil remains and can excavate them safely.

Large numbers of fossils are now being found in Mongolia and China, and in 2010, the skull of an enormous sea creature, a pliosaur, was discovered in Dorset, England and is thought to be over 150 million years old.

FACT FILE

This skeleton of the early reptile Dimetrodon is unusually complete. Most fossil remains consist only of fragments, which must be pieced together.

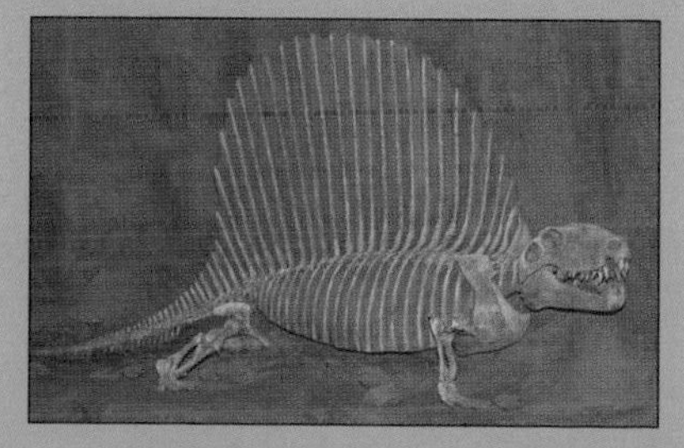

HOW DID LIFE BEGIN ON LAND?

Plants were the first living things on our planet, starting with very simple plants such as algae. Then mosses and liverworts developed, followed by ferns and other larger plants. Animals did not leave the sea until plants had become fully established, otherwise there would have been no food for them.

Next were relatives of the spiders and scorpions which were probably the first creatures to leave the sea and actually colonize on land. Later they evolved into larger and more complex forms of life. Amphibians multiplied rapidly, and the word actually means 'living on land and in water'.

FACT FILE

The first mammals lived alongside the dinosaurs, but in comparison with reptiles they were tiny and insignificant like the *Glyptodon* below.

How did some fish become land-dwellers?

Around 400 million years ago fish began to creep out of the water onto land. The main reasons for an animal to change its habits would be to obtain fresh food supplies and to escape from its predators. Many fish were able to just wriggle along on land, but in order to lift their body clear of the ground ordinary fins were not strong enough. One of these fish is the *coelacanth*, a large fish up to 1 m long with strange leg-like fins. It was found to contain bones that were very like those of land-living vertebrate animals. Relatives of the *coelacanth* had leg-like fins reinforced with bones, which allowed them to slither along like a modern crocodile. Many ancient fish developed simple lungs which they used instead of their gills when they were out of the water.

FACT FILE

Baryonix is the only known fish-eating dinosaur, and uniquely it had huge claws on its front limbs.

How do we know what dinosaurs were like?

Although dinosaur remains are few, we know we can deduce quite a lot from their fossilized skeletons. We can calculate its weight by studying its bones. Heavy animals have massive bones to support their weight, while swift-moving hunters have very light, hollow bones. Muscles are firmly attached to bones, and although no trace of the muscles are left in the fossils, the points at which they attach can still be seen on the bones. These facts tell scientists how big the muscles must have been.

We know that a large digestive system is necessary to digest vegetable matter. The herbivores would have had massive barrel-shaped bodies, while carnivores would be slimmer. The shape of the teeth tells scientists what type of food the dinosaurs ate.

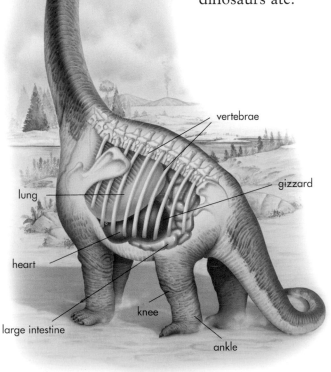

FACT FILE

Much is presumed and guessed about dinosaurs. Looking at the *Carnotaurus*, it had weak jaws and was not well equipped for hunting, so it was assumed that it only fed on small prey.

HOW DID DINOSAURS EVOLVE?

Dinosaurs were reptiles that evolved into the most varied kinds of any living creature. They ranged from tiny bird-like animals to monstrous beasts that were the largest animals to ever live on land.

The dinosaurs survived for about 150 million years. They were not all meat-eating killers as often portrayed in books and films. Most dinosaurs were peaceful, browsing animals about the size of modern farm livestock.

FACT FILE

Some dinosaurs had characteristcs the purposes of which are unknown, as in this *Saurolophyus* that had a large bony ridge on the top of its skull.

The main thing that distinguishes dinosaurs from other reptiles is the way their body is supported by their legs. The legs of ancient and existing reptiles stick out sideways, so the body drags on the ground for most of the time. It is raised briefly when the animal runs. The skeletons of dinosaurs developed so the legs were beneath the body, raising the whole body off the ground.

How similar were dinosaurs to mammals?

As dinosaurs multiplied they became more diverse. Among them were mammal-like reptiles called the synapsids. One of these, *Dimetrodon*, had a sail-like structure on its back. The sail may have helped control the body temperature. By turning the sail to face the Sun these cold-blooded reptiles could absorb heat.

Other mammal-like reptiles called dicynodonts are thought to have become warm-blooded to gradually evolve into true mammals.

Another group of reptiles called Archosaurs appeared during the Triassic Period. Most of them were predators, and they gave rise to animals such as dinosaurs and crocodiles. The archosaurs were a group of animals in which the modification to the hips and legs developed. This led to the animal being able to support their own weight and to stand upright.

FACT FILE

Triceratops had a resemblance to the modern rhinoceros and probably lived a similar lifestyle. It was one of a large family of plant-eating dinosaurs which all had spiked skulls and a frill of bone covering their necks.

How clever were dinosaurs?

Troodon

It is difficult to assess the intelligence of an extinct animal. But we do know that the intelligence of dinosaurs must have been sufficient for their way of life, otherwise they would not have survived for millions of years. Some of the plant-eating dinosaurs certainly had very small brains in proportion to their size. However, a large brain is not important in an animal which is too enormous to be attacked and has little to think about except eating. On the other hand some of the predatory dinosaurs had quite large brains, because they needed to think quickly as they went after their prey.

The cleverest dinosaur was the *Troodon*, which was only about the size of a large domestic dog. Its brain was very large in proportion to its size. It could run very fast, swerving and ducking to catch its prey. It had all the right physical attributes to have evolved into an intelligent form of life, but it became extinct with all the other dinosaurs.

FACT FILE

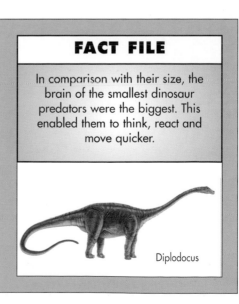

In comparison with their size, the brain of the smallest dinosaur predators were the biggest. This enabled them to think, react and move quicker.

Diplodocus

How many different types of dinosaur were there?

There were thousands of different species of dinosaur and we have only discovered a small proportion of them. It is important at this stage to realise how rare fossils are. There were a few dinosaur species that must have been very common, like *Iguanodon*, which left many fossils. Others were probably scarce when they were alive or lived in regions where fossilization was unlikely, and so there are few remains of these dinosaurs.

Herbivores often lived in groups or herds, but carnivores were usually more solitary and their fossils are therefore more rare. Many of the interesting dinosaurs are known from a single fossil, or one or two bones, and scientists must deduce the shape and size from these.

FACT FILE

Although in many ways the *Ouranosaurus* was a typical plant-eating dinosaur, it had a remarkable sail-like crest running down its back and along its tail. Its exact function is not known.

How big were dinosaurs?

Dinosaurs vary in size enormously. Some were only about the size of a chicken, or even smaller. *Compsognathus* was only about 70 cm long and was very slightly built. It was an agile and fast-moving creature and is thought to have lived on insects and small animals. The skeleton of this dinosaur is very similar to that of a modern bird.

Scientists cannot agree on the maximum size of giant dinosaurs. But it is usually said that *Brachiosaurus* is the biggest, and is thought to have been about 30 m long and to have weighed as much as 130 tonnes. This would make it by far the heaviest land animal to have ever existed. The *Sauroposeidon* has been described as being as high as 17.2 m, making it three times the height of the tallest giraffe.

FACT FILE

The biggest mammal to have lived on Earth actually preceded dinosaurs. It was called the *Indicotherium* and was big enough to push over trees which were too tall for it to graze upon.

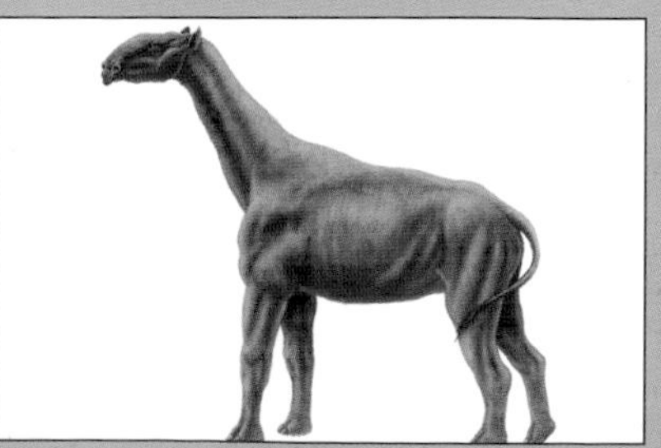

How did dinosaurs communicate with each other?

There is very strong evidence that some plant-eating dinosaurs could produce a lot of noise, although we cannot be certain about this.

Many duck-billed dinosaurs had a large bony structure on their head, which was probably used to amplify sound, rather like the body of a guitar. Hollow air passages in the bony structure allowed the dinosaur to produce low, booming cries.

In some species, the shape of the crest and the sounds produced varied between individual animals, helping herd members to locate each other. Males probably used individual sounds in their mating displays. The extraordinary crest carried by the *Parasaurolophus* appears to have acted as an echo chamber, giving this dinosaur a very loud booming cry.

FACT FILE

It is believed that the plates on the back of some dinosaurs were used in display to rival animals. The sharp spikes along the edge of the body of *Sauropelta* would have stopped any predator from getting at its soft underbelly.

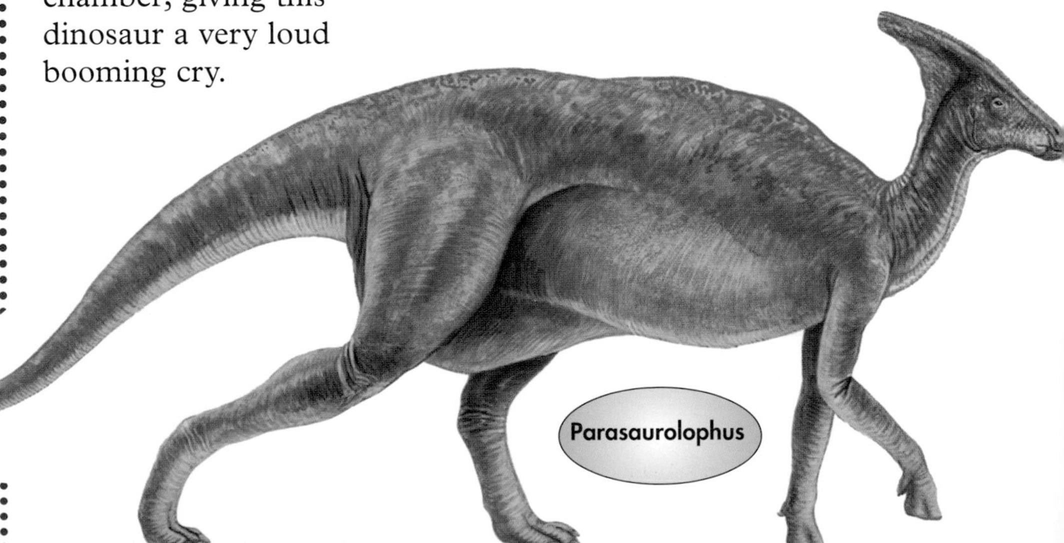

Parasaurolophus

HOW COULD SMALL DINOSAURS ATTACK LARGER ONES?

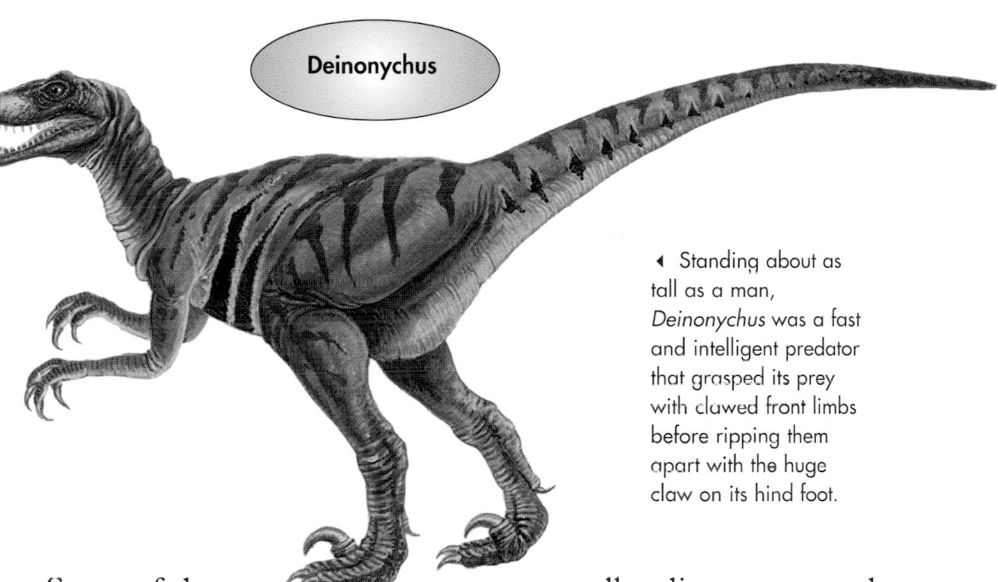

◂ Standing about as tall as a man, *Deinonychus* was a fast and intelligent predator that grasped its prey with clawed front limbs before ripping them apart with the huge claw on its hind foot.

Some of the smaller dinosaurs may have hunted in packs, like modern wolves. By working together they would have been able to kill much larger animals.

The *Deinonychus* was lightly built so it could run extremely fast. This hunter had a very stiff tail which it probably used to steer itself and change direction quickly while chasing its prey. It also had very sharp teeth, and powerful arms with grasping claws. The most unusual feature was a large upturned claw on its foot which could be swivelled downwards so that it could slash its prey with its muscular hind legs. This would probably have killed the prey due to loss of blood.

FACT FILE

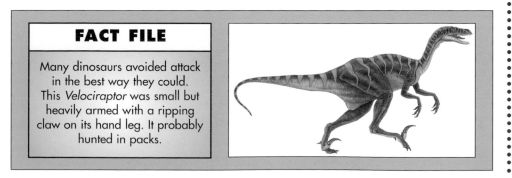

Many dinosaurs avoided attack in the best way they could. This *Velociraptor* was small but heavily armed with a ripping claw on its hand leg. It probably hunted in packs.

How did carnivorous dinosaurs catch their prey?

All meat-eating dinosaurs were roughly the same shape, but they all varied in size a great deal. They all belonged to a group called theropods meaning 'beast feet'.

The giant dinosaurs like *Tyrannosaurus rex* probably ambushed their prey, charging at them with jaws wide open. They could run at a speed of 32 miles per hour, although probably for only a very short distance. The impact of seven tonnes of dinosaur hitting its prey with a jagged mouthful of teeth would likely kill most animals outright.

Many smaller dinosaurs retained powerful front limbs and claws, and could cling to their prey while biting it.

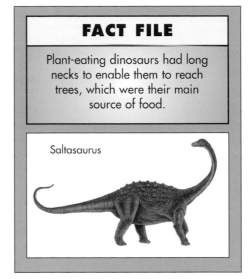

FACT FILE

Plant-eating dinosaurs had long necks to enable them to reach trees, which were their main source of food.

▼ *Tyrannosaurus rex,* usually just called T-rex, was the largest and most fearsome land-living predator ever to have existed.

How did plant-eating dinosaurs find their food?

▲ *Hadrosaurus* was a large plant-eater that walked sometimes on two legs and at other times on four.

The type of food that plant-eating dinosaurs fed on depended on their type of mouth. Some had broad mouths like a duck's bill and they probably grazed on a mixture of plants. Dinosaurs with narrow jaws, most likely selected particular plants to eat.

FACT FILE

The diets of some dinosaurs are a complete mystery. For example, the *Segnosaurus* could have eaten termites, fish, or plants.

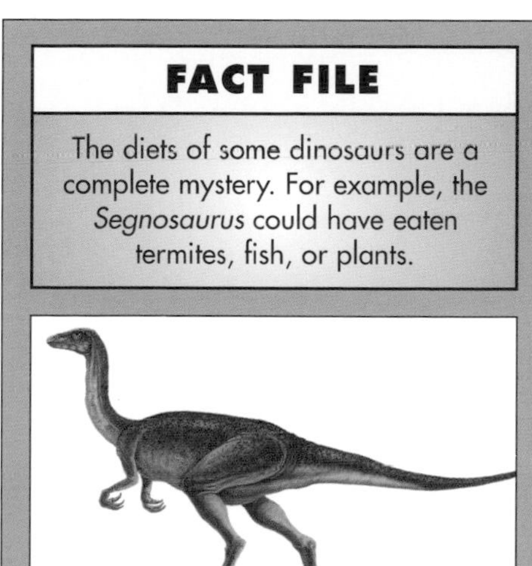

The long-necked sauropods probably grazed on leaves and shoots. Large herds of sauropods would have caused tremendous devastation by feeding in this way and may have used their great weight to push trees over so they were easier to reach. A herd would have cleared great areas of trees, creating large expanses of open ground where smaller dinosaurs could graze. Dinosaurs with cutting beaks would have been able to crop vegetation short.

How did dinosaurs look after their young?

▸ Very large numbers of remains of *Protoceratops* have been found in the Gobi desert, including eggs and nestlings. These animals seem to have nested in very large groups and probably cared for their young.

It was thought at one time that dinosaurs laid their eggs in isolated places. But in 1978 a remarkable find was made in Montana, USA. Fifteen *Maiasaurus* babies were found scattered around a large mound-shaped structure, together with many broken eggshells. The babies were not newly hatched because their teeth were partly worn away. The nest itself was about 2 metres across and covered with vegetation.

In the Gobi desert, the pig-sized dinosaur *Protoceratops* dug holes in the sand and buried her eggs. She left them to hatch in the heat of the sand while she guarded them from predators. The eggs were arranged in careful circles, in layers. Presumably the mother dinosaur turned herself above the nest as she laid each egg.

FACT FILE

The eggs of *Orodromeus* have been found broken open from the inside as the young hatched out. The baby dinosaurs are thought to have foraged for their food while being guarded by adults.

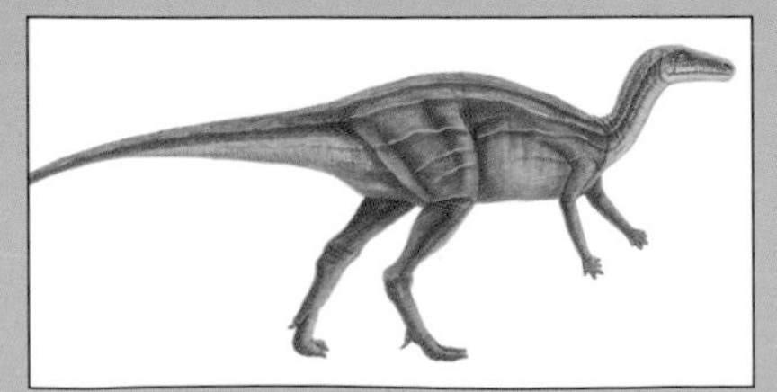

How big were dinosaur eggs?

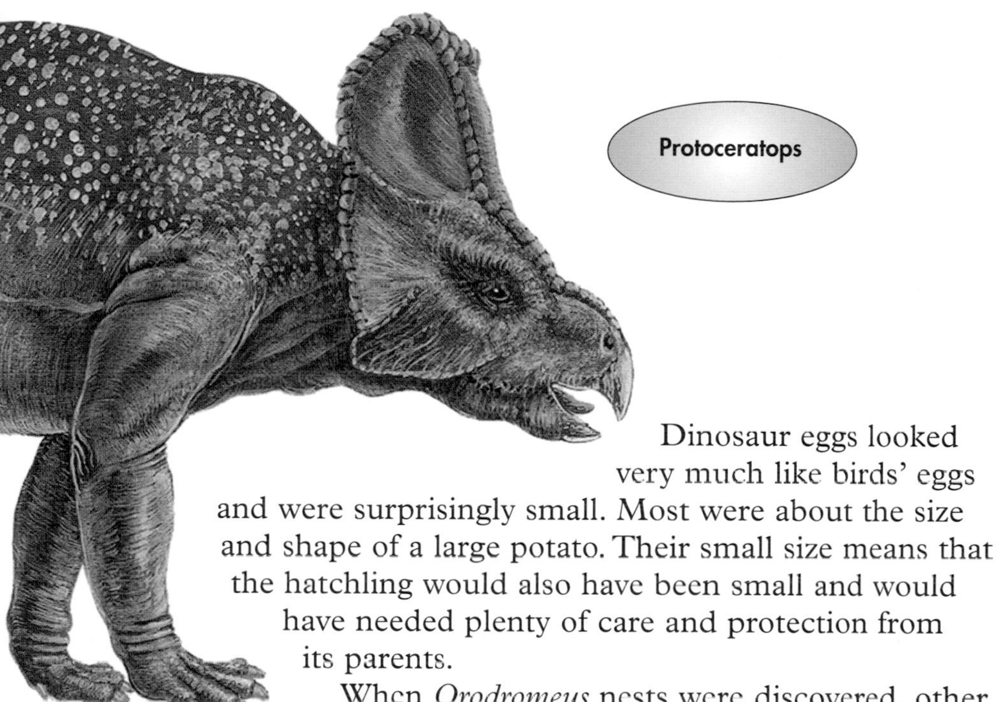

Protoceratops

Dinosaur eggs looked very much like birds' eggs and were surprisingly small. Most were about the size and shape of a large potato. Their small size means that the hatchling would also have been small and would have needed plenty of care and protection from its parents.

When *Orodromeus* nests were discovered, other dinosaur eggs were found between them. These eggs were smaller and were laid in straight lines. It has recently been found that they are the eggs of a small predator called the *Troodon*. It appears to have laid its eggs in the *Orodromeus* colony to gain protection from other predators. This habit is similar to that of modern cuckoos and their relatives, although they also use another species of bird to raise their young.

FACT FILE

The Oviraptor was an odd dinosaur that may have lived entirely on the eggs of other dinosaurs. It was bird-shaped, with a powerful beak for crushing eggs and did not have any teeth.

HOW DID DINOSAURS PROTECT THEMSELVES?

Dinosaurs had various ways of protecting themselves. Firstly they might just have been too big to be brought down and eaten. Secondly, some dinosaurs could run very fast indeed which meant they escaped their predator. Thirdly, a slow-moving dinosaur may have been covered with spikes and horns to help deter attackers.

FACT FILE

Although the sides of its body were less heavily armoured than many of its relatives, the underside of the *Minmi* was well protected by being covered with tough bony plates.

▾ As well as being covered with jointed armour and defensive spines the *Euoplocephalus* carried a massive club on the end of its tail which would have crushed any predator.

How did dinosaurs use their armour?

FACT FILE

Although some dinosaurs could not run very fast at all, they had other ways of defending themselves. The *Shunasaurus* had a tail club that it could wield in defence.

Several theories have been put forward as to why some dinosaurs had armour on parts of their body. The plates on the back of the *Stegosaurus* could have been used to display to rival animals, or perhaps help to regulate body temperature. It has even been suggested that the plates could have folded flat to make a sheet of armour over the animal's back. The whole head of an Ankylosaur was covered with protective plates and this cover even extended over the eyes. Others wielded their tails in defence.

HOW DID FISH EVOLVE?

◂ As fish developed jaws, they were able to hunt other animals. Soon they evolved into large creatures, sometimes with armour to protect themselves. The most fearsome fish grew to 9 metres in length.

Fossils show that the first fish occurred in the Ordovician Period which began about 460,000,000 years ago.

These fish were jawless, and the most primitive of all. Their mouths were a simple opening, suited to feeding on the tiny animals that lay hidden in the mud.

Next came fish with jaws. Jaws allowed fish to explore various food sources and to feed more efficiently. Early fish with jaws are called placoderms. The jaws actually evolved from a set of gill arches that were present in the jawless fish. Gill arches are the bony supports of the gills.

From these placoderms came our present-day fish, the sharks and bony fish.

FACT FILE

Ammonites were relatives of the modern octopus and squid. They secreted a hard shell, living in a small compartment. A new compartment was added as they grew larger, eventually producing a spiral shell.

HOW DID MARINE REPTILES LOOK?

The *ichthyosaurs* looked very much like modern dolphins but were totally aquatic reptiles that gave birth to live young.

Mesosaurus was a small ancestor of the crocodile. Its remains have been found in both North and South America.

Many reptiles returned to the sea. Some of the most familiar ones are the plesiosaurs, large animals with a barrel-like body and a long snaky neck. They did not have a flexible body, they rowed themselves along by waving their fin-like front and rear limbs up and down.

Pliosaurs were relatives of the plesiosaurs but had shorter necks and massive skulls armed with enormous teeth. They were the largest and most powerful predators ever known.

Turtles also developed at about the same time. Unlike modern ones, the early forms did not have a complete shell.

FACT FILE

Although looking at them you might think a crocodile is a dinosaur, you would be wrong. They both evolved from the same type of ancestors and crocodiles have changed very little over millions of years.

HOW BIG WERE PTEROSAURS?

Various reptiles have developed the ability to glide, but the pterosaurs were the only ones to develop true flight. Their arms were quite short and their wings were supported by an enormously long fourth finger, leaving the other fingers free to function as a hand. A thin, skin-like membrane was stretched from the elongated finger to the sides of the body, and sometimes to the hind legs.

The whole body was extremely light with hollow bones. Many pterosaurs lived a similar life to the modern seagull and albatross. One pterosaur discovered, the *Quetzalcoatlus*, had a wing span greater than 15 metres, which is larger than that of many light planes.

FACT FILE

The *Pterodactylus* was a very small flying reptile, smaller than a modern pigeon and much lighter in build. It had a wing span of 40cm across which means it would have been a fast and agile flyer.

▲ Scientists were astounded when the remains of Quetzalcoatlus were found. It proved to be the largest flying creature ever to have existed.

How did pterosaurs fly?

▾ *Rhamporhyncus* was a moderate sized pterosaur with a 1.75 m wing span. Its long tail was tipped with an unusual diamond-shaped piece of skin which may have helped stabilize it in flight.

It was believed at one time that the pterosaurs were unable to flap their wings and fly like a bird. They probably launched themselves off cliffs and glided on upward currents of air.

More recently, however, it has been suggested that pterosaurs were actually very efficient flyers.

Some of the smallest types would not have been very effective gliders and must have fluttered their wings like modern birds. This would not have been possible for the giant pterosaurs, which must have been pure gliders.

Pterosaurs did not have feathers, because their large wings were more like those of a bat than a bird. However, pterosaurs did have fur! This seems to suggest that they were warm-blooded, as there would be no point in the body of a cold-blooded creature, such as a modern reptile, being insulated.

FACT FILE

The small predatory therapod dinosaur *Campsognathus* resembles *Archaeopteryx* so closely that the remains of the two animals have sometimes been confused. This seems to prove the dinosaur ancestry to birds.

▼ *Pteranodon* was a large and efficient flyer. Its head carried a huge backward-pointing crest of uncertain function, though it might have been used as a rudder during gliding flight.

HOW DID PTEROSAURS MOVE ON THE GROUND?

Scientists are not really sure how pterosaurs moved about on the ground. We know for certain that their huge wings could not be folded away as neatly as those of a modern bird, and they would have been very ungainly on the ground.

Most palaeontologists think that pterosaurs probably scuttled around on their hands and on the feet of their hind legs, with their wings folded and trailing behind them.

Another view is that some pterosaurs may have scuttled about upright, running on their hind legs. Some people think that they may have been scavengers like vultures, but it is hard to imagine this because of their size and ungainliness.

FACT FILE

Some of the giant birds, like the *Diatryma*, were unable to fly. They were important predators and could tackle almost any prey with their massive beaks.

How similar were pterosaurs to birds of today?

Despite their apparent similarities, pterosaurs were quite different in structure to birds, and they never developed the powerful breast muscles needed to beat their wings in the same way as birds.

Similarly, they could not fold their wings away like modern birds, so would always have been clumsy when moving on the ground.

Modern birds never have teeth, and their tail is reduced to a small stump; the 'parson's nose'. Fossils of a whole range of feathered dinosaurs are now being found in many countries and especially in China. All these creatures were built along the same lines as birds. Some were undoubtedly dinosaurs and would have used their feathered forelimbs to help them run rather than fly.

FACT FILE

The ungainly and primitive hoatzin lives in South America. Its young show their reptile ancestry by having claws on their wings with which they clamber about in branches.

◂ *Archaeopteryx* is a strange mixture of reptile and bird, leading some scientists to think that its fossilized remains were perhaps a fake.

FACT FILE

Huge meteor craters still exist, though most become eroded after millions of years and are not as obvious as this crater in Arizona, USA.

HOW DID DINOSAURS DIE OUT?

Dinosaurs lived for an enormously long time – some 150 million years – before they died out about 64 million years ago. During their time on the Earth they dominated the land, while other reptile relatives were the dominant forms of life in the sea and in the air. Before the dinosaurs finally disappeared there were two mass extinctions when a large number of species died out. The dinosaurs survived, however, until the end of the Cretaceous Period.

Many people believe that dinosaurs became extinct as a result of climate change after a huge meteor or a small asteroid struck the Earth.

The other theory regarding the extinction of the dinosaurs is that it coincided with a period of high volcanic activity, which could have wiped out the whole population.

However, it was not only the dinosaurs that became extinct. At the same time most marine reptiles and pterosaurs also died out. Also, tiny plankton whose shells form chalk deposits, ammonites and the remaining species of trilobites. It is very difficult to imagine the exact causes of this extinction. For instance, how did turtles manage to survive?

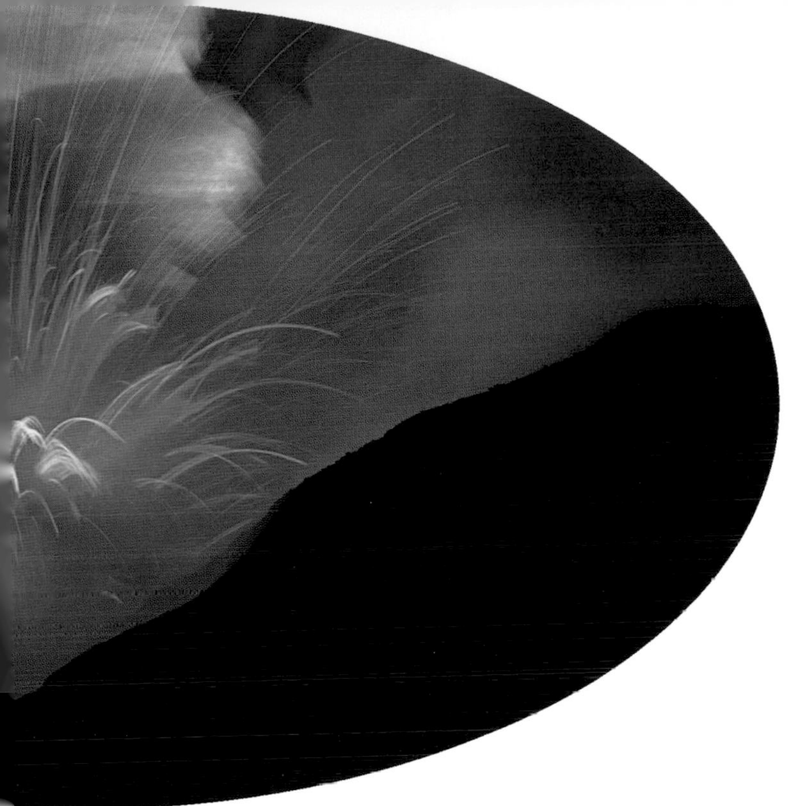

◂ High volcanic activity could have contributed to the dinosaurs' extinction.

HOW DID CLIMATE AFFECT DINOSAURS' SURVIVAL?

During the late Cretaceous Period the world's continents were drifting into new positions. This constant shifting within the crust led to a huge increase in volcanic activity. Volcanoes spewed out hot lava and gases, which could have built up in the atmosphere to such high levels that they affected dinosaurs and their plant food.

Other climatic changes like the Ice Age may have wiped out many species of dinosaur that were unable to adapt to the extreme cold.

FACT FILE

The Earth went through some incredible climate changes during the era of the dinosaurs and one of the theories regarding their extinction would have been the Ice Age. There are very few plants or animals that could have survived this extreme cold.

How did mammals evolve?

A group of mammal-like reptiles preceded the appearance of the dinosaurs. These early mammals gradually disappeared, however, during the Triassic Period and were replaced by the true mammals.

It is hard to decide exactly which of these extinct animals was a reptile and which was a mammal. It is quite probable that the later reptiles had hair and other mammal-like characteristics. The first mammals were small and were vulnerable to all the fierce dinosaur predators. Once the dinosaurs died out the mammals were able to develop properly and evolve. Eventually the mammals grew into forms that were almost as gigantic as their dinosaur predecessors.

Thylacosmilus

▲ *Thylacosmilus* was a typica example of the sabre-tooth ca with long canine teeth that we used to stab their prey.

FACT FILE

Mammoths closely resembled modern elephants but were covered with thick, coarse hair and were adapted to live in the cold tundra regions. They survived in northern Arctic regions until well after the appearance of man, who hunted them to extinction.

How similar are marsupials to the first mammals?

It is said that marsupials, like the kangaroo, are actually primitive mammals because they give birth to tiny, undeveloped young. The young are raised in a pouch until they are developed enough to live on their own. There are two kinds of mammal, however, that still lay eggs like their reptile ancestors. Both the duck-billed platypus and the spiny anteater, or echidna, live in Australia. They lay eggs and the hatchlings are placed in a primitive pouch on their mother's stomach. Unlike the young of reptiles, these babies are nourished by their mother's milk. These two very unusual animals give us some indication about how the earliest mammals may have developed.

FACT FILE

Also known as *Zeuglodon, Basilosaurus* is the most commonly found of the ancient fossil whales. It was a predator like modern dolphins. When whales die their remains usually sink in deep water where they are unlikely to form fossils.

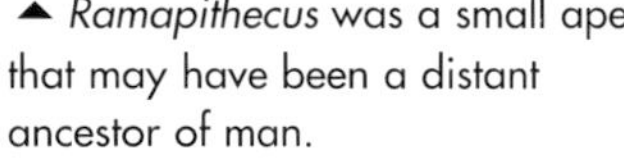

▲ *Ramapithecus* was a small ape that may have been a distant ancestor of man.

▲ *Australopithecus* was an early ancestor that walked upright but still had many ape-like features.

▲ *Homo habilis* was an early form of man that began to use simple tools like flints.

HOW DID HUMANS EVOLVE?

Early ancestors of humans were called hominids, and they appear to have evolved in Africa where many of their remains have been discovered.

FACT FILE

The large skull of a Neanderthal man. These people lived alongside modern humans during the last Ice Age.

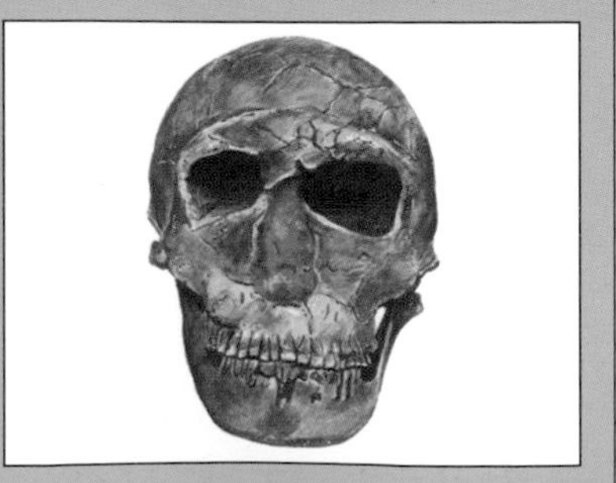

The earliest remains of what were probably our ancestors are those of human-like apes called *Australopithecusm*, which date back more than three million years. These creatures walked erect and looked similar to us, but their brain capacity was very small.

All the forms found were much shorter than modern humans, and their teeth showed that they had a vegetarian diet. The first true human appeared around two million years ago.

▲ ***Homo erectus*** was the first of our ancestors to walk completely upright, and he looked very like modern man, though with a heavy jaw and bony eyebrow ridges.

▲ The Neanderthals lived alongside modern man. They were heavily built but probably just as advanced as modern man. They soon died out.

▲ Modern man probably appeared first in Africa, and spread rapidly throughout Europe and Asia.

HOW SIMILAR ARE WE TO THE APE FAMILY?

Human beings belong to a group of mammals called primates. It includes apes, monkeys and several much smaller animals. As much as 50 million years ago, back in the Eocene Period, there were traces of primate-like animals.

Very early man was rather ape-like with long arms and walked upright. This was replaced by *Homo erectus*, which looked much more like us. It had a heavier jaw, bony ridges over the eyes and a sloped-back forehead. *Homo erectus* appeared around 1.6 million years ago.

FACT FILE

These are examples of Stone Age tools. The hand axe and scraper were made from flint and the spear head from deer antlers.

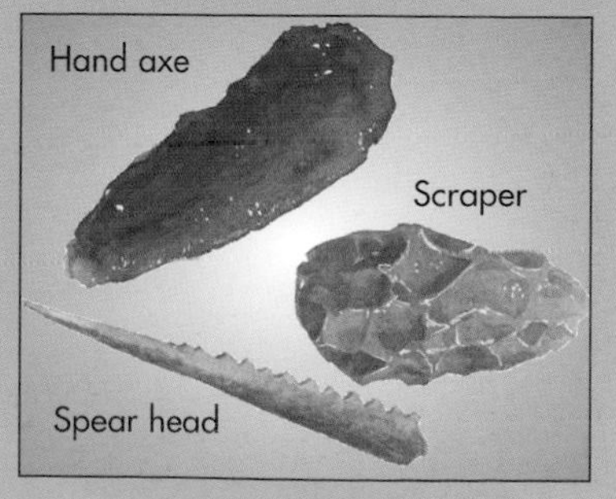

Historical Times

CONTENTS

How do archaeologists reconstruct the past?

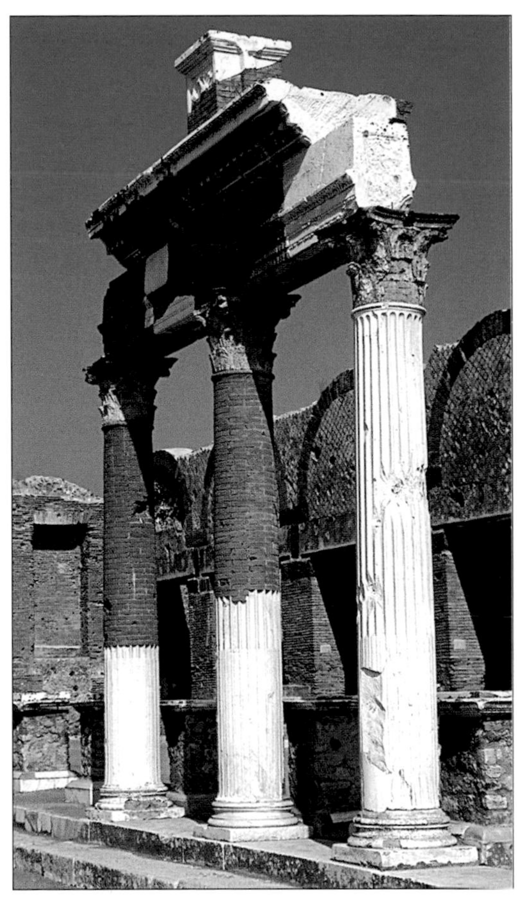

An archaeologist reconstructs the past by studying buildings and objects that have survived. Sometimes historical remains are astonishingly well preserved, for example the Roman cities of Pompeii and Herculaneum which were overwhelmed by the eruption of Mount Vesuvius. Many tiny aspects of Roman life were preserved, including graffiti on the walls. Such perfect preservation is very rare.

Archaeologists usually need to make a painstaking reconstruction, carefully excavating the remains of ruined buildings. Sometimes only the post-holes of a wooden building are left, but even they can provide useful clues about the type of building. The oldest archaeological remains come from the Stone Age. The remains of flint tools and weapons have survived, together with bones that show which animals were hunted and eaten.

FACT FILE

Trajan's column. This is part of a giant monument that the Roman emperor Trajan built to record his deeds. It also shows the day-to-day tasks of the Roman army.

Newly cut wood begins to lose its radiocarbon

After 5,700 years it has lost half its radiocarbon

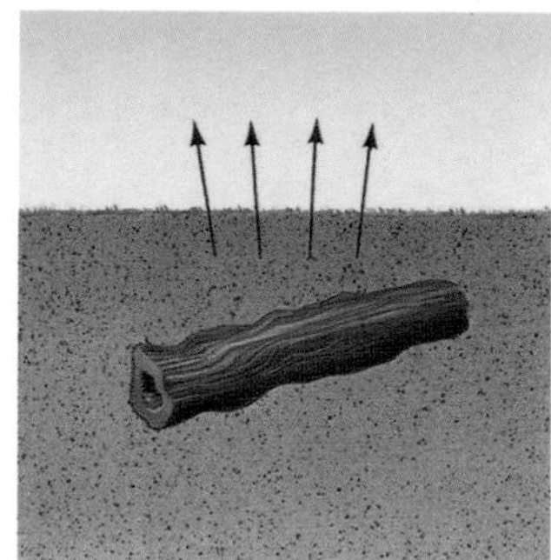

After a further 5,700 years it has lost half as much again.

Carbon that forms a part of living things loses its radioactivity at a steady and predictable rate. Archaelogists use this information to determine the age of organic remains. After about 70,000 years organic material has lost all of its radiocarbon. Carbon dating is used by archaeologists to help determine the age of artefacts.

HOW DO ARCHAEOLOGISTS KNOW WHAT THEY FIND?

An archaeologist doesn't always find the things he needs to build a complete picture of a people or a way of life. After all, what he finds is only what people left behind, usually everyday objects. These might be remains of houses, tools, jewellery, dishes, toys and also bones of animals used for food. However, important objects made of leather, wood, cloth, wool, or straw usually decay and leave no trace. But, despite this, the archaeologist can still tell us a great deal. He first finds out the order in which early towns were built, one upon the ruins of another. Then he must know the town in which each object was found. Each object is labelled, photographed, measured and so on. If the site belongs to historic times, the archaeologist must know the ancient writing used in that place. There are many experts who help archaeologists such as geologists, botanists, zoologists, and others, all of whom help identify and analyse what they have found. Sometimes it takes years of work and study before the archaeologists are ready to publish a work about what they have found.

FACT FILE

This iron helmet was part of a series of treasures and artefacts unearthed at a burial site called Sutton Hoo (in England).

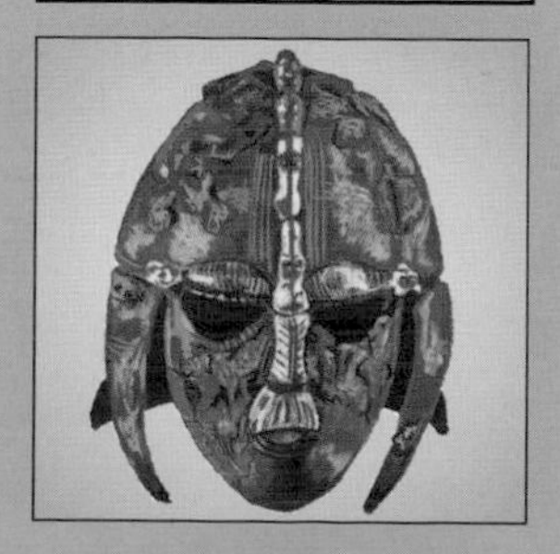

How were the Egyptian pyramids built?

Pyramid building developed slowly in ancient Egypt. The first pyramids were simple structures called *mastabas*, which were platforms built over the tombs of important people. Over the years further levels were added, until a structure called a step pyramid was produced.

In later pyramids, like those at Giza, the steps were filled in to produce the iconic, smooth, conical shape.

Pyramids were vital in the burial rites of the rulers, to ensure their smooth passage to the afterlife. The pyramid builders used complex mathematical calculations, a system of levers and a vast workforce of slave labour in the construction.

FACT FILE

Civilizations sprang up at similar times in different parts of the world. One very advanced civilization was in the Indus Valley, in modern Pakistan and India. The remains of Harappa have been excavated, revealing a large city, with multi-storeyed buildings and carefully laid-out streets.

How were hieroglyphics understood?

No one really knows how the first writing system developed because no records remain. The earliest known writing was recorded in the form of picture symbols on clay tablets by the ancient Sumerians around 3500 BCE.

Hieroglyphics was a system of writing used by the ancient Egyptians around 3000 BCE, using drawings rather than the shapes we use in modern script. They gradually became more stylized to resemble modern forms of writing.

It was the discovery of the Rosetta Stone which contained the same inscription in hieroglyphics and in Greek, that allowed the meaning of the complicated pictures to be understood.

It is likely that all writing started this way before shapes and letters were used to indicate sounds.

FACT FILE

Ancient Egyptian hieroglyphic writing had long been indecipherable. The discovery of the Rosetta stone provided the key to understanding the ancient script.

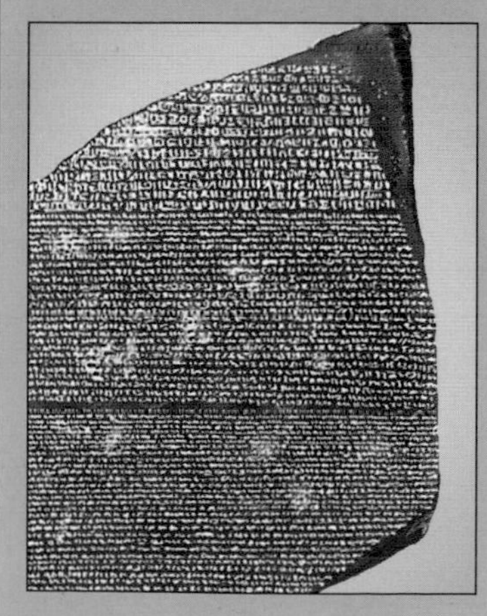

How did the Olympic games begin?

The Olympic Games started as a religious festival held in ancient Greece in honour of Zeus, the king of the gods. The festival was held at Olympia, below Mount Olympus, the home of the gods, every four years.

The first staging of the Olympic Games that we know of was in 776 BCE. People came from all over Greece to take part in or watch the Games. The winners of sports such as running and discus were rewarded with crowns of olive leaves.

The Games continued until CE 393 when the ruling Romans banned them. They were revived during the 1800s after archaeological finds renewed interest in Greece. The first of the modern Olympic Games were held in 1896 in Athens, Greece.

The modern Olympic Games are divided into winter and summer events, which take place two years apart.

FACT FILE

The Greeks also introduced culture, with actors performing plays on a flat platform called the orchestra. Audiences sat in the open air on a hillside and may have seen as many as four plays in one day.

HOW IMPORTANT WERE GODS TO THE ANCIENT GREEKS?

The Greeks believed in a complicated family of gods and goddesses. They believed the gods could and did interfere in human affairs, bringing success or disaster.

Each one was believed to have a particular role in heaven. Aphrodite, for example, was the goddess of love, while Artemis was the goddess of hunting. Poseidon was the god of the sea and is often seen carrying a three-pronged spear called a trident.

The Greek religion was not based on formal written rules, so there were considerable local variations in what people believed and how they worshipped their gods.

The one common element in all Greek religion was the ritual of sacrificing animals to their gods.

FACT FILE

Zeus was king of the Greek gods. The first Olympic Games were held in his honour. Zeus was the head of a family of gods and goddesses called the Olympians.

Poseidon

HOW WAS ROME FOUNDED?

According to the legend, Rome was founded in 753 BCE by twin brothers called Romulus and Remus. The babies were raised by a she-wolf, having been abandoned by their uncle on the banks of the River Tiber. They were eventually rescued by a shepherd.

By 509 BCE the original Etruscan inhabitants of Rome had been driven out, and by 275 BCE Rome controlled most of Italy. The Phoenicians were great rivals of Rome, and they were finally defeated by the Romans in the Punic Wars (261–146 BCE). After this, the Romans were able to extend their empire with little organized resistance. The Celts, the Seleucid kings, the Greeks and the Egyptians all fell before Roman power. Only the Parthians in the east and the Germanic tribes in northwest Europe defied the mighty Roman army.

FACT FILE

Part of the complex of Roman baths in the city of Bath in England. Romans would visit the public baths to bathe in hot and cold pools, and also to relax and talk with their friends.

HOW VAST WAS THE ROMAN EMPIRE?

FACT FILE

The disciplined Roman armies developed special weapons and techniques to overcome the tribes they encountered as the empire expanded. This 'tortoise' formation proved impregnable against their Celtic foes.

At its peak, the Roman army extended all around the Mediterranean Sea and most of the rest of Europe. Much of what is now England and France, Belgium and the Netherlands, Spain and Portugal, Switzerland, Austria, Hungary, part of Germany, Romania, Bulgaria, Greece, Turkey, Israel, Syria, Arabia, Tunisia, Algeria, and Morocco was ruled by the Romans from their base in Italy.

A huge army was needed to maintain control over these regions, and the costs were tremendous. There were continual minor wars and skirmishes along the edges of the Empire, which meant that large garrisons of soldiers had to be maintained.

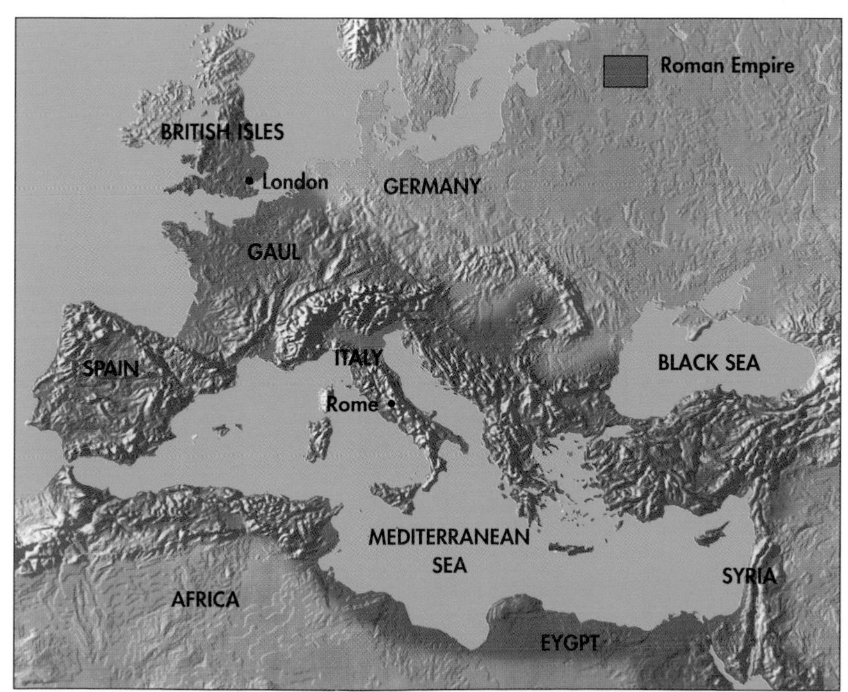

HOW SUCCESSFUL WERE VIKING ATTACKS?

The Vikings came from Scandinavia (Norway, Denmark and Sweden). Their homeland of mountains, fjords and forests offered little spare farmland for a growing population, so many Vikings went abroad in search of new lands to settle.

They were fierce warriors and their first impact on western Europe was a violent one. Norwegians and Danes began to sail across the North Sea in the late CE 700s, raiding the coasts of Britain and mainland Europe. They raided churches and towns, carrying off loot and slaves. Their raids caused panic and rulers tried to buy off the invaders with gold. This only encouraged the Vikings to come back for more.

In Britain the Vikings were finally defeated by Alfred, the king of Wessex.

FACT FILE

Religion was important to the Vikings. Their most important gods were Odin, Thor and Grey. Odin, the god of battle, was the leader of the Norse gods, who lived in a place called Valhalla.

HOW FAR DID THE VIKINGS TRAVEL?

FACT FILE

The Viking longships were fast and strong enough to cross oceans. They had a long, slender hull with a single mast and sail.

At a time when sailors dared not venture far from the coasts, the Vikings boldly sailed out far across the Atlantic in their small open longships. Viking trade routes took them throughout Europe and beyond. The Vikings travelled as far east as Baghdad and Istanbul, and as far west as Greenland and Canada.

Wherever Vikings landed they mingled with local people, and they began to set up colonies in Iceland and Greenland and sailed on to North America. Traces of Viking settlements have also been found in Maine, in the United States, and in Newfoundland in Canada. However, these colonies soon vanished, together with the colony in Greenland. Other Vikings sailed around the Mediterranean, trading for goods from places as far away as China.

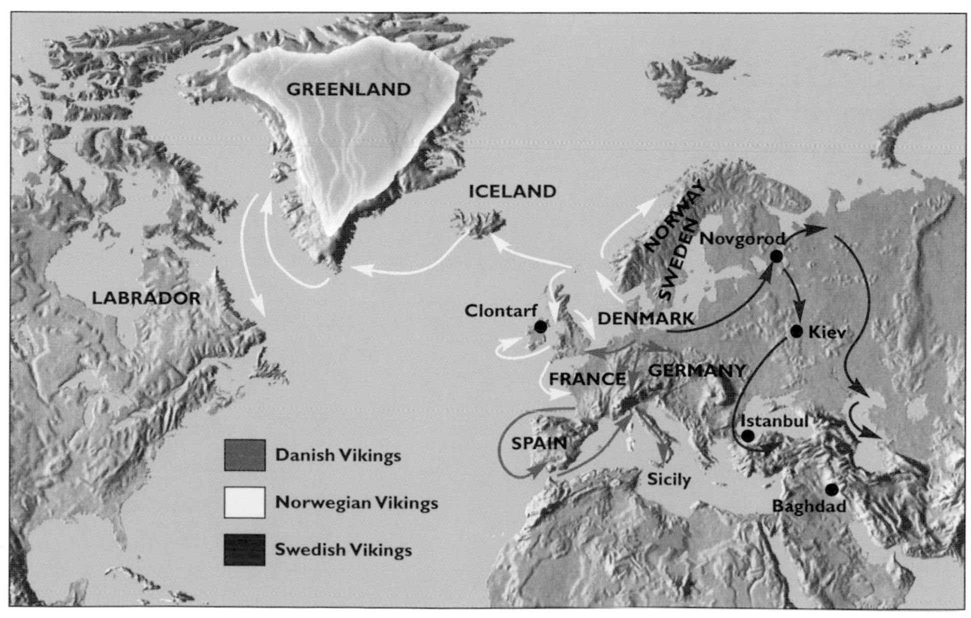

HOW DID THE NORMANS CHANGE BRITAIN?

The Bayeux tapestry records the Norman victory over the Saxon King Harold, who is shown here receiving the fatal arrow in his eye.

The Normans introduced the feudal system, in which the king owned all the land, some of which he gifted to barons, in return for services to him. The baronial estates were taken from the English earls. The barons paid taxes to the crown and supplied soldiers for the king's armies.

The barons gifted smaller portions of their land to knights, for which they received military service, and who let even smaller parcels to farmers (villains) who had to provide fresh food.

Society was thus divided into easily controlled units. The Normans brought mediaeval French into the language and built many castles and churches.

FACT FILE

Knights were soldiers in the service of a Norman lord. They owed their loyalty to their lord and had to fight for him whenever asked. This meant that the knights were called upon in times of unrest.

How does the Domesday Book help historians?

The Domesday Book

Once the Normans had secured their hold over their new territory, they wanted to know exactly what it was worth. In CE 1085 William I ordered a survey of land in England. The findings were written down in the Domesday Book (Domesday means 'Day of Judgement'). It is the best record we have of life in England between CE 1066 and 1088, naming about 13,000 towns and villages.

This book listed every single town, village, farm, who owned what, and how much each holding was worth, so that taxes could be applied. This book is still in existence today.

FACT FILE

Conwy castle, in north Wales, is typical of the castles built by the Normans. It was built to give defending archers an uninterrupted field of fire against any attackers, and could withstand a long siege.

HOW DID THE MONGOLS LIVE?

The Mongols never settled permanently but lived in large circular tent-like prefabricated homes called yurts.

These were carried with them during their migrations and invasions, and are still used today. They are made of felt, which is fastened over a light wooden frame. The whole structure can be quickly dismantled and carried by horses as the Mongol tribes migrate across the steppes, or grassy plains, following their grazing flocks.

The Mongols were feared for the ferocity of their unpredictable attacks on cities throughout Asia and the Middle East. Genghis Khan was a famous Mongol who unified the scattered tribes and began the conquest that resulted in the Mongols controlling nearly all of Asia and threatening to destroy Europe. After the death of Genghis' grandson, Kublai, the Empire proved too large to govern and began to break up.

FACT FILE

This is an example of a Mongol home called a yurt, which they carried with them during their migrations and invasions.

HOW EXTENSIVE WAS THE MONGOL EMPIRE?

FACT FILE

Marco Polo was one of the first Europeans to travel through Mongol territory. His reports helped to establish trade routes there.

Genghis Khan was a Mongol warrior whose conquests built the greatest land empire in history. His vast empire stretched across central Asia from the sea of Japan to the Caspian Sea and occupying most of modern Russia. The Mongols succeeded against established armies because they were unpredictable. They charged into battle on horseback, relying entirely on speed and surprise, and taking no prisoners. The Mongols were remorseless fighters, developing fighting machines that enabled them to break into the cities they besieged. They were merciless towards those people who resisted them and sometimes they slaughtered entire populations. Most cities surrendered immediately, rather than risk being massacred!

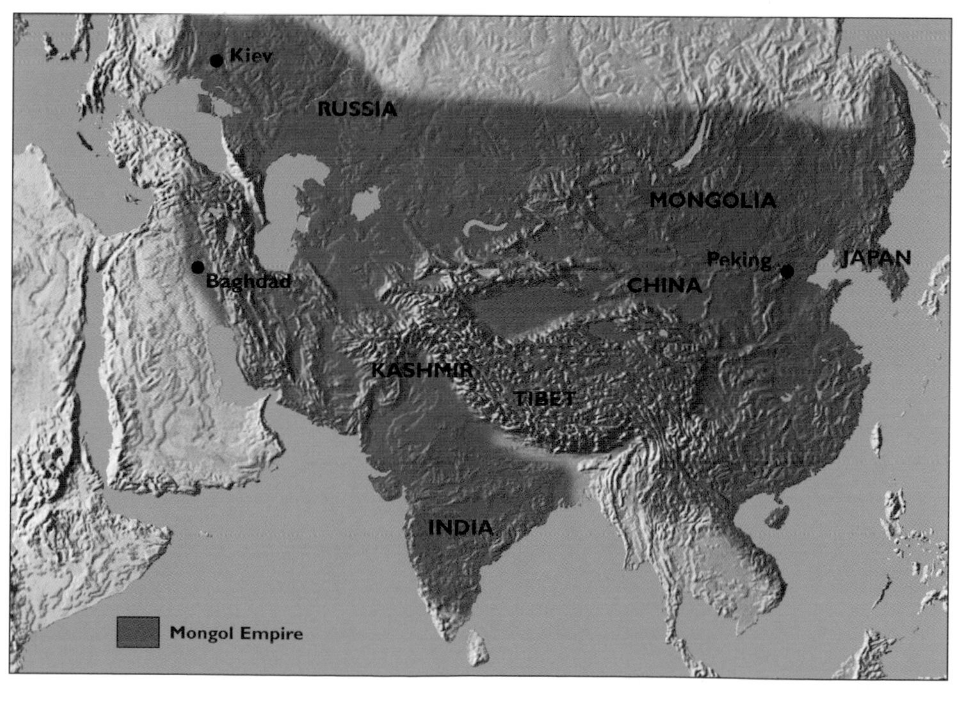

HOW LONG WAS THE HUNDRED YEARS WAR?

The Hundred Years' War began in 1337 and continued for more than a century. It was not a single war but a series of skirmishes between England and France. It began when the English tried to dominate France, and the French in turn tried to confiscate lands occupied by the English.

The English invaded France and won a great battle at Crécy. The British archers with their longbows defeated a much larger army of knights, marking the beginning of the end for mounted knights. Further battles followed, but in 1396, Richard II of England married the daughter of Charles VI of France, establishing a 20 year truce that finally ended the fighting.

FACT FILE

The two branches of the Plantagenet family battled for the throne in the Wars of the Roses. The name comes from the red rose of Lancaster and the white Rose of York.

How widespread was the Black Death?

FACT FILE

The Magna Carta was a document signed by King John in 1215, guaranteeing feudal rights to the barons. After his death the barons renegotiated the charter with his son and it became part of English law.

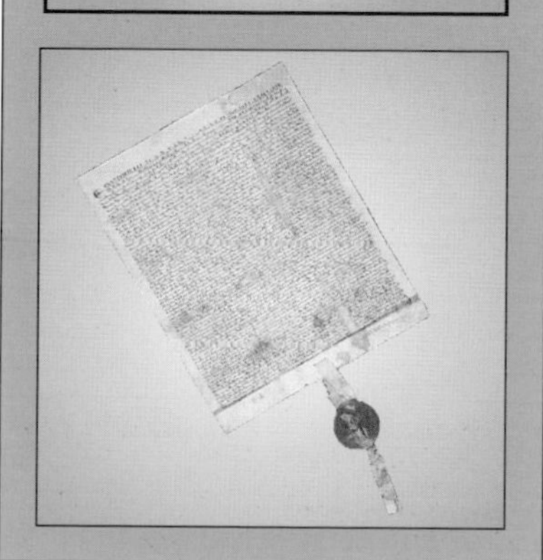

The Black Death was an epidemic that permanently changed the face of medieval Europe. It killed more than one-quarter of the population, causing thousands of villages to be abandoned and subsequently to disappear.

The Black Death probably arrived in Europe from Central Asia by way of Mongol raiders. It first caused epidemics in Italy in 1347, spreading rapidly through the rest of Europe.

The disease was spread by the bite of fleas from infected rats, but because its cause was not understood the infection raged unchecked. The resulting fear led to a great wave of religious hysteria. A shortage of manual workers led to the collapse of the long-established feudal system.

How did the Spanish empire develop?

After the discovery of the Americas, Spanish adventurers set out to seek their fortunes. They sent expeditions to South and Central America and to Mexico in search of gold and treasure. In Mexico a group of Spanish soldiers attacked the capital of the Aztec Empire. The Aztecs had been expecting the god Quetzalcoatl to return to Earth and believed that the leader of the raiders, Cortés, was this god. The Aztecs offered little resistance, so Cortés captured Montezuma, the Aztec emperor, and ruled in his place. In Peru, the adventurer Pizarro took advantage of a civil war to conquer the Incas, murdering their rulers.

FACT FILE

Other nations expanded their empires in the same way as the Spanish. Many British people sailed to America to establish themselves and settle on this newly discovered land.

Several factors made it easy for a small group of Spaniards to conquer these great civilizations. Though vastly outnumbered, the Spanish had horses, armour and guns, which gave them a huge advantage over the native warriors.

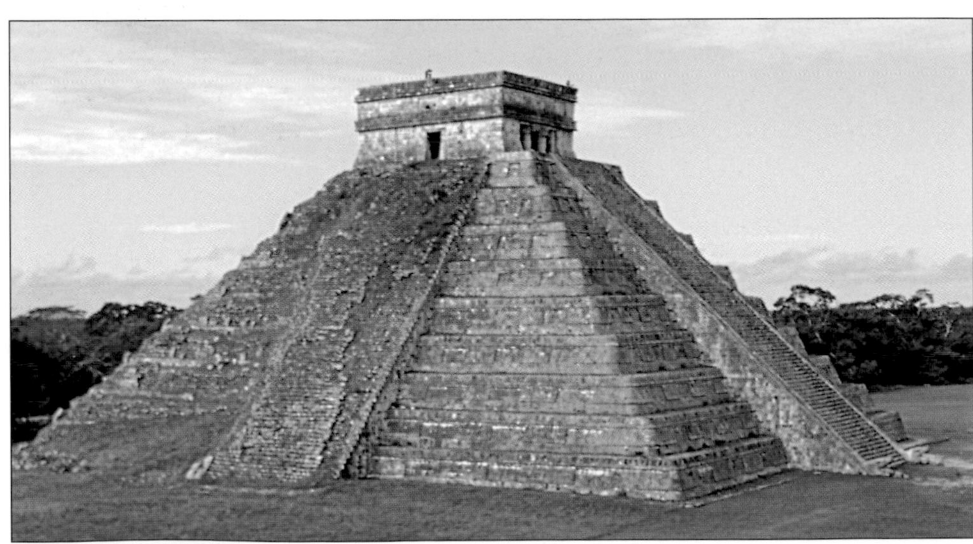

How was the Spanish Armada defeated?

The English were envious of Spain's rich colonies in South and Central America. During the reign of Elizabeth I, the English raided Spanish ships carrying gold and silver to Spain. The Spanish suspected that the English Crown supported these privateers, which angered them. To make matters worse, an English army helped the Dutch who were fighting against Spanish rule. In 1588 Phillip of Spain sent the Spanish Armada to invade England. The Spanish came very close to actually conquering England at this time. Their Armada, however, was scattered by storms, then harried and destroyed by English ships.

FACT FILE

Ships such as these were also responsible for the voyages of pilgrims, in search of a new life, heading from England to America. This particular ship is called *The Mayflower*.

HOW DID AMERICA BECOME INDEPENDENT?

Resentment against taxes imposed on the American colonies by Britain finally led to the Declaration of Independence, and in the following war, the Americans finally gained full independence of British rule.

The new American nation consisted of 13 states (this has now grown to 50). It had a president, who would be elected every four years, and was run by a Congress. This same structure exists to the present day.

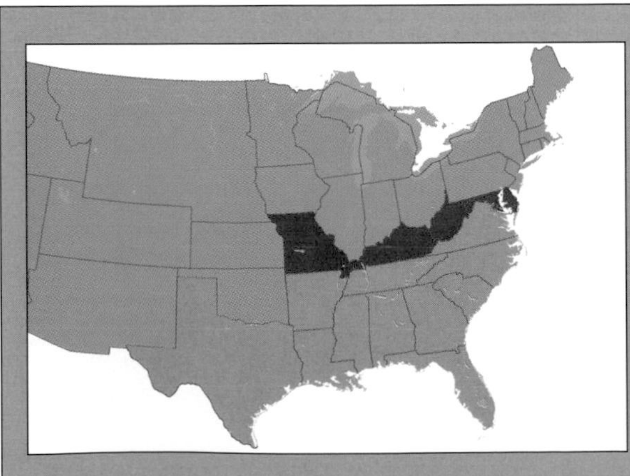

FACT FILE

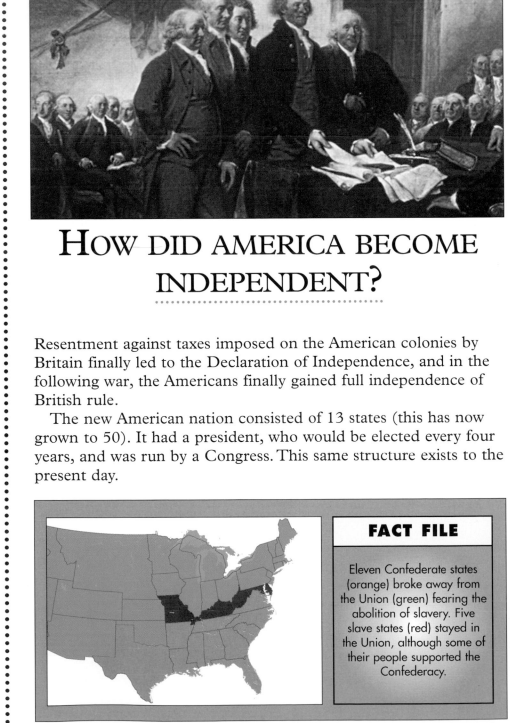

Eleven Confederate states (orange) broke away from the Union (green) fearing the abolition of slavery. Five slave states (red) stayed in the Union, although some of their people supported the Confederacy.

HOW DID THE NATIVE AMERICANS LOSE THEIR LAND?

The Native Americans understandably resented the numbers of settlers who swarmed onto their traditional hunting and grazing lands. As the population of the United States grew rapidly, the Native Americans were forced to migrate to the south and west. Soon they had nowhere left to go and began to fight back.

The US government reacted by forcing the Native Americans into reservations on land that was not wanted by the settlers. Many died fighting trying to save their land, or from starvation and disease. The huge herds of buffalo on which many depended were hunted by the settlers, depriving them of their main source of food, clothing and shelter.

FACT FILE

The American flag was originally designed with thirteen stars and thirteen stripes to represent the original colonies that signed the Declaration of Independence. With each new state, another star is added to the flag.

How did Africa become colonized?

The central regions of Africa were not properly explored until the middle of the 1800s. As the continent was explored, it was colonized by European countries seeking territories to exploit and bring them riches.

The British, Dutch, French and Portuguese all established colonies near the coast and later inland. The slave trade had destroyed the structure of many once-powerful African nations, and they were unable to resist the Europeans with their modern weapons. Germany, Belgium and Italy all joined in the scramble to capture new lands in Africa.

FACT FILE

Powerful tribes such as the Zulus mounted strong resistance to the invading colonial armies.

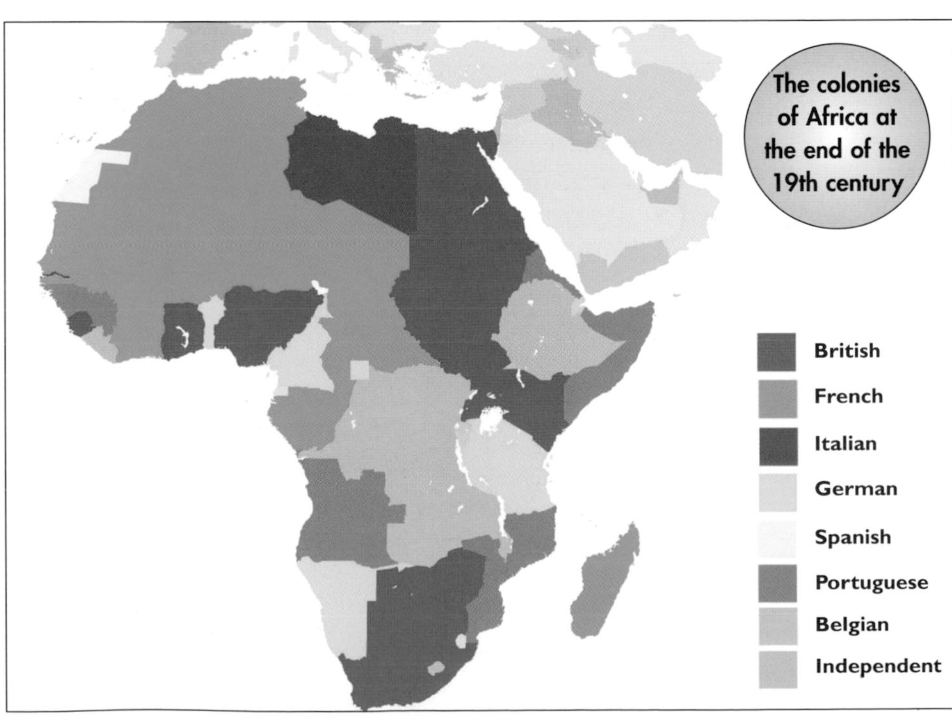

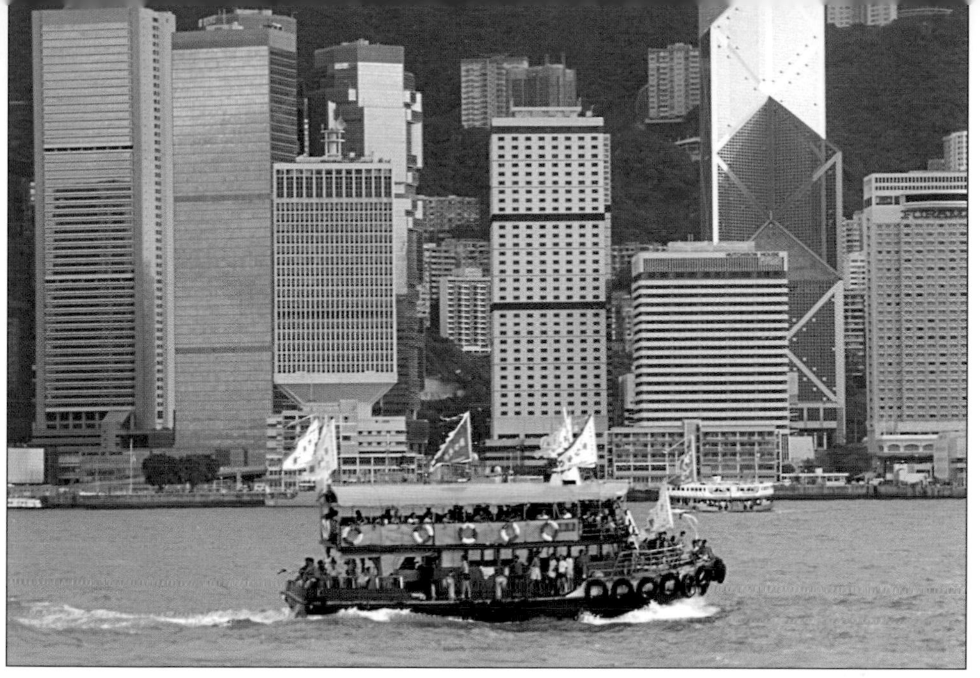

How did Britain gain Hong Kong?

For centuries China was a closed country and foreigners were not encouraged to explore it. European traders smuggled huge amounts of opium into China so that people became addicted, paying for the opium with silver. The Chinese government tried to stop this opium trade and the British sent the navy to threaten them. From 1839 to 1842 the British and Chinese fought over access to the Chinese ports. The Chinese were defeated and the British forced them to grant trading rights. Five ports were opened and Hong Kong Island became a British colony. In 1898 Britain was given Hong Kong on a 99 year lease. On July 1, 1997 Britain finally returned Hong Kong to China.

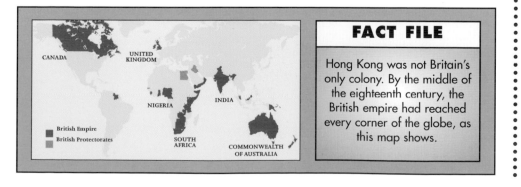

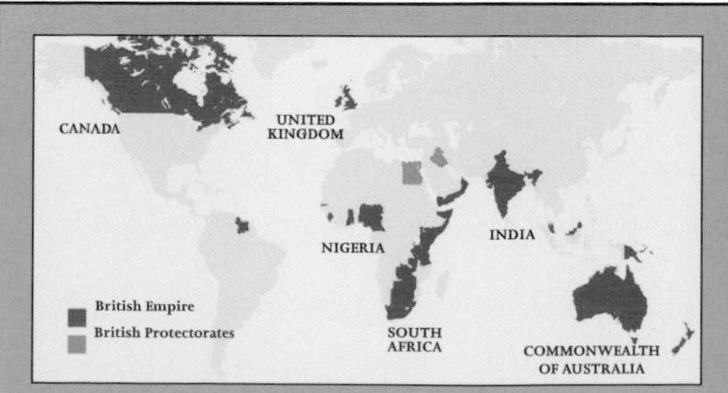

FACT FILE

Hong Kong was not Britain's only colony. By the middle of the eighteenth century, the British empire had reached every corner of the globe, as this map shows.

HOW DID THE FRENCH REVOLUTION BEGIN?

▲ On July 14, 1789, a mob attacked the royal prison in Paris, the Bastille. Although only a few prisoners were released, this event marked the end of royal power in France and the beginning of the Revolution.

FACT FILE

Napoleon was a very effective military leader and politician. He ruled France for fifteen years, expanding their empire abroad.

During the 1700s France was not prosperous. The government was short of money and needed to raise taxes. Louis XVI could only do this by recalling a traditional assembly, which promptly demanded political reforms. He responded by trying to dismiss the assembly, but the citizens in Paris revolted in support of the assembly.

The new National Assembly showed its strength by introducing fresh laws in 1791, insisting on freedom and equality. The royal family was imprisoned for a while, then tried and executed.

HOW DID THE GUILLOTINE BECOME SO FEARED?

The French Revolution was opposed by neighbouring countries who feared that unrest would spread across Europe. A Committee of Public Safety was set up in France to defend the revolution, and they executed any person who might oppose the committee. In fact thousands of people who were thought to threaten this new regime were put to death by the recently invented guillotine.

This period became known as the Reign of Terror. It lasted for about a year and during this time around 18,000 people were put to death. The French aristocracy was almost entirely wiped out, together with any political opponents of the regime. The Reign of Terror finally came to an end when the head of the Committee of Public Safety, Robespierre, was accused of treason.

FACT FILE

Marie-Antoinette, wife of Louis XVI, was an influential woman in the court. She met a gruesome death, sentenced to beheading at the guillotine.

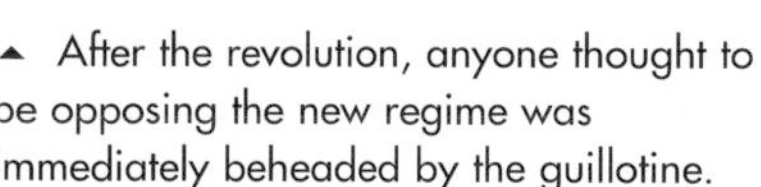

▲ After the revolution, anyone thought to be opposing the new regime was immediately beheaded by the guillotine.

How did the Industrial Revolution change Britain?

Back in the early 1700s, Britain was still a large agricultural nation. The few manufactured goods were made in small workshops or at home. As a result of Britain's world trading, the cotton industry developed and everything changed.

At first water power was used to drive spinning and weaving machines, and factories and mills were set up. New towns were built to provide homes for the workers. Steam engines were adapted to provide power to factories.

The railway and canal system were developed. The other key development was the smelting of iron using coke rather than wood. Britain was able to exploit the raw materials from her overseas empire to become one the world's most prosperous industrial nations.

FACT FILE

Trade with the Far East involved a long voyage around the tip of Africa. The Suez Canal provided a quick route through the Mediterranean and the Red Sea.

HOW SIGNIFICANT WAS THE INVENTION OF THE STEAM ENGINE?

Steam locomotion also made overseas trading possible. One of the most important exports was tea, which was in great demand in Europe.

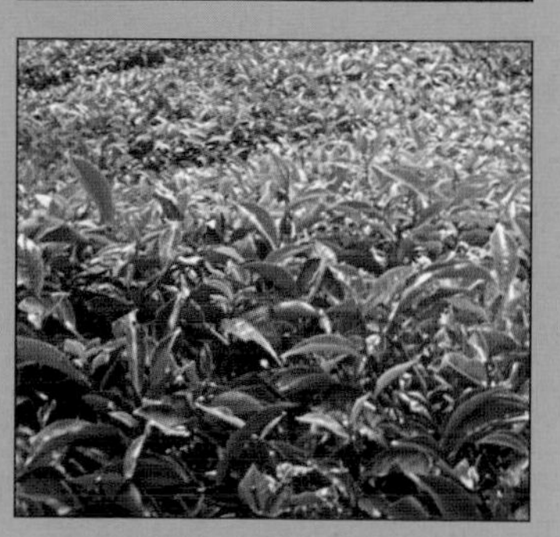

The invention of practical steam engines was the most significant advance in the 1700s, providing power for the Industrial Revolution. The first steam engines were massive stationary devices that pumped water from flooded mines, but they were soon adapted to power vessels.

The first steam locomotives appeared in the early 1800s. They carried goods and allowed people to travel to the factories where they worked. Trains were an important means for social change because, for the first time, people could travel quickly and visit areas that were previously too far away.

HOW DID WORLD WAR I BEGIN?

Continual trouble in the Balkans led to the formation of several complicated military alliances throughout Europe. The continent was eventually split into two groups. Britain, France and later Russia joined to form the *Entente Cordiale*, while Germany, Austria-Hungary and Italy formed the Triple Alliance. In 1914 Archduke Franz Ferdinand of Austria-Hungary was assassinated in Serbia, activating the alliance agreements.

First Austria declared war on Serbia, Russia sided with Serbia, and then Germany declared war on Russia. Germany invaded Belgium, bringing the British and French into the conflict.

FACT FILE

The Versailles Treaty ended World War I, but its terms were so severe that Germany suffered economic collapse and this caused resentment that was to build up and eventually contribute to the causes of World War II.

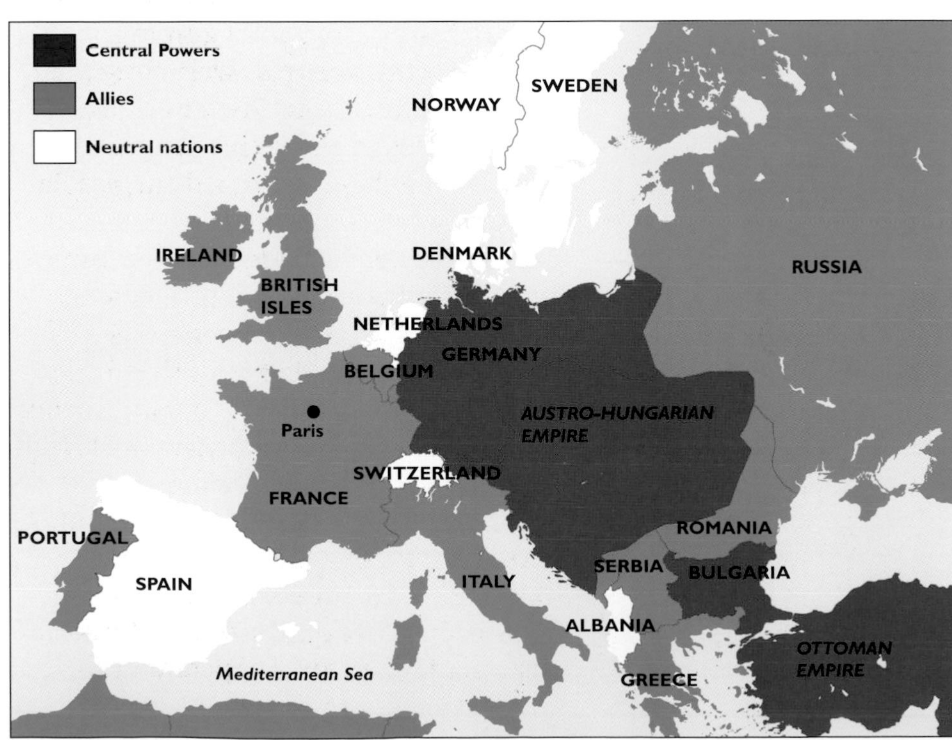

HOW DID NEW TECHNOLOGY INFLUENCE WORLD WAR I?

FACT FILE

The Great War of 1914–18 brought the first appearance of armoured tanks in battle. They were able to break through enemy lines and create openings for troops to advance through. Earlier use of tanks could have saved lives and helped shorten the war.

World War I was the first mechanized war in history. In the beginning fighting was similar to wars fought in the previous century. But new and terrifying weapons were introduced which completely changed the whole style of warfare.

Aircraft were used for the first time to observe the enemy and to locate suitable targets for the long-range artillery. Later on, fighter planes began to shoot down the spotters, introducing aerial warfare. Aircraft and Zeppelin airships were used as bombers.

The most terrifying new weapon was poison gas which was used by both sides. It caused millions of deaths and terrible suffering. Tanks also made their first appearance.

How did World War II begin?

As in World War I some international alliances were activated following the German invasion of Poland. As a result of this Britain and France declared war on Germany.

When the Germans attacked Poland, the Russians also attacked the country and it was divided.

The Germans went on to invade Denmark, Norway, Belgium, The Netherlands and France in quick succession. They crushed any resistance with overwhelming armoured forces.

World War II killed more people than any other war in history. The fighting spread to nearly every part of the world and included nearly 60 nations.

FACT FILE

Britain was led through World War II by Winston Churchill. He is remembered for his great wartime leadership qualities. He is also remembered for his famous 'V for victory' sign.

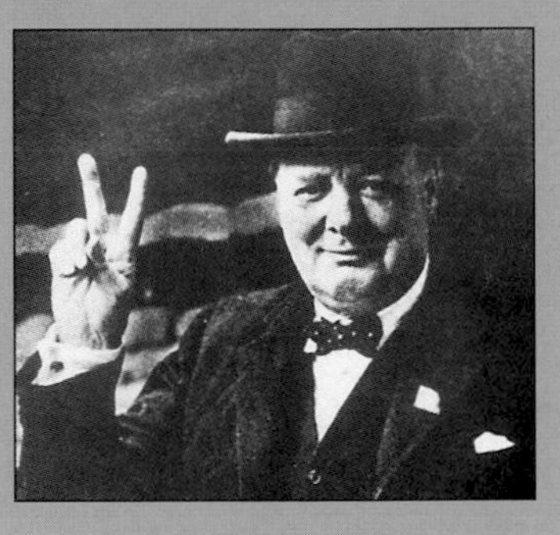

The Americans entered the war in 1941 after being attacked by Germany's ally Japan. At this time a huge military build-up began in England.

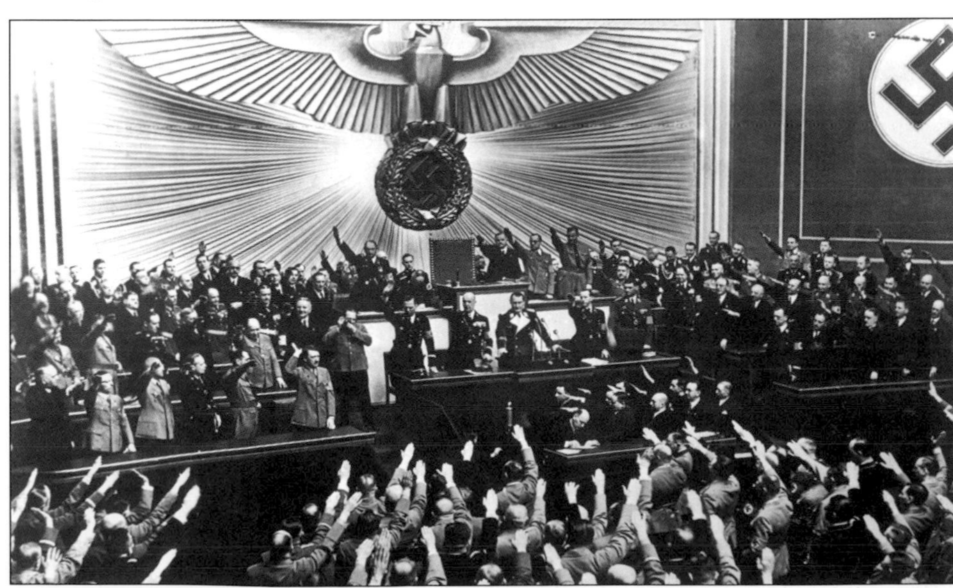

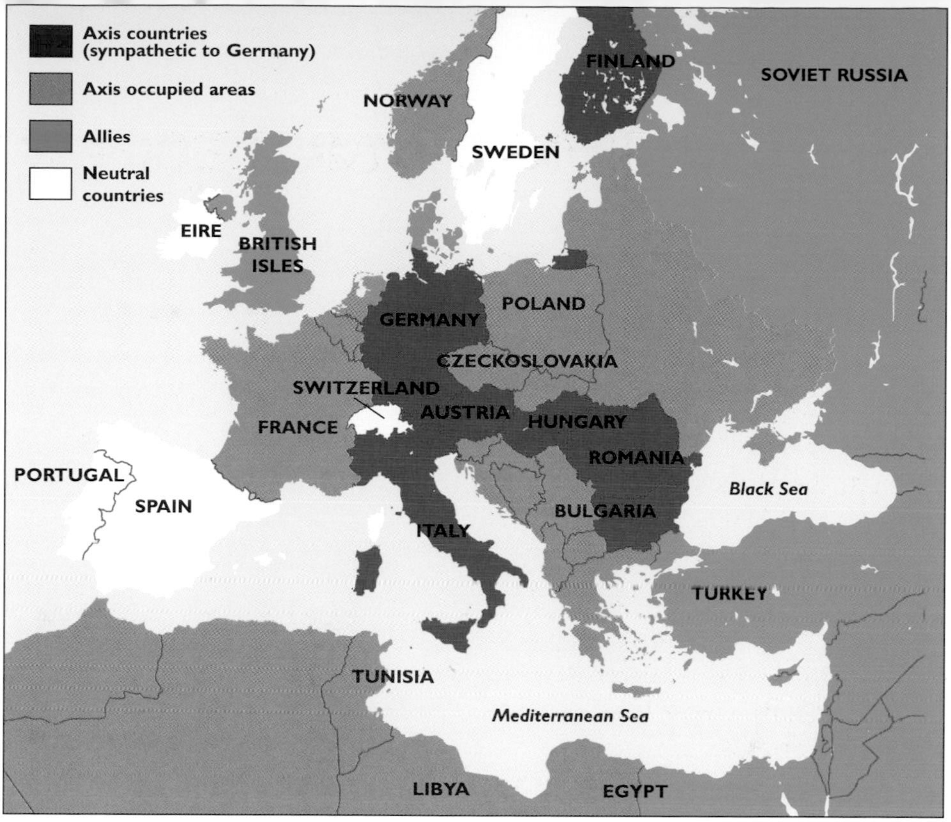

HOW STRONG WAS NAZI FIGHTING POWER?

FACT FILE

The greatest military operation ever carried out was the invasion of Europe by the Allied forces in 1944, when millions of troops were ferried across the Channel and landed from floating harbours on the shores of France

When the Germans realized that the British defences were too strong for their aircraft, they tried to destroy British industry. They hoped to damage the morale of the British population by night bombing of the cities. The German Luftwaffe, which was considered to be far superior to the RAF, set out to bomb the British airfields and shoot down their aircraft. The Luftwaffe finally abandoned its attempts to defeat the RAF when they realised they were flying too far from home and ran short of fuel. As part of their policy to 'purify' the German race the Nazis had a deliberate plan to exterminate the Jews.

How did the United Nations begin?

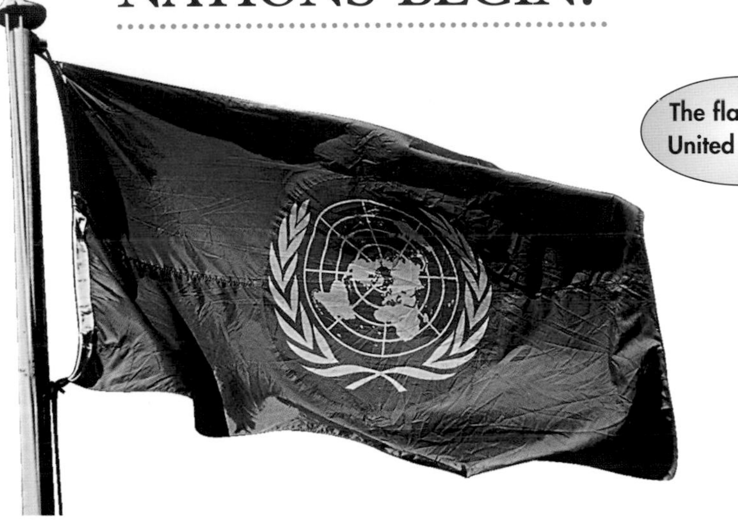

The flag of the United Nations

During World War II the Allied nations referred to themselves as the 'United Nations'. In 1942 they agreed that they would not make any separate peace agreements with Germany.

It was the Potsdam Conference in 1945 that really laid the ground for the foundation of the United Nations to prevent future conflict and also set out procedures for the prosecution of Nazi war criminals. Twenty-seven countries signed this first agreement and in 1945, after the war, the United Nations formally came into existence with an initial membership of fifty countries.

The United Nations (UN) is led by a powerful Security Council, which can intervene in international disputes that might lead to conflict. Today the UN is also involved in many economic aid programmes around the world.

FACT FILE

Early in 1945 the Allied leaders met in Yalta in the Crimea to decide on the post-war shape of the world. Churchill, Roosevelt and Stalin decided on how Germany was to be split up once the war was won.

ICELAND
NATO countries
Warsaw Pact
Neutral countries
FINLAND
NORWAY
SWEDEN
BRITISH ISLES
DENMARK
EIRE
NETHERLANDS
BELGIUM
RUSSIA
POLAND
EAST GERMANY
LUXEMBOURG
WEST GERMANY
CZECHOSLOVAKIA
SWITZERLAND
AUSTRIA
ROMANIA
FRANCE
BULGARIA
PORTUGAL
YUGOSLAVIA
SPAIN
ITALY
ALBANIA
TURKEY
GREECE

HOW DID THE COLD WAR AFFECT INTERNATIONAL RELATIONS?

A lot of tension grew between East and West after the war. Soviet forces suppressed attempts by Czechoslovakia and Hungary to obtain independence. However, nuclear war between the East and West did not happen. Instead, they sponsored wars and political unrest in other countries, destabilizing governments of which they disapproved.

The closest the world came to nuclear war was in 1962 when the Soviet Union moved missiles into Cuba, directly threatening the United States. The missiles were eventually removed, but only when the Americans threatened retaliation.

FACT FILE

The Berlin Wall was constructed to prevent people escaping to the West. It finally came down in 1989 as the Soviet system collapsed.

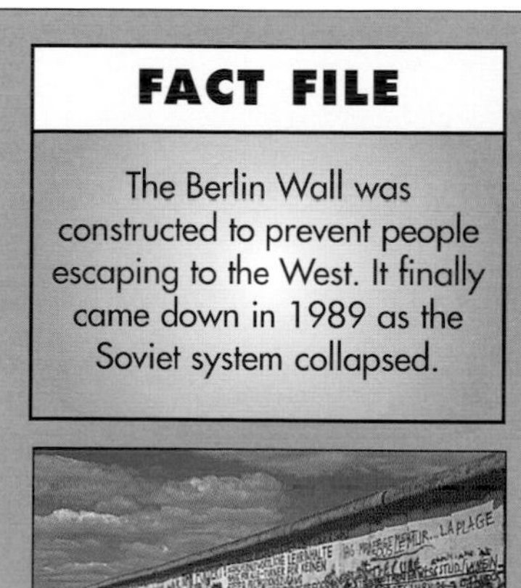